HACKER, MAKER, TEACHER, THIEF:

ADVERTISING'S NEXT GENERATION

EDITED BY
Daniele Fiandaca,
Ana Andjelic and Gareth Kay

CREATIVE SOCIAL

Thanks

Thanks to everyone who has supported Creative Social since its inception. Every speaker, all our sponsors, industry bodies and fellow collectives, the journalists who continue to write nice things about us and every single Social who has contributed to our ongoing success. You all continue to be an inspiration.

Thanks to all our authors for investing time to contribute your words of wisdom to this book. Thanks to Simon Scott for designing our amazing cover as well as the lovely Louisa St. Pierre of Bernstein & Andriulli for making it happen (again!).

In addition, a massive thanks to our amazing Creative Social team. To the lovely Elle for continuing to drive Creative Social forward with very little support. To James for singlehandedly building a community on twitter and the blog with such ongoing engaging content. And for all our helpers – Anna, Charlotte and Natasha. Thanks

And hello to Jason Isaacs.

Contents

About Creative Social

When we founded Creative Social over ten years ago, we really did not realise what it could become. The initial premise was to simply get some of the world's most pioneering, interactive creative directors and business owners together in one place and to see what happened. Since then we have held Global Socials in Amsterdam, Antwerp, Barcelona, Berlin, Beirut, Florence, Helsinki, Las Vegas, London, Montreal, New York, Paris, San Francisco, Sao Paolo, Seattle, Shanghai, Stockholm and Tokyo. We have published two books (Digital Advertising: Past, Present and Future being our first). Creative Social Sydney is still going strong (great job Ben, we promise to make it there sometime soon). Readership of the blog (www.creativesocialblog.com) continues to grow, as does our twitter following (@creativesocial). And our UK event programme is ever-expanding – in 2014 we expect to have over 10 events in London.

However this book is not about the past but about the future. It is really our view of what is going to drive the next 10 years of this wonderful industry we work in. We hope that you enjoy it, and if we inspire a single reader to do something that shapes the next 10 years, it will have been worthwhile.

We are as committed as ever to deliver on our goal of representing a platform for progression for all creatives and creative business leaders. And we hope that this represents a worthy addition to the tools we use to do that.

Mark Chalmers and Daniele Fiandaca, Co-founders, Creative Social

Introduction

An interview with Ana Andjelic and Gareth Kay by Daniele Fiandaca

"Everything but nothing has changed" – this probably best summarises the way I feel since we published our first book in 2010. On one hand the phrase "digital advertising" has finally died, digital Creative Directors are now simply ECDs (rather than digital ECDs), innovation seems to have been given more prominence and the best work finally feels truly integrated. On the other there are still way too many ad agencies whose first solution is a TV ad, there is still an unhealthy fixation within the industry on awards and we are still talking about the future of advertising.

And when we started plotting the next book, we in fact defaulted to looking at the future of advertising (the first proposed book title was 'The future of advertising…. Is advertising'). But then we realised that you cannot really know what the future of advertising really is. We made some predictions in our first book – some were true and others were completely wrong (yes I did talk about the death of TV advertising).

What we loved most about our first book was that when you asked people about their favourite chapters, they were all very different. It reminded me how different we all are, which fundamentally is the joy of our industry. There are no set formulas. Things are constantly changing. And we have no idea most of the time where things are going to go.

We are extremely lucky in that, in truth, we fell into Creative Social and have since had the pleasure of hearing some truly amazing speakers and rubbing shoulders with some of the top talent in advertising, as well as visiting some quite amazing cities. But what is it that makes our speakers and Socials so bloody interesting and (most of the time) inspiring? Apart from the lack of egos (the first rule of Creative Social), it is their passion, be it for advertising, creativity, sneakers, architecture, fashion, music, film or vinyl toys.

We realised that if we could bottle this passion, we might have the opportunity to actually inspire those people who will fashion the future of advertising over the next decades.

So this book simply collects a series of essays from those people who have inspired us over the years – Socials, Speakers and friends of Creative Social. And talking of friends, it was to two such people that I turned to when I was looking for my fellow Editors of the book, Ana Andjelic and Gareth Kay:

So Ana and Gareth, what were your first thoughts when you were first asked to co-edit Creative Social's second book:

GK: To be honest, slightly intimidated - the prior books have been so good it feels there's a high bar to jump over. Luckily, when we began to see the contributions you could feel the weight lift as there's terrific diversity and quality and generosity in all the chapters.

AA: I don't believe I was asked! I recommended myself for the role of the East Coast Editor, and it turned out it was a fantastic idea and a wonderful opportunity. I am really, really glad I seized it.

Ana, you actually came up with the name of the book. Tell us where this came from and how it relates to the book?

AA: It was a moment of inspiration. The name is an obvious play on the movie titled "Tinker, Tailor, Soldier, Spy." But the more I thought about this (movie) title, the more it made sense for the context of the book: today's best advertising talent are not one thing, but can assume multiple identities, sometimes at the same time. It's a diversity of disparate perspectives held together at any given moment that has become the key for success in our profession. So I came up with "Hacker, Maker, Teacher, Thief" to summarise the kaleidoscopic identities that advertising's "next generation" is inspired (and forced) to assume. Teacher and thief refer to a strong educational role that we have in relation to our clients and our organisations; and we are all thieves as we take inspiration, ideas and knowledge from each other - transparently and freely - and recombine it. This exchange is the core of digital culture. Hacker and maker are more straightforward and capture the shift towards designing consumer experiences and service systems vs. just communicating messaging, and working - hacking - with consumers to make them compelling and useful.

So given that the book is about the next Generation of Advertising, why do you think the chapters submitted by the authors so naturally seemed to fit into six distinct sections – Advertising, Creativity, Culture, Education, Innovation and the Future?

GK: I think they're the big issues we are wrestling with as an industry – they're certainly the ones I feel the majority of passionate conversations are around. The interesting thing to me is how many of the chapters lie at the intersection of two or more of these categories. I guess the interesting stuff always happens at the intersections.

AA: Ha, the agenda of this question seems to be that these six categories *are* the future of advertising! You are probably right, however. The way I see it is that these topics are like concentric circles: at the very centre we have advertising and creativity. Around them is culture, and then further around education. Innovation is the next layer, and then the future. So we can explore all these different layers, all the while staying focused on the business and creativity of advertising as our playing field.

If we were to go again, is there any topic you would have liked to have seen in there (e.g. technology)?

AA: Technology, to me, is not a separate topic; it's an inherent part of advertising, creativity, culture, education, innovation, and the future. I don't think these areas can be explored and understood without exploring and understanding technology. Similarly, I am not sure how we would study technology without thinking about all the values, rules, intentions, purpose that went into its design.

GK: I would have liked to have seen something around the future of business – how we think business, and its associated models, need to change.

What has personally most surprised you from editing and reading the book?

GK: The diversity of thinking around these areas. Some essays almost feel contradictory and I like that. There isn't a single right answer after all.

AA: A lot of people working in advertising aren't quite happy with advertising right now. Then again, this may be an artefact of having to write about it: it's always much easier to criticise something, to write about problems and what is going wrong, than to write about solutions and ways to improve things. Hopefully the future is brighter than some envision.

Given each chapter is distinct, how would you best recommend people read the book?

AA: I think the readers won't make mistake if they start from the beginning, going back to my concentric circles analogy. It makes sense to start from pieces belonging to advertising and slowly make one's way toward the future.

GK: Select a chapter at random and dive in. More seriously, I'd try and read a section together if possible. You'll get more that way about the diversity of thinking around each topic.

And finally have you been inspired by the book and if so how?

GK: Absolutely. I've been provoked, challenged and inspired. It's made me think differently about a few things, made me want to try and do things differently and overall raise my game.

AA: There are a lot of good ideas and great thinking compiled in this book. There is enough diversity and enough convergence for readers to recognise that advertising creatives - no matter where and who they are - are grappling with similar issues. It's encouraging to see this diverse community come together.

Thanks Ana and Gareth. I hope that our readers enjoy the book as much as I have editing it with you guys.

Now over to you, the reader. Enjoy....

ADVERTISING

Tomorrow Today

By Gareth kay

"Prediction is very difficult. Especially if it's about the future".
– Nils Bohr, Nobel Laureate Physicist

People are rightly nervous about making predictions about the future. As Ray Amara famously observed, we have a nasty tendency to overestimate the short term impact and underestimate the long term impact of new things. In our strange, little world of advertising and marketing this tends to lead to hyperbolic, sweeping assertions about how a shiny new thing will lead to the death of the thing before (apparently TV advertising should have died a few years ago and there shouldn't be radio ads any more) rather than how it might alter and begin to transform the existing status quo. The slow stuff matters more than the shock of the new.

However, I feel more comfortable writing about how the advertising agency business needs to change and how it might look in the future. And that's for a simple reason: advertising, as we know it, is simply not working. It has failed to change as fast as culture and as a result is becoming increasingly irrelevant to people, business and the talent we need to attract and retain. If we don't change today, then there is not going to be much of a future to predict.

The march to irrelevance
People are not seeing the difference between brands and ads. As far back as 2000, Copernicus Consulting discovered that people saw the brands in 4 out of 5 categories as being increasingly homogeneous and only 7% saw a

1

difference in ads. And not only are they not seeing difference but they are increasingly seeing little usefulness in the notion of the brand. Havas Media Lab has recently fielded global research that has shown that the majority of people couldn't care less if 3 out of 4 brands disappeared tomorrow and only 1 in 5 brands are seen to make a positive and noticeable contribution to people's lives. So we are failing in delivering on the most basic needs of marketing: to forge differentiation and be useful and valuable to people.

As a result of this, clients are beginning to question the efficacy of marketing. One in four clients believe marketing is not boosting corporate profitability and in the world of packaged goods, for every dollar spent on brand building three dollars are being spent on price promotions. They are also aware of the lack of change in the advertising industry itself: only one in ten clients think the industry is doing a good job in evolving their services for the digital age.

Finally, the industry is not attracting or retaining the best talent. Talk to people who perhaps a decade ago would join the industry and they'll tell you that it just doesn't feel that exciting to them. It's not the strong cultural force it once was and it isn't about solving the 'wicked problems' that exist in other industries. So, the best talent is no longer joining the industry and the talent that does isn't being invested in the way it should to be able to grow and flourish and be remarkable. Andrew Bennett highlighted this by discovering that Starbucks spends more per head training their baristas than we spend training our talent.

Quite simply, in an era of massive cultural change (from putting a man on the moon, to the Berlin Wall coming down, to us walking around with our faces stuck in supercomputers) we have changed little, if at all. It's unsurprising, as a result, that we need to change now if we are to have a healthy tomorrow. What follows are three of the most important things I think we need to do in order to build a healthier and more relevant industry for today and tomorrow.

1. Close the commercial gap

The great failure of the advertising industry to transform itself has been down to the fact that we're excellent at the wrong type of innovation. We relentlessly pursue and celebrate the latest new and original ways of doing what we have done before. But it is rarely about imaginatively and daringly finding new types of things to do with our creativity and new ways to get paid for them.

Laurence Green, a Partner of the agency 101, summed this up brilliantly: *"The task of any imaginative agency, any creative company, is to understand and serve its client's business problem. Too often, our business has sliced and diced its tasks in the style of a sub-prime mortgage bundler. A corporate task set by the chief executive, reframed as a comms task by the marketing director, refined by the brand consultancy and reduced by the ad agency to the stuff advertising can do: grow awareness, nurture engagement. Too many links, too indirect and weak a connection between commercial possibilities and creative resolution."*

To do this we need to break the muscle memory of seeing every business problem as something that can be solved by the act of advertising.

Clients are asking us to grow their business and solve big, tough, complicated commercial problems. Yet our default behaviour and niche obsessions with the ad makes the link between the commercial imperative and the creative solution far too weak and indirect. We have to become more obsessed by the outcome we create rather than the output we make.

Perhaps even more damningly than this there is, I would observe, an increasing lack of understanding about how business really works today. The industry tends to only understand business through the lens of advertising and, as a result, has little to no understanding of how companies really make money. There's been tremendous innovation in business models that will be invisible to most agency people because they see the world in simplistic and outdated ways.

2. Put real people at the heart of everything we do

I sometimes wonder if we might be the most narcissistic industry on Earth. We look at award show annuals for inspiration. Our references in meetings are other ads. Competitive reviews are ads and nothing else. We even make behind the scenes films thinking we are making the next Quentin Tarantino movie when we're not.

We think the world revolves around us. It doesn't. It revolves around people. And those people really don't care much about brands and the stuff we make on their behalf. They're much more interested in their family and how their day has been, what's for dinner, what's on TV, how their job is going, what the football score is, etc.

So maybe we would be better off if we try to understand what people are interested in and work back from there. Maybe do something interesting around things they are interested in, rather than trying to wring out the last bits of commercial value from what we think is important.

This means we need to help brands have a point of view on the world, not just a position in their category. It means being people positive, not media neutral. I'm increasingly using a very simple yardstick - that of the bridge - when evaluating ideas. Great communication ideas act as a bridge. A bridge between what people are interested in and care about and what you make/ sell. A bridge between your world and theirs; real life/culture and commerce.

(By the way, you may notice that this piece uses the word 'people' rather than the more common marketing-ese of 'consumers'. Give it a go. I guarantee you'll start doing things that are more welcome in their lives just by treating them as real people, not actors whose sole role in life is to consume stuff).

3. Get experimental

Peter Sims wrote a fantastic book called 'Little Bets'. In it he outlines the reality of how great cultural ideas are formed, from Chris Rock's standup to Google's innovation process. It's not about arriving at a perfectly formed idea, but rather a willingness to stumble upon greatness. And this mindset is something at odds with an industry constrained by the tyranny of perfection.

Let's compare for a moment how two different types of creative companies work. Let's take Pixar, the maker of amazing movies that push the boundaries of what's possible with technology, and an ad agency. Let's call the agency Sterling Cooper Draper Pryce. Now Pixar has a simple motto that guides them: 'from suck to non-suck'. They are driven to be wrong as fast as you can; to go from suck to non-suck as quickly as possible. They accept that mistakes are an inevitable part of the creative process, so they get right down to it and start making them. Their process is built around this and is perhaps best exemplified by their use of show and tell dailies where anyone can comment on progress and the day's work, regardless of how rough the day's work is. They fail forward. As John Lasseter, their creative supremo put it: "Every Pixar film was the worst motion picture ever made at one time or another. People don't believe that, but it's true. But we don't give up on the films."

Now compare that to the process inside an ad agency or a marketing department: a siloed relay race, where we spend 90% of our time on the last 2% of craft.

In today's ever accelerating culture we are setting ourselves up to fail every day we walk into work. We don't move at the speed of culture and thus are becoming irrelevant. We have to try and remove the pointless quest for perfection.

A brighter future lies in us becoming hackers of commerce and culture

Quite simply, I believe that we are at our most valuable when we behave less like advertising people and more like a hacker. Now when you think of hacker, you often still think of people who break stuff and live outside the law. But that's not what hacking is about. It's about something much more powerful because, at it's most fundamental, a hack is *the most ingenious and effective solution to a problem*. I believe orienting ourselves around this is more powerful for five simple reasons:

I.   Hacks, by definition, are more effective. They take big complicated problems and break them into smaller problems that can be more easily solved, whatever form that solution takes. As a result, they remove the gap between the commercial imperative and the creative solution;

II. Hacks tend to be people positive. They solve real problems for people and make their lives in some way better. So we make stuff people care about;

III. Hacks simplify things for people and get out of the way. They don't feel they have to interrupt you or get in your way in order to be noticed;

IV. Hacks are forward looking and imaginative; they have an inherent disdain for the tired solutions of today. They are true to the etymological meaning of technology: "a better way of doing things"; and

V.   Hacking is about a predisposition and bias towards speed. It's about solving a problem in a better, faster and easier way. It fights the tyranny of perfection that far too often slows us down. It lets us move and experiment at least as fast as culture (Lorne Michaels, the Producer of Saturday Night Live, captured this brilliantly: *"the show doesn't go on because it's ready; it goes on because it's 11.30pm Saturday night"*).

We need to rediscover our healthy disregard for advertising

To become relevant today and thrive tomorrow, we need to have a healthy disregard for advertising, at least as we know it now. We need to break out of our paint by numbers mentality. A healthy disregard for advertising has always been a common thread in the best advertising people and clients: Phil Knight famously spoke about how much he hated advertising, Google run a million miles away from stuff that 'feels like an ad' and I'm convinced that the best work we do in the industry stems from people who don't see themselves as advertising people. We need to rediscover this disregard. Somewhat perversely, we need less advertising people in order for advertising to flourish.

We face today two interlinked problems. First, we are a cultural laggard - we're less interesting and progressive than the stuff that surrounds what we do. As a result, we are less meaningful to people and less vital to brands. Second, we have forgotten how to understand and serve our clients' business problems; we only know how to make the stuff we've grown up making.

The confluence of this means we are currently making the slow walk to irrelevance. If we're to stop this and seize the amazing opportunities open to us, we need to stop being advertising people, and we need to become much more like hackers.

Or, as Mark Shayler says much more succinctly: *"It's not sufficient to do things better. We need to do better things."*

You Lucky B***ards

By Patrick Collister

For God's sake, don't tell my mother I work in advertising. She thinks I play the piano in a brothel.

It's an old joke but descriptive of how adland was regarded not so long ago. When I started as a copy trainee way back in the late 70's, a number of my snooty pals thought I'd sold out.

Even my brother. And he worked for Plessey, designing gadgets to give our chaps advantages in the theatre of war.

Pah!

The educated middle classes wanted to use money, not make it. So they became academics, teachers and civil servants.

Advertising was despised for being of no social benefit whatsoever. It interrupted the best TV programmes and was, for the most part, witless. It followed that the people who created it were shallow all the way through.

Today, though, I would argue that if you're in advertising, you've never been so important. You have much to contribute.

Hell, you might even be the ones to save us all.

One, you can change behaviours.

Two, creativity is crucial.

Three, you can reach the world from a desk in Shoreditch, Brooklyn or Mumbai.

Frankly, there's never been a more exciting time to be in this business. The pace of change is amazing. It's allowing new opportunities for imaginative, inventive people to pop up across the media landscape like meerkats in 'Wildlife on One'.

The cause of all this?

Digital.

And the web.

And it's still in its infancy.

Malcolm Gladwell, author of 'The Tipping Point' et al was asked why he has no Facebook page. He replied that he didn't tweet, he didn't post, he did nothing online because the digital revolution hasn't started yet. When it does, he will consider his options.

When I arrived at Google in April 2013, I thought I understood how advertising was changing. After all, I had started what I believe was the first digital creative unit of any ad agency in the UK. And, for seven years, I had published Directory magazine, a showcase for innovative ideas in communications. I had reported on great new ideas in the digital space from dynamic new agencies such as Akestam Holst and Lowe Brindfors in Sweden, Shackleton in Spain, Buzzman in France, Duval Guillaume in Belgium and, the daddy of digital, Crispin Porter + Bogusky in the USA. Ha! It turns out I knew nothing.

To get myself bedded down at Google NACE (Northern & Central Europe) I asked my team to help me work on a Re:Brief.

25 years ago, I'd written a TV commercial, which, while it never won awards had gained a certain sort of playground traction.

In the commercial, two kids come in from playing football. One offers the other a drink.

"Milk, yuck" says his mate.

"It's what Ian Rush drinks," says our little freckled hero with a Liverpudlian accent. "And he says, if I don't drink enough milk, when I grow up, I'll only be good enough to play for Accrington Stanley."

"Accrington Stanley? Who are they?"

"Exactly."

The important thing to take from the commercial is it's positioning milk as a drink for growing kids.

So, how would we do that today?

Well, first thing: we'd bring back Ian Rush.

And we'd bring back the Milk Cup, last played in 1993 before milk was privatised in the UK and the National Dairy Council wound up.

In those days, it was a match played at the beginning of the season between the winner of the FA Cup and the winner of the league.

In our version, it's a match between men and boys. Between Accrington Stanley and a team of boys selected by Ian Rush.

The way it would work is ads on milk cartons and banner ads online would invite parents to make videos of their kids showing off their football skills and upload them to the Milkcup YouTube channel.

Not only can kids now compare and contrast their own skills with others of their own age, but Ian Rush can start selecting young players to come to his special 'boot camps'.

These might be three sessions involving, say, sixty hopefuls at each. Here, the 180 lads would get coaching from Jamie Carragher and Stevie Gerrard. More videos of the coaching sessions would be uploaded to the YouTube 'hub'.

By this stage, there could be hundreds of videos.

And, who knows, maybe one of them might attract millions of views. Why not? The video of 'A new Messi, Haitem, 8 years old' has had two million views in a year. Young Hassan Ayari has accumulated many millions of views. One video alone has over six million views.

So, Ian Rush selects his squad.

Now we need a 'hero' video, a piece of advertising that will get viewers to watch the match live on YouTube.

Maybe we organise a flashmob at a Premier League game. Our squad of young stars invades the pitch at half time. The stewards are simply unable to catch them as they kick a ball between them. It's funny, it's amazing, is it real?

Who knows but it drives traffic to the match.

Now, if Samsung can get nearly two million people to watch the live unveiling of their Galaxy Gear smart-watch, we must be able to get a similar number to watch our team of pint-sized champs whup Accers? Surely?

Here's the thing, back in 1989 when I wrote the original TV commercial, I changed one life. The kid in the ad, as a result of the experience, decided to become an actor. Carl Rice, for that is his name, pops up regularly on the telly. I think he's been in Casualty, a well known UK medical drama, very recently.

In 2014, I can change the lives of dozens, maybe even hundreds of kids. I can get them out playing football.

And, at a time when parents are increasingly worried about obesity, milk can become synonymous with a healthier alternative to sugary drinks.

As schools distance themselves more and more from sport, milk (or a milk brand) can become a valuable and valued partner to parents who want a more active life for their little 'uns.

In 1989, I created 40 seconds of content.

In 2014, we may end up with 4 hours of video. Or more.

Today I am in the business of creating advertising. But not advertisements. People don't choose to watch ads about products and their attributes. But they may choose to watch video about people and brands whose interests and values are in synch with their own.

At this stage of the creative process I was feeling rather pleased with myself. We'd re-imagined the milk ad in a way that seemed to make sense both of Google's platforms and of the way that social media works.

Then one of the planners came to me.

"I've been looking at the numbers," she said. And I groaned. Numbers have never really done it for me. Not in the past, anyway.

"Look, the numbers show that while kids are still into football, they aren't as crazy about it as they used to be. What they are interested in these days are individual sports like swimming and cycling."

Now that is a real insight.

Of course kids are more into cycling and swimming. First Beijing and then London with all the medals and all the knighthoods.

"But, get this," she said. "The trending sport in the UK right now is…."

"What?"

"Dance."

Wow! And there it is. The numbers show the interest. It's the Billy Elliott effect. It's Diversity winning 'Britain's Got talent', it's the rather successful Step Up trilogy of films, it's dance competitions in community centres every weekend, troupes of kids gyrating, spinning, acrobatically bouncing around in choreographed togetherness.

What this meant, of course, was we had to go back to the drawing board and reimagine the whole campaign again. But spot the difference. This time, with girls. In the new iteration, groups of boys and girls would be invited to create their own dance routines. The winning group would get to perform at The Royal Variety Show. With Beyonce.
(Hey, there has to be an incentive!)

So, going back to the beginning, why are you so lucky?
Well, people can edit advertising out of their lives entirely now.
That means you have to create ideas they actually want to engage with. In other words, creativity has never been so important.
But it's not just that ideas need to be more thoughtful, more human and more remarkable than ever before, but they need to be based on shared values.
If people are going to buy a company's products today, they want to buy into the company first.
In a world of massive over-supply, they can afford to be picky.
Brands, then, need to sell themselves to their customers not on *what* they do or even *how* they do it – but *why*.
Steve Jobs believed that people bought into Apple because Apple understood that they wanted not the tools to do a better job but the tools to create a better world.
For me, for any brand to survive, let alone thrive, it needs to mean something to the people who buy it.
For creative people, that means creating ideas rooted in human truths rather than ideas rooted in product facts.
Think about whisky for a moment.
Many whiskies talk about how they are made. The earthy, smoky flavour that results from Scottish rainwater seeped through heather and peat.
Then there's Johnnie Walker, who talk about 'Keep Walking.'
About moving forwards. Having a goal. Picking yourself up and starting all over again.
You can't have a conversation about peat.
Well, not a very long one.
But you can have a conversation about what success and reward means to you.

And that's why you're lucky. You are being invited to have ideas about people. About what they really do and think and say, which brings you closer to being artists than advertising folk have been before.

There is also an added incentive. If you are able to come up with these new, engaging ideas then you are also able to change behaviours.

Changing behaviours.

Urgh. It's become a new advertising cliché, which is a pity because the future of our planet depends on people changing how they do things.

For instance, how can you persuade people to be less wasteful with energy?

How do you get people to use less water?

How do you get people to shower less often?

To do the laundry with just a litre of water?

How can we curb the greed that is leading to the deforestation of the Amazon basin? To the disappearance of cod from the North Atlantic?

How can we get people in the first world to see that they have a responsibility for what goes on in the third?

Sir Ken Robinson, educationalist, author and all-round top bloke, has argued with startling coherence that the population of the world is currently 7 billion, set to reach 9 billion.

If everyone everywhere was to enjoy the same standard of living that we do in London, New York, Paris and Berlin, the globe can support a population of 1.5 billion.

It is a problem of unimaginable proportions.

Sir Ken argues that what we need now are ideas. He is concerned that we start to teach our children in new ways to free up their imaginations so that they can find a way out of the mess their forebears have made.

I argue that there are already people out there who can make a difference. You.

Creative people – young or old.

With ideas, which, through new digital platforms, can reach the world.

Some of the ideas I've seen in the last year or two which give me hope include:

Kony 2012. Jason Russell made a film about the leader of the Lord's Resistance Army. It got 100 million views on YouTube. Many NGOs attacked the film as simplistic but the film led directly to President Obama enacting legislation aimed at bringing Kony to justice. 100 combat troops were sent by the US to the Central African Republic to offer help.

iFold. A young creative team working in Ogilvy Mumbai noted that people were sending letters in envelopes the same size as the sheet of paper inside.

They thought, imagine how much paper we'd all save if we folded our letters in half? Or even in half again?

They made a film, got Vodafone to support it, posted it onto the internet and started saving 800 trees a month.

Pepsi Bottle Light. In the Philippines, creative director David Guerrero saw that an ingenious problem-solver in the slums of Manila was bringing light to the shanty towns by putting a mix of bleach and water into Pepsi bottles.

David got his client, Pepsi, to start bringing light to more parts of the country. After Typhoon Haiyan hit, the Pepsi lights brought more than light to devastated areas but hope.

And so on and so on.

All are new kinds of idea and none of them what you might call an advertisement.

Like the milk work I developed with my team. Advertising, yes, but carefully constructed little stories about the product, each neatly packed into a specific time-length, 20, 30, 40, 60 seconds, no.

Content.

TV advertising isn't dead. There will always be a role for the tent-pole commercial. Especially when brands have news they want to share. It's just that it can't really change behaviours on its own. Together with digital and experiential media, however, it can help get people to change what they do and how they do it. And maybe, just maybe, to start looking out for each other as well as looking out for this fragile world of ours.

The list of great behaviour-changing ideas is getting longer by the year. Cannes has been giving a Grand Prix for good since 2006 (I think). And two years ago, through the Cannes Chimaera, the festival partnered with the Bill and Melinda Gates Foundation to give cash prizes to help pay for the development of great ideas.

D&AD has a similar scheme, the White Pencil initiative, to encourage creative people to generate real-world ideas for worthy causes.

Thanks to the digital revolution, advertising people have become relevant. Not just to marketers with brands to sell but to people.

You are creating apps that help kids with diabetes regulate their medicine. You are creating apps that automatically shut down your smartphones so you can't text and drive.

You are creating ideas to help prevent online bullying.

You are using Minecraft as a place to talk to kids in real-time about how daft it is to start smoking.

You are creating YouTube channels to try to prevent the destruction of the environment.

You are creating maps of 'Where the bankers live' to hold to account the invisible folk who have brought the world to the brink.

You are bringing people together in communities. You are starting movements.

And you have the future on your side.

In two years time you will be using tools and platforms we can't imagine today.

You are the change-makers. The what-iffers, the experimentalists. The creative geeks. You are making a difference.

And that is why you are lucky b***ards.

What the Fuck do Clients Know About Great Advertising?

By Scott Morrison

"Is it me or are there loads of shit ads out there at the moment?"

The words of my friend Chris last week at my birthday curry. He's your typical bloke - Sun on Sunday, Jaguar with Corinthian leather seats, loves a pint and watches X-Factor. He loves ads - he reels off his favourites with the sing-song voice and gusto of a market trader selling you an extra bowl of mangoes that you really didn't want - "Monk-ay" he Northerns, "Follow the Bear", he doths an imaginary hat, "he's got an 'ology'" he shrugs. He even gives me the van-full-of-builders rendition of 'We hope it's chips it's chips" as someone chimes in 'Fried onion rings' from the restaurant kitchen. I can't believe for one minute that these very same conversations aren't happening around the table at O'Blarney's in Brooklyn where they lament the demise of the great American 'Madvertising' of the 60s or indeed, at the BierKellers of Berlin or the RSLs in Sydney.

"You're in the game incha mate. What the fuck happened"

And I sat there amongst the party hats, cracked poppadoms and chutneys trying to work out what HAD happened. Wasn't there a time when Advertising would look this type of disdain squarely in the face and, Maximus Decimus style, shout 'Are you not ENTERTAINED' to the non-believers who were hoovering up oven chips, cheap booze and tea bags. There was no internal dialogue, no soul searching, no remorse - advertising was once unstoppable. A crazy, everyday art form that squished its powdered nose into our lives through a Sony Trinitron in the corner of the room or swaggered through the letterbox on a Sunday morning, pushing aside breakfast plates and cereal as people made room for the glossies and the supplements. It belched through lunch and didn't say pardon. It pushed hats off policemen, wore monocles to meetings and lost it's car for days on end. It was bigger than the banks (when it wasn't trying to buy them) and was the place that I, as an 11 year old boy transfixed on the BA advertising, knew I had to work.

So, whilst nicking a couple of extra mint imperials from the bill plate, I started to think who, or what, was to blame for this demise. Why *were* there so many shit ads out there? Why was my professional integrity being challenged? Did we tip appropriately?

Halfway home, it hit me - it's the client's fault. What the fuck do they know about great advertising? Of course, that's it. Nailed on.

Tell me, what do clients know about great advertising? Much of what my friend Chris sees is a classic product of 'Shit in, Shit out'. Read trade press descriptions of what a campaign was looking to achieve and be amazed at how the client is expecting a piece of advertising to deliver 3 or 4 different KPIs - then marvel as the ad is a derivative, pseudo-ironic, line by line execution of the brief. You know the kind - for 'prevents irritating bowel' read, 'Packaging lands on CGI-humanoid-bowel poking people with a stick in the street'.

Or clients, unfamiliar with their brand values and heritage, plump for Sunday-People-front-page-in-the-making celebrities, whose whiff of desperation at getting 250 TVRs on repeats is almost as strong as the client's need to use framed pictures of the shoot 'meet and greet' to lavish their small, open plan hamster cage at Plonk.Inc

Someone once told me that only 10% of a client's working time was available to work with agencies. And, boy, is it starting to show. The other 90% of time is heavily involved with talking to The Street, managing politics, writing reports, meetings, P&Ls and budget cutting. It's little wonder that when it comes to managing the ad process, many clients either palm it off to the junior or prescribe to the latter what it is they expect to see - all through the lens of 90% of their working life. Ads end up trying to do so much with one execution because they're being filtered through the unrealistic demands of every other department in the business. Advertising is glorious - it is the sexy part of the job - it's shoots, lunches, celebrity, parties, Soho, booze - everyone wants to have a piece of it - every department wants their 15 seconds of fame - and with 30 seconds in an ad, do the math (oh, of course Mrs.client, we can deliver a 120 second version and run it at 3am on S4C).

The Client, as David Ogilvy once said, is "getting the advertising that they deserve". Lazy, ill thought through, democratic, vanilla wallpaper. Where are the Clients that bought the old BA ads? What happened to the team that welcomed the baked-bean headed Tango man into their fold. Or those fun lovers at Hamlet and Carling who signed on the line for 2 of the most well remembered end lines of all time? Where did they go? What kind of hapless, hoofwanking suckers are deserving of the soulless pulp that adorns our screens (dual or otherwise) most nights now?

It really can't be as simplistic as that can it? In other words, can the Yellow-pencilled, Armani suited espresso-atti of adland wash their well-manicured, Aesop-lubed hands of any association with the disappointment of my friend Chris.

I think not.

You see, all of the greatest ads ever have outstanding ideas at the heart of them. Ideas with their clackers swinging in your face like a badly strapped ladyboy at Pride. They challenged society, insidiously changing language, behaviour and even media consumption. They spawned a myriad of playground, pub and dinner table spin offs. People would joke that they 'watched the ads more than they watched the TV'. And somewhere, we lost all of that. It's as if Advertising folded it's balls back into its Paisley Y-fronts and stopped challenging. For fear of failure; for fear of losing business;

for fear of political correctness, somewhere along the way, the advertising industry lost its balls.

Agencies have been complicit in this - they let some daylight into the magic. They promised to do things cheaper, to charge less at the pitch and to allow 'THOSE' changes just this once so that they could get an ad out of the door. Instead of telling the Client that it's not acceptable to 'know what you want when you see it', they've wimped out and instead, passive aggressively turned it into a cute little meme and pasted in on Facebook with 20 other 'Nightmare Client Comments' like some etch-a-sketch bully in an iPad world. They mothball bottom drawer ideas for fear of upsetting the apple cart and have diversified into every other discipline from 'retailtainment' to 'youthmatising' whilst doing exactly what they tell their clients not to do - losing their heartland…heart stopping, tear-welling, finger-lickin' idea generation.

Advertising is becoming a caricature of itself - desperately finding award after award to indulge in for mediocre work or for real outliers that, in decades gone past, would not have even graced their showreels. Whilst, in the digital world, clients can engage their own audience far more efficiently, cleverly and contextually with their own in-house expertise. They can tap into the smaller, nimbler, more creative agencies at will and capitalise on their own audience and reach to create stronger ideas, better and more convincing messaging and creativity. The big Agency model has lost its swagger. It's losing its heartland and is being eaten from within as smaller, more agile models come to light. The client is eating at the once sacred table and this is perpetuating the power clients have over the creative process.

It would appear that Advertising is getting the clients it deserves.

Chris wasn't interested in my stats on the way home. I told him I'd seen somewhere online that 89% of ads are not remembered. 7% are remembered and not liked and only 4% are remembered and liked. Why oh why (he said) be satisfied with being one of the 89%. Why aren't agencies and clients working together to get their ads in that magic 4%?

The dynamic of blame is what undermines trust, which in turn destroys creativity. The tea-bagging lunacy that was Advertising in its heyday was born of clients and agencies working for a common purpose in symbiotic relationships - a creative Yin, a commercial Yang, spooning each other in a loving, trusting marriage, not rutting like 2 Alpha teens in the back of mum's Ford Ka. The 10% was more like 50% and getting to understand your client's business wasn't test-driving the car for 20 minutes at the test track before tucking into a 6 course lunch - it was working with the mechanics at a service centre until you found that tiny rock that got polished into a creative diamond. Deserving work that sold on the premise of real insight, not a lazy interpretation of a poor brief.

Don't get me wrong, there are some recent examples of outstanding work where the relationships have been long-standing and the results are incredible. The diversity of media means that even more now, a well-formed idea has to be the bedrock of the creative output and then blown out across all channels. Weak ideas quickly fail and are ridiculed and 'turkeyed' faster than ever across social media that preys on those at the arse end of the Buffalo herd - those in the middle order enjoy the relative safety of the crowd but are one push away from the crocodile's jaws at the river crossing. Those at the front, the 4%, continue to lead, seeing the clear path ahead and forging their destination. They don't look back - they couldn't care less about the lions or the crocodiles. Their balls swing free.

As we opened the door to my flat, Chris said -

"So, you've sensationalised the start of this conversation to draw me in by slagging off clients and now you're telling me it's the agencies fault - make up your CRUNTING mind son"

"No", I said. "Well yes. And, shit, I've been both."

"You ought to know a thing or two then son - give me a few top tips"
he segued nicely.

It's not rocket surgery but it takes discipline, collaboration and real joint energy to make great ideas fly. In my experience, great ideas and advertising has, at its heart, disruption. The power to make you cry, buy or die (laughing, not literally - although that would be truly disruptive). That disruption has to be rooted in truth and executed aggressively. No half measures.

Firstly, there's no getting around it - Client and Agencies must work together to ruthlessly define and own the outcome they wish to see from the idea - it *has* to link back into some deep-seated truth about an opportunity that the business has seen to disrupt the status quo. Make their colleagues, consumers and competition squirm either with joy or fear as they focus solely on doing something incredibly powerful with the idea.

After that, Clients and Agencies need to embrace the idea of Wicked Problem solving, the sort of thing Stanford calls Radical Collaboration. That means getting together and interrogating what it is about the idea that is truly disruptive, ironing out problems, talking through incredible solutions, how it could permeate the business, impact different areas, provide brilliant solutions. I remember working with our lead agency on a project to better understand the customer journey for our brand. Once, collectively, we reframed it from a 'customer journey' to a 'customer's adventure', the play field suddenly opened and we were able to build incredible ideas for content, engagement channels and purchasing opportunities that shaped the way we would build ideas and business in the future.

This joint relationship has to crave simplicity - ask anyone who has done a TED talk - my friend told me that the crux of his 18 minute speech could be distilled into 8 words by the end. Great ideas and advertising does that and because it's so single minded, people get it every time.

Together, this unbreakable partnership needs to fight for creativity that powers business. George Lois will always tell you that a great idea is a great business tool - so often, either one of the parties forgets this, discipline slips and the execution of the idea loses the power that was bestowed upon it at the Wicked Problem stage. It becomes too generic, loaded with messages or just plain flabby. The creative thrust has to be as sharp as the disruptive truth that gave it birth - the combination of the 2 delivers the end result. It also needs to live and find homes across the business. Not as a bastard child but as a fully embraced newborn with whom everyone has an affinity. We would often create a manifesto for campaigns that would become ways of living the brand through the campaign - they'd permeate the business, changing people's views on how to make things happen, to communicate with customers or to live their lives. They became rallying cries, resonating and uniting an organisation across the world and bedding the ideas and advertising that followed with a series of fellows who had already fully embraced the passion of the single minded approach - I'll never forget how powerful Be Stupid became in reframing our Diesel business in that respect.

Finally, both parties must be hungry for results, feedback and the responsibility that brings. So many times I had been in meetings and there was a lack of visibility on both sides of each other's respective businesses models, expectations of results and joint ownership of both. Clients looking for huge upswings in sales revenue (the ads aren't working!) and agencies looking to run some extra 'films' for awards. When everyone's clear what constitutes success (as they should be from the start) then it makes absolute sense for everyone to want to celebrate that mutually earned and respected achievement.

So, in many ways there needs to be a disruption of the way clients and agencies operate in order that great, disruptive, behaviour changing ideas can be released. It's happening - 'Accelerator Units', small, agile networks that operate outside the hierarchy of the main business and that draw on outside, best in class thinkers, is an approach that some big clients are using. This is a great kicker to get the space required to do some of the stuff above that brings about disruptive work.

There's no hero or villain here. The simple truth is the real losers are those who see great ideas as part of the make up of society. Great advertising, like great beer, is the hallmark of a country. It mirrors, fuels and fucks up in equal measure the psyche of the nation. It is a benchmark for our humour, intellect and emotional state. It's light relief and social glue. It deserves, no demands, a return to the brave, fearless and downright crazy approach that delivered the greatest work. Advertising and marketing is not a place for the faint-hearted, the weak or the undeserving.

Of course clients know great ads, as do agencies. They both just need to give a fuck more often about what they put out.

"I couldn't give a shit" said Chris. "Where's the beer"

The Great Escape

By Seb Royce

I'd like to tell you something you probably already know but almost certainly don't do enough of.

It's a really simple, common sense thing. It's also an area that has been written and spoken about many times before, by people far wiser and more experienced than me. But perhaps precisely *because* it's so obvious and so simple to do, we often forget to or fail to make time for it.

And it's important to remind ourselves of why it's a good thing - and why it will always remain important for the job we do, in generating ideas, no matter how the world moves on or how advanced technology becomes.

It's all to do with inspiration and where best to look for it.

Ironically, if you work in advertising it is likely to be far more of a challenge for you. Because whilst a career in the creative side of the industry can be a hugely fun, stimulating and rewarding experience, it can also be an all-consuming job, confined by briefs and brand values - artful and agonising in equal measure. And it can be difficult to mentally switch off from that – which in turn can adversely affect the quality of ideas we have.

Each of us is only as creative as our imagination allows. We need to continually both feed that imagination and give it room to breathe, because it's really easy not to.

Advertising is still rapidly evolving for a whole host of well-documented reasons. In the last few years, there has been a lot of hand wringing about the 'death of industry'. It has sometimes been its own worst enemy - insular, derivative and at times shockingly self-reverential.

There was initially an apparent resistance or reluctance to change from the industry's more traditional ranks. This has been coupled with a perceived creative brain drain to more progressive start-ups or businesses. Although there is some truth in all of this, there are now pockets of genuinely progressive thinking within advertising.

As the industry continues to experience a fundamental shift in how it is planned, executed, delivered and received, one thing has remained the same - the need for great ideas.

What makes an idea 'great' is of course, a matter of opinion and endless debate.

Advertising builds its heroes by measuring and evaluating their ideas in relation to others within the industry. We love to judge each other's work. For a relatively small sector, we have an incredible number of awards ceremonies and competitions.

But in a broader world context, very few advertising ideas would make people's 'greatest ideas' list. And why would they? Generally speaking we are shifting product, which although critical in a business context, is not often doing a great deal to improve the world or promote a deeper purpose.

In relation to advertising ideas that are deemed to be great, we are still in an era where one of the central themes is Innovation. We have created 'Innovation Directors', 'Labs' and 'Hack-a-thons' to encourage innovative thinking in our work. We are utterly enthralled by new technology because we have come to the consensus that innovation in advertising is inextricably linked with that particular field. But of course, that isn't always the case.

If an innovation is understood as the introduction of something original or new and important, then how do we get to 'new, original and important' ideas that move beyond simply using technology in a different way?

If your frame of reference is mainly based on advertising and the usual sources of inspiration that everyone else in the industry is accessing, then your ideas will invariably be in danger of becoming derivative.

Equally, being preoccupied with what has already been created by your competitors, you are increasing your awareness of what already exists – and potentially even inhibiting your own creativity by an over focus on developing comparative or similar ideas.

Where's the creativity in that? Those ideas and executions are already out there. You won't find inspiration to be creative if you're only looking at things that have already been created.

The fact that the cliché marketing-speak phrase 'thinking outside the box' has been around for so long is quite revealing. It suggests the need for a continual reminder to think laterally.

I think we have created an industry that has become 'the box'.

We need to free ourselves from thinking about 'the box' at all. Escape. Let our minds wander, stop inhibiting and limiting ourselves by too much focus on ourselves and our peers.

If we shifted our gaze and broadened our perspective more often, beyond the industry and into the wider world – we would see with real clarity the introspection, navel-gazing and unhealthy judgement our industry can be affected by.

The real, jaw-dropping, eye-opening creativity is not happening in advertising at all – but it is happening elsewhere.

Leo Burnett said, 'Curiosity about life in all of its aspects… is still the secret of great creative people'. There are fantastically inspirational people and practices in hundreds of professions from art and architecture, to Fashion, Food, Music, Science, Sport and beyond. How much time do we really take to try and immerse ourselves in those worlds?

The natural curiosity that so many of us have by nature can be completely stifled and deadened by the 'production line' style demands of many briefs. Shorter and shorter deadlines, the pressure to produce ideas on demand, the expectation you will work insanely long hours for extended periods – no wonder it's tempting to take 'short cuts' when it comes to getting inspiration.

If we took the blinkers off for just a few seconds, I truly believe that we would not only realise what we've been missing, but create more genuinely innovative, engaging and effective ideas too.

This is not new thinking – far from it. But it is particularly important and pertinent in an age where the pace of change is being driven at incredible speed. And it is a real challenge for anyone working in an industry where the bubble we create for ourselves is at risk of becoming further and further out of touch with what is actually going on in the real world.

If you want creative 'greatness' look further afield. So many great ideas have been created when people take inspiration from outside their own field of interest.

It's a random example, but take underarm deodorants. They were inspired by the way ballpoint pens work – using a ball system to deliver an even flow of ink. This idea was adapted and used to provide an even flow of liquid deodorant, a development preferred to the old style sticks and sprays.

The ball deodorant revolutionised its industry, even though the kernel of the idea came from a completely different sector.

This lateral approach was something that Steve Jobs believed in.

"A broad set of experiences" he said "expands our understanding of the human experience. A broader understanding leads to breakthroughs that others may have missed".

If you have ever read anything on Jobs you'll know that he found inspiration in everything from a phone book, the fine details of a Mercedes-Benz, a food processor, The Four Seasons hotel chain, Zen meditation and India.

He didn't 'steal' ideas from them as much as use them to see things differently - to inspire his own creativity. In doing so, he consciously made the great escape from a narrow minded, heads-down approach, adopted by many of his peers – to a 'heads-up, look around you' approach, which as we all know, worked out pretty well for him....

Even with his passing, it seems that Apple continues to subscribe to that way of thinking. The hiring of the CEO of Burberry, Angela Ahrendts, at the beginning of 2014 illustrated that the company are looking to the fashion industry for inspiration, with Ahrendts bringing her considerable digital and social media knowledge to the company.

And when it comes off, the rewards can be great. The author Bob Roitblat wryly noted, 'Adopt a best practice from within your industry and you may be accused of industrial espionage. Borrow from another industry, and you are considered a creative genius'.

Back in ad world, there are now hundreds of vocational University degrees being offered. The danger of 'schooling out' creative inspiration or wrapping students in an advertising bubble right from the outset is more present than ever. Speaking about screenwriting and directing, Terry Gilliam (of Monty Python fame) said, 'There's so many film schools, so many media courses which I actually am opposed to. Because... you only know about cameras and 'the media', ... it's better learning about philosophy and art and architecture and literature, these are the things to be concentrating on...then, you can *fly*'.

So how and where to broaden your experience and be inspired to greatness? These days it all seems so easy. Search online for virtually anything and you can read up on it, watch videos, view galleries, see reviews, share it all, so that everyone else can see the same thing too. But this is predominantly information, not inspiration - and there is an important difference.

The Internet is not and never will be a substitute for the inspiration you can get through real world experiences, although it is tempting to think that it can be. Of course there will be times when we are going to use the Internet for inspiration. But the danger lies in simply marinating your brain in high profile advertising blogs and conversations day after day - because that is what will serve to dull your own creative angles. And when many of your peers are similarly watching and unintentionally mimicking the same few people, blogs, ideas and conversations, you'll end up with a head full of the same kind of content.

So have as much variation as you can via your daily feed, follow interesting people who have nothing to do with your job or your industry and read blogs and watch content that showcases highlights from across different industries.

For what it's worth, I'm currently hooked on @djhistory, veteran DJ Bill Brewster's brilliant and growing collectable dance music ecosystem of recommendations, discussions, parties and podcasts. I get daily inspiration from The Retronaut site @theretronaut. It's an awesome photographic 'time machine' of images and video with a new picture posted every hour. I have followed supersonicart.com for a while now. Really inspiring work from all over the world, all simply and cleanly presented. Fast Company's selection of blogs, feeds and sites are all well known. My favourite of them is fastcoexist, their environmental, energy and future facing section. @dailymash still has the capacity to make me laugh out loud. @shinyshiny gives me a light tech fix.

Vice still nails longer form topical video content…..

But getting out there and do things for real matters too.

Viewing a Picasso through Google is not the same as getting up close to the brush strokes in a hushed gallery. Watching a streamed football match at your desk is not the same as being in the stands surrounded by the energy and passion of thousands of fans. Checking out a music video is not the same as being at the gig for real, the air thick with smoke and beer and sweat dripping off the ceiling.

My humble view is that the best kind of inspiration comes through real, visceral experiences - not from those that have been streamed or downloaded. But you need to make time for these experiences and in order to do that you need to be pretty bloody-minded about it.

Your job will take all of your time if you let it. Ask anyone who has ever worked in advertising and they will tell you that there is no limit to how long or late you can work. The easy thing to do is to roll over and accept it as the way things are. But it isn't the way things have to be. Any forward-thinking creative boss should understand the need for their people to be creatively inspired. And if they don't, well you might want to find someone/somewhere that does. Lack of time for something that is going to make you better at your job is just not a valid argument.

Many ways of getting inspired involve minimum effort or time. Walk if you need to think. Turn your phone off, look up occasionally. See what's around you. Listen to music you know nothing about. Make a list of classic films you want to see and watch them on your commute. Cook a totally random recipe. Volunteer....

These have all worked for me, but anyone who believes that it is important to stay inspired will have their own ideas and things that work for them.

My advice is simply to try and do everything you can to make sure you explore people, places and experiences that are unfamiliar.

Of course we can all stay within our comfort zones and still get along fine, but our ideas will inevitably diminish in their impact and originality over time if we do. So keep an eye on your sources of inspiration, escape regularly from what you already know, learn new things and see how great your ideas can really become.

For a Handful of Change

By Jana Savic Rastovac

In recent years, it's become a rule that at least one Cannes Lion statue gets to travel to the Balkans. Make your pick: Romania, Macedonia, Serbia, Krakozia ... (ok, maybe not the last one. That's where "The Terminal" was set).

The campaigns that get to take the Lion home are bold, charming, and just a little bit exotic. Just like a wonderful safari ride. You never know when the monkey's going to make a cameo and steal your lunch.

The sceptics may attribute this democratisation of creativity to a whim of judges or to the ever-growing political correctness of advertising. Something along the lines of the gender-equal juries (ha), fair competition and "one world, one heart" policy.

Here's another thought: maybe the best and the brightest in advertising have grown tired, predictable and rigid. Some would even say that the soul, that indescribable thing, is missing.

All the while, it seems that there's a ton of soul brewing in the Balkans, among those god-forgotten, second-world, no-one-thinks-about-them-ever and no-one-mentions-them countries. It just happens that exactly there, in between Ceauşescu boulevards, cobblestone streets of Sarajevo and the provincial air of Ljubljana, is where the action is. Just because they have so little to lose, both in terms of reputation and next year's marketing budgets, creatives from the Balkans have become the bold and the beautiful of advertising.

This isn't a matter of global economic crisis, budget downsizing and never-ceasing questioning of the agencies' strategic and creative outputs. It's a matter of risk management.

High risk and great uncertainty sometime leads to great and groundbreaking innovations (think military strategy). Often, it leads to paralysis and a "let's not rock the boat" attitude. It leads to the culture of fear, conformism and aversion to doing anything new and different. It's the culture of change-phobia.

Fear, risk aversion, and conformism breed complacency and mediocrity. Complacency and mediocrity are the ultimate enemies of creativity (along with those gnarly account managers).

Big, global clients, with big, global markets don't help here. They are under this same economic pressure, and they seek solutions that will help them stay in the same excel spreadsheet column as the last year. Status quo is more desirable than doing worse.

We are witnessing a big money shift in advertising. It's very unlikely that the budgets would go back to the level of the legendary Pepsi commercials with Britney and Michael Jackson before her. The industry will just need to adapt.

But what happens to the long tail of this industry, which never had the budget for Britney Spears? This long tail has been for years working in markets so tiny that they needed to be bundled under the name of 'Eastern Europe' in order to make sense, profit-wise. The advertising professionals in this long tail know that their audience is so poor that only every fifth person will be able to afford the products they are advertising, shrinking their market even further.

Yet, they don't give up. They push and stretch their minuscule budgets, keep their brands on life support but alive, endlessly translate global brands into local copy, they are fast and nimble and stubbornly persistent. In recent years, they've done more than that.

They started winning. Constraints are the best friend of creativity. The can-do attitude is alive and well in the Balkans.

So, what's there to learn from the creatives working in Romania, Serbia, Croatia?

1. Think of a small budget as a blessing and an opportunity to stretch your creative muscle. If you have a big budget, ask: what would I do with the budget half this size? Then reduce it to half again, and see what you come up with. For example, McCann Belgrade promoted the Suicide Prevention Center's SOS line by projecting the message "You are not alone" onto the shimmering surface of the river Sava, which runs through Belgrade. This is an ultimate "moment of truth" advertising: the SOS number ended up right in front of the eyes of those who needed it. The campaign won a Bronze Lion in 2011.

2. Think of your team as a small, guerrilla force in the big jungle. Find your team's unique creative voice (a warrior chant) and start fighting against complacency. But never head-on. That's why you are guerrilla. Guerrilla's are sneaky: they find the holes, the hide behind the bushes, and they jump out to surprise everyone. Be a positive surprise factor in your agency, even if you often feel discouraged. For example, Y&R in Skopje organised a joint prayer of Muslims and Christians in the same room to promote tolerance amongst nations in Macedonia, a country where national and religious issues are of such high importance that this seemed almost impossible. Until it was made possible, in modest production value, by Y&R Skopje and awarded with Titanium Lion in 2013.

3. Always dare. Dare yourself first, then dare others. What's the worst thing that can happen? The client can decide that it's too risky. Find another client. You won't starve, daring work never goes unnoticed. But daring is best tested on smaller clients. Try that first. For example, think of a prank that McCann Romania won a Grand Prix for in 2012, where they put an American flag on the most popular chocolate bar in Romania. "Americanising" the iconic national brand for a short period of time was made possible

with a limited budget, unlimited trust between an agency and a client and the creative urge to make something extraordinary out of an ordinary tactical brief.

If this sounds too optimistic, that's because it is. If there's one thing to learn from us creatives in the Balkans, it's our relentless optimism. If we can bet against all odds, so can you.

We are also hungry. Unlike global well-awarded and well-known creatives, their Balkan colleagues are hungry for attention, for recognition, for being seen and heard. That's why we work harder (just like Avis). Maybe because we appeared so late on the global scene, we still have this great desire to prove ourselves to the world, and the entrepreneurial spirit to match. Just like any creative, we are mesmerized by the very act of creation. We strive to tell good stories, come up with great ideas to drive positive change, and yes, to win some more awards.

The difference between you and us is that we're desperate to be heard and seen. And you know what they say of desperate men and women ... they'd perform miracles for a handful of change.

CREATIVITY

The King is a Copycat [Too]

By Mark Earls [Part 1] and Dave Bedwood [Part 2]

Part 1

"There have been a lotta tough guys. There have been pretenders. And there have been contenders. But there is only one king." Bruce Springsteen

"He was a unique artist - an original in an area of imitators." Mick Jagger

Of all the icons of musical creativity in the 20th Century, Elvis Presley remains an original: from his early Rockabilly days with Sam Phillips' Sun Records, through his Hollywood period, to his gloriously overblown Vegas years, Elvis remains distinctly original and not just as a white man playing the blues (there were a number of those around Young Elvis' Memphis). The great classical composer and conductor, Leonard Bernstein was unstinting in his estimation of Elvis' impact, in his view:

"Elvis is the greatest cultural force in the twentieth century. He introduced the beat to everything - music, language, clothes - it's a whole new revolution. The '60s comes from it."

He changed the course of popular music with his musical choices and his vocal stylings – the Reverend Al Green, one of the greatest soul and R&B writers and performers of all time, suggests that:

"Elvis had an influence on everybody with his musical approach. He broke the ice for all of us."

And as both James Brown and Jackie Wilson noted, his act became the template for many black artists whose music he loved:

"A lot of people have accused Elvis of stealing the black man's music, when in fact, almost every black solo entertainer copied his stage mannerisms from Elvis."

Rod Stewart sees a more direct influence:

"People like myself, Mick Jagger and all the others only followed in his footsteps."

The one and only
Elvis' physical appearance – be it as the beautiful Sun-era hoodlum, the mid-era cheesecake (Warhol rightly picked out Gunslinging Elvis to play with) or the bloated jump-suited beast of the latter years – still seems so unique. Most of us have at some time tried out an Elvis move and vocal mannerism (an "uh-huh" or a "vair march") and most of the time our efforts are rewarded with recognition. Impersonating ("paying homage") to the King is no new phenomenon – France still just about has it's own Elvis (Johnny Halliday) and Britain has both Cliff Richard, whose early career was built on Elvis impersonation, and a host of others (including Cardiff's own Michael Barrat AKA Shakin' Stevens who styled himself on Truck Driver Elvis, wobbly leg and everything). You don't have to look far to see Elvis in today's leading performers – Alex Turner, frontman of the Arctic Monkeys has recently (like so many before him) restyled himself as a young Elvis-a-like.

Even today some 37 years after his death, Elvis remains one of the favourite fancy-dress choices around the world and the basis of many a night-club act: at various times and in various places, I've seen Chinese, Sikh, Jamaican, Bangladeshi and Thai Elvis impersonators. Recently the "Elvies" (an annual festival of Elvis impersonation held in the South Wales holiday resort of Porthcawl) managed to break the world record for the simultaneous performance of 942 Elvises (singing "Hound Dog" of course).

Copycat Elvis

You'd think then, that for Elvis to be "The King", to be "The Original", "The One and Only" he'd need to be, and do, original and different at every turn.

Interestingly, the truth is otherwise: Elvis wasn't even his mother's only son – he was one of a pair of identical twin boys to be delivered to Gladys Presley on January 8th 1935. Sadly Jesse Garon Presley was born stillborn and Elvis remained an only child for the rest of his life.

His music was far from original – the early swampy mix of blues, country and gospel emerged from the stew of all those gamblers, hustlers and musicians drawn from across the Mississippi delta to downtown Memphis. Indeed, the story goes that on his first session at Sun Records, it was only by accident that the hard-paced rockabilly sound was spotted. Elvis, Scotty Moore & drummer Bill Black were mucking around while a tape was being changed, racing through a fast cover version of the old country tune, "Blue Moon of Kentucky". "That's it", came a voice from the control room – "that's the sound!" Over the years, his love of gospel styles (learned especially from family visits to the Tupelo Assembly of God *Church*) became more and more clear and visible, as did his love of sentimental ballads of all sorts.

While in later years, his management twisted the arms of songwriters to hand over a share of publishing credits to the Big Man for him doing the favour of recording their tracks (including, unsuccessfully the stony-hearted Dolly Parton) Elvis was essentially a covers artist – using other people's music as the basis of his art. For example, while you may think "Hound Dog" as a Presley tune, it was written 4 years before Elvis' cover by 19-year-old songwriters Jerry Leiber and Mike Stoller and was a hit for blues singer Willie Mae "Big Mama" Thornton in 1953, spawned a handful of country-style covers and a bizarre selection of "response" and spoof records (including "Bearcat" with re-written lyrics by Sun's own Sam Phillips).

It appears that Elvis was particularly taken by the tempo and the verve of the version played and recorded by Vegas lounge act Freddie Bell & the Bellboys: "When we heard them perform that night, we thought the song would be a good one for us to do as comic relief when we were on stage. We loved the way they did it." noted guitarist Scotty Moore. So Elvis and the boys copied it and made it their own.

His clothes were not especially original or novel either: from his earliest days hanging around in Memphis, Elvis' loved the street fashion he saw from the cosmopolitan, and somewhat shady crowd that gathered on Beale Street. Local shopkeeper and tailor Bernard Lansky dressed Elvis throughout his career – as he got more famous, Lansky and his brother either closed the original Beale Street shop so that Elvis could shop unmolested by his fans, or took armfuls of "real sharp" threads up to Graceland for the King to select his own. Lansky's influence on Elvis lasted nearly 25 years: "I put his first suit on him and his last suit on him," he boasted. Over that time, Lansky introduced him to the latest street-sharp looks in Downtown Memphis. From the peg-leg pants and boxy jackets of the early days through the leather jumpsuit of the '68 comeback TV special and the white all-in-ones of the Vegas and Hawaii era – all of these looks Lansky borrowed from what hustlers and gangsters were wearing in that one small Southern city. And helped Elvis to do the same, too.

It's not even that his name is all that original (although it may seem now to us that there could never be another Elvis): it's no "moonunit" (the name Frank Zappa gave to one of his unfortunate children). Indeed, analysis of the historical record suggests that the name was already in decline in the US when Elvis was christened. And as our own Dylan Thomas impersonator, Rory Sutherland, points out, Elvis is a Welsh name. It is the name of the bishop who baptised the future patron saint of God's Own Country, St David. This is why the original Church of St Elvis is not to be found in Memphis or Vegas, but on a windswept Pembrokeshire hillside, within reach of the city of St Davids and in sight of the Irish Sea.

"Before Elvis, there was nothing" *John Lennon*

So what does all this Elvisology have to tell us about creativity and originality?

Well, first and most importantly, it's clear that copying and originality aren't polar opposites: being original and doing original work is often best achieved by using the power of copying. Elvis was a covers act, whose musical stylings were borrowed and honed through practice and accident. His iconic appearance was the result of borrowed fashions and styles. Even his name – perhaps the most "unusual" aspect of the piece – turns out to have a long, borrowed history. Elvis is not a fake but he is a copycat and that's what makes him and his music so original.

Other creative minds have long appreciated this simple truth about making original things: Sir Isaac Newton may possibly have been the most self-regarding of all physicists but even he was forced to admit that Descartes and Robert Hooke's work on the science of Optics had provided the basis of his own much acclaimed work.

"If I have seen further than most it is because I have stood on the shoulders of giants."

The Scientific Method – with its focus on experimentation, transparency, peer review and verification through experiment – has enabled science to advance by providing a reliable way for scientists to use each other's work (rather than just rely on authority and reputation).

While in our world we tend to disdain people who copy and work that is clearly copied from other work ("derivative", "pastiche" or "rip-off"), there are folk like the brilliant Faris Yakob who have challenged this: Faris' blog puts the famous Picasso dictum that 'talent copies, genius steals' to work to champion and explain "remix culture" and sampling.

Take the Amen break – a 4 bar drum sample from the b-side of the 1969 single by the Winstons, titled "Amen Brother" (sic) which is probably the most sampled piece of music ever. It was originally shared by hip-hop pioneer DJ Breakbeat Lenny on the first of his Breakbeat sample compilation albums in 1986. Slowed down, it became the basic rhythm track for early hip-hop; speeded up, it's the template for dubstep and drum and bass, and in between it became a mainstay of 90s dance music, even getting sampled by the Gallagher brothers. Taking a piece of someone else's stuff and using it, collage-style, is one way of using copying to create something new that is now an accepted part of contemporary culture.

But another – more important and more widespread – use of copying to create original work is described by the poet TS Eliot. All poets copy, but it's how you copy – not if you copy - that signals the poetry's quality:

"One of the surest tests is the way in which a poet borrows. Immature poets imitate; mature poets steal; bad poets deface what they take, and good poets make it into something better, or at least something different."

On the one hand, there's Single White Female copying – where accuracy of replication seems to be important; then there's what you might think of as "sort of" looser copying. This has a really important scientific basis: when a copy is looser, it creates error and it's in the error and variation that the value for a creative person or enterprise emerges. Mistakes in copying – like Elvis's speeded-up "Blue Moon of Kentucky" – are where the juice is.

This is clear in genetics and evolution: when your parents bumped uglies to create the amazing unique individual that is you, they produced a mixture of their own genetic material – or rather, copies of their genetic material. It's the miscopying in this that is responsible for your uniqueness (and as far as the species is concerned, the variation that makes it possible for the evolutionary forces of selection to operate – without variation, selection becomes a very black and white affair).

If you've ever played the "Chinese whispers" line game with me, you'll know how rapidly copying a simple gesture along a line can create innovation and transform the original thing.

Of course, this is not what we normally mean by "copying" – we tend to think about copying either as deceit (think of forger Tom Fielding's "Sextons" or of George Harrison's "My Sweet Lord" which – so the circuit judge thought – was unconsciously copied from Ronnie Mack's original "He's so fine"); or, think about copying in terms of producing the same old, same old. The business school notion of "benchmarking" tends to produce just this kind of bad copying result: again and again, when key players in an industry benchmark themselves against each other, this will tend to commoditise the market, producing interchangeable products, processes and services.

What's needed is looser copying – copying making errors – rather than Single White Female copying.

Far far away
The other way to access this power of looser copying is to copy from far away. Again, T.S.Eliot put it clearly:

"A good poet will usually borrow from authors remote in time, or alien in language, or diverse in interest"

Rather than copy from your immediate peers, copy from as far away as possible. If everyone's copying Korean filmmakers, look at Argentinian or African sources – anything to get away. If everyone's design is aping Apple, who are you going to look for as your source material?

In my work, I've turned this into a whole approach to solving problems: together with my collaborators, I've collated some hundred different types of strategy, each of which has been successful in a particular context (from Frederick the Great teaching the Prussians to eat potatoes to Apple making their users advertise the popularity of their music players by using white earbuds).

Rather than following the traditional reductionist approach (where there must be only one answer to the client's unique problem), we ask first *what kind of problem* is this and then use the 25 or so strategies appropriate for that kind of problem to act as start-points. This pushes the thinking as far as possible away from the problem we're thinking about and whatever rules might be the norm for people working in the space.

And if my observations about how people use this archive is correct, it seems that having several potential sources is important in making the copying looser. In innovation projects, my chum John Willshire does the same thing with a game he calls "popular thing – broken thing", which encourages problem solving by using a whole range of different successful answers – sometimes at least, we need to shake off our habitual solutions and force ourselves to look at a wider range of source materials.

This is where that old practice of scrap-booking is so useful: noticing and recording things you find interesting and useful, and then forcing yourself to apply them as source material to any problem that comes your way, creates the opportunity for error and variation. The more different things you can copy from and the further away they are from your problem, the better because you're creating more error.

Alex's top tips:

My friend and co-author Professor Alex Bentley first opened my eyes to the importance of copying, so I thought it only appropriate to ask him for his tips on copying and creativity (one of the core subjects of his Anthropology and Archaeology studies). And for me to pass them off as my own.

1. Get over the idea that copying is cheating.
    Yes, when you discover all of the movie plots identical to Avatar, it's hard not to think worse of the movie and its creator. But loose copying and copying from far away really do create error and variation and it helps you see the problem from new angles rather than the same old way. It's also something that humanity have long done – Anthropologists distinguish between "invention" (what we would normally think of as creativity) and "innovation" (using copying to create variation and error and thus new 'stuff').

2. Get over the idea that copying makes you a cheat.

   Copying is a natural as breathing – we do it from the moment we are born and it becomes our species' #1 learning style. The ability to use the brains and behaviour of those around us – to outsource the cognitive load, as the scientists put it - is one of the central evolutionary advantages that our species has. Just don't be a Single White Female.

3. Not copying is cheating yourself.

   In his recent Reith lecture, transvestite ceramicist Grayson Perry points out that "Originality is for those with short memories". All those ideas and suggestions are out there in the world, waiting for you to use them – why ignore them and insist that you have your own idea. Is it really worth it? Yes, you may be a genius but even then it's probably a better bet to start elsewhere.

Ask yourself this: if copying is good enough for Elvis, why isn't it good enough for you?

Part 2

Note on part 2 from Dave Bedwood.

My chapter is a riposte to Mark's. Mark has talked about copying and originality and how error and copying from a distance allows interesting ideas and shapes to emerge.

So we decided that I'd take his essay and copy it.

I introduced error by copying it and then copying it from memory, adding to it, slowly erasing Mark's original, and copying it again, putting it all through Google translate several times and then rewriting it to make that nonsense make some sense again.

200 OK

{
    "data": {
    "translations": [
       {
              "translatedText": "He kissed hard, there have been
contenders, but I love the King " [Bruce Springsteen]

He urinated on Fred - [Mick Jagger]

Elvis Presley did innovation in bucket loads of original music for the 20th century, from rockabilly with Sam Philips, to singing loudly.

Elvis was playing the blues in Memphis for 10 cents a ride. Classical train conductor Leonard Bernstein exerted the influence of Elvis: "From my point of view he was a football fan, a beautiful women from Brazil on a tricycle. Thanks to the introduction of blow and its greater strength in the 20th century - a new revolution comes in the 60's: language, music, clothing and knives".

The author Reverend Al Green suggests Elvis is one of the best artists of the R & B and soul category at any time, redefining the landscape and that includes Marty Pellow:

"If Elvis was a sandwich he'd be a bowl of hot soup instead."

James Brown and Jackie Wilson were able to create an Elvis model out of Angel Delight. This was copied by Michael Jackson and Prince, who Elvis loved. He often listened to Smooth Criminal whilst playing squash, even though it hadn't been written at the time.

Some say Elvis stole black music and never gave it back. But Kenny Everett sees a more direct influence: "I wouldn't of copied Rod Stewart if he hadn't of copied Elvis. In that sense I was following in Elvis's footsteps, but with an inflatable arse"."

},
    {

        "translatedText": "The one and only

Chesney Hawkes wrote this song staring at his Dad (original title: I'm not even an e-mail sample like all the rest). From the Sun-era hoodlum, to bloated white jump-suited beasty (brilliantly played by John Candy in the never to be released: Eating Baby Elvis) Elvis appears unique, and paying homage to the King is nothing new.

Johnny Hallyday was so French popular, he became property of the French Government, who then sued the Elvis estate for copyright infringement. Front man Anthea Turner of some frothy band had an Elvis gilet. Finally, Cliff Richard, a bus driver in the UK, quit his job for a shot at singing nothing like Elvis at a rain drenched tennis installation.

Yesterday, 137 years after his death, Elvis was the number one costume worldwide. I found an Elvis in China, Japan, with Sikhism, Jamaica, Bangladesh and a Thailand parody. South Wales has its own world record each year with 98.3 % of its population performing "Hound Dog" simultaneously. However 0.213 people were murdered via botulism by the neighbouring village. It had been attempting to make the world's biggest cheeseburger."

},
    {

        "translatedText": "Copycat Elvis

You'd think then, that Elvis is "The King" by dint of creative willpower; by being original and different at every turn. The truth is quite different: Elvis was not even the only son of his mother. He was an identical twin. Sadly Jesse Garon Presley was born stillborn and Elvis remained an only child for most of his life.

Someone said that his music was also scared of originality. It had been around forever, the ingredients cooking in huge pot that was sat just above the boiling Mississippi river. The pot fed most of the population but Elvis was the one that got scolded with the thick stew of blues, country and gospel. According to legend Leather Elvis and his band - 'the Jock-straps' were bang out of cash in the studio, so they played faster. They thought they'd made a pigs ear out of it (Memphis slang for "bollocks").

Sam Phillips was in the control room shooting billiard balls with a revolver called John Wayne. When he heard this new sound he put the revolver down and began to cry into his beetroot.

Later that day Elvis went to church and had his ears flushed with gospel. Church was popular back then, before the second coming of Richard Dawkins. This Gospel juice was injected into Elvis, much like hedge fund management being injected into babies of today.

In later years, his management twisted the arms of songwriters. Only a few were ever hospitalised, and no records of these can be found. All shared their publishing credits with the Big Man.

Even his biggest song "Hound Dog" was a stolen treasure. Written by two buff offenders as a nursery rhyme for their prison warden's deceased dog. The warden would whistle the tune whilst beating up, and was overheard by another inmate, who in turn sold it to a very large lady called Paul. Once Sam Philips heard this version he put down his revolver and cried into his beetroot.

But copying also took a more direct root. Archeological dogs revealed that Elvis loved the tempo and the verve of the version recorded by the boy band Las Freddie Bell and Bell boy Elvis. "We heard what they were doing. The behaviour of the comic scene at a time, and the only good thing is that I love the way they did it". Said a totally pissed guitarist Scotty Moore. So the guys copied the way Las Freddie shook it and Elvis had an act!

His clothes were also not the original. You see all types of hustler spoofing, shake if you want to hang in stores near Beale Street, Memphis. One man, for the first time, configured this mixture to achieve the President of sewing: Samuel Lanksy. Elvis and his 'myopia' Samuel was short with blindness, but long on style kindness. Lanksy wanted to create something new in fashion again. He knows how to use the first and the last, and the fact that Elvis was neither. Black on the edge of a sports car? Just normal Lanksy. He had a hand in all the Elvis costumes, especially the black 66 iconic Hawaiian word for skin. On the other hand, it wears well at 80.

Elvis' threads were about as original as his name. It certainly is no "Terraferma" (the name Frank Zappa's son Moon Unit gave to one of his unfortunate daughters).

You should look at history, the name Elvis was in slow decline by the time of his birth. We think this was to do with the rise in mercury in the water, which makes it difficult to pronounce the 'issss' sound. Designer Issay Miyake to this day, when visiting the Memphis region, believes people cannot hear or understand him.

In fact, honoured member of the advertising world is Sir Rodney Dangerfield, remembering for us that Elvis is actually the original name of Wales. It was also the name of the head of a religious man, who played squash with the church vegetables, his favourite, of course, being squash. After the house of a straw man, and the spirit of the game, religious education is very high in the Pembrokeshire Coast."
},

{
        "translatedText": "Before Elvis, there was nothing" [John Lennon]

Even now originality, creativity and Elvisology are inseparable. Is it possible to not live in the shadow of an idea by someone else?

Now, for starters, it's clear that copying and originality are not complete opposites. Some of the most original work uses the power of copying. Elvis was a cover artist, but later on became covered.

Thus, repeating again and again, like a Xerox, becoming faint, corrupted, damaged, gaps appearing for a variety of new ideas and opinions to seep in. This happened with his fashions, his name, his songs, his photocopier. Elvis is not a fake a foogayzi a fugarzi, he's a copycat, but one with the correct intent and this makes him so original. He's not trying to be a carbon copy. That's why his imitators are so unoriginal today. He was taking stuff, combining and moving it to a sparkly box that we decided to label 'originality'.

Sir Issac Newton a physicist and inventor of the Issac C5 appreciated this. He admits his work at Apple could not have happened if it were not for Descartes and Captain Robert Hook - inventor of the touch screen.

"If I have seen further than most it is because I have stood on the solar plexus of Andre the Giant".

Which Noel Gallagher stole for his band Oasis' fourth and best flavoured water.

Let's not forget that the Scientific Method focuses on experimentation, transparency, peer review and verifiability through experiment. Which has enabled it to advance by providing a reliable way for scientists to use each other's work. Rather than relying instead on the power of Stephen Hawking's thinly veiled threats.

Alas in the world of advertising, there is a tendency to focus on those that have copied, and hate them. But there are folk like the brilliant Faris Yakult (he accidentally created healthy pots of bacteria whilst trying to invent the post-it note) who have challenged this. To maximise the talent of copying check the famous adage by Picasso: "Picasso, engineering, master, and blog describing knight exhibitions. Steal and love remix Culture!" Music songs take the Amen break Sample, a 4 bar drum sample from the b-side of the 1969 single by the Winstons (title "Amen Brother" sic). Which is probably the second most sampled piece of music ever. The first being the 'Oooh Danone!" global sound stamp.

>data error:

But then - there is a broader and more important point - explains T.S Elliott. All poets copy, but it's how you copy – not if you copy - that signals the poetry's quality. This is not a copy:

"Test, it is a sure way to make a tradition of poet immature poet, but the poet is excellent, the bad poet to destroy and steal ... it takes a mature poet not to, repeat. But steal". Which aptly enough, is sort of what Oscar Wilde said.

On the other hand, it is all possible infertility. This can be seen in the 2042 meta-classic remake of the 1992 film Single White Female. The director copied every single frame of the original film, which was about a girl copying her roommate. Nothing is added – just accuracy of replication is important. Then there's what you might think of as "Sort of" looser copying. This has a really important scientific basis: when a copy is looser, it creates error and it's the error and variation that the value for a creative person or enterprise emerges. Mistakes in copying – like Elvis's speeded-up "Blue Moon of Kentucky Fried Plantation" – are where the juice is. Ride that Xerox copier until it prints out a page with the words MERCY! written across it in 72pt Aerial bold.
This program is an important step. Including copies with lack of effort by the minimum resistance, to ensure the safety and health. Show your loyalty and give a choice in this world. But all I can get is the right to clean everything in a blender, and others think that vomiting is nothing new.

This is clear in genetics and evolution. When your parents played hide the sausage to create the amazing unique individual that is you, they produced a mixture of their own genetic material. Or rather copies of their genetic material. It's the miscopying in this that creates the unique individual that is you. And as far as the species is concerned, it's this variation and error that allows Jeremy Kyle IX to create such a vibrant televisual show and parliament.

Another example of this is the game Chinese whispers. I did one in a school where a gesture was rapidly copied from one person to another, something simple. Each translation and turn the gesture changed. Michael took the painting of my friend, but try a bowl of Yakult suspended by the teacher. Ironically, after the invention of the class teacher. The result is something original, nothing like the first sentence and completely unrecognisable.

I think in the 80's Philip Scholfield tried to look like Tom Cruise in Top Gun depression. I think the game or boring in terms of production and the same old, same old. They tend to be the roof of the Faculty of Business Administration of the poor to produce "model" long-copy only: Branchenreferenzgegeneinanderals and very important player in commoditise comes on the market, however, on several occasions, it is the services that I produce and processed beats I eat.

What's needed is looser copying. Copying with errors, that take thoughts and ideas all over the place, rather than Single White Female copying (meta masterpiece aside)."
},
        {
                "translatedText": "Far far away

Copy loose mother fucka! How can you make this shit juice happen? Intent is one way, when a person is seeking to be original, even if we know that that is not possible, the intent to keep digging, finding new connections will result in a looser copying and more error.

One way is to copy from a great distance. Keep on digging till you are far far away. Eliot again put it clearly:

"A good poet will usually borrow from authors remote in time, or alien in language, or diverse in interest"

Or more profoundly but with less sense: "Reporters for another loan to keep the author or a foreign language at a time"

Include as much as possible, please never copy your closest friends. If someone copies Koreon filmmakers then copy Peru or Africa or goats and Egyptian traders. Anything to pull you away, and when you drag it back into your problem your kaleidoscope will have more fractures in it, and more chance of making interesting patterns. If everyone has just Apple Inc in their kaleidoscope, add a few shards of something else, an architect like Ludwig Mies van der Rohe or a pipe maker from Dudley.

In my professional life I've and be able to amass an arsenal of 100 strategies, from the Russian King who made a lot of people eat a lot of potato chips. To Apple and its white headphone 'earvertising' massacre.

I take these strategies and apply them to new problems. It forces new thinking, and takes us far away from the usual ONE ANSWER approach. It's copying in a loose way, error leading to cupid in an apache helicopter outside a speed dating convention.

If in doubt, sit down, undo your top button and ask yourself "What would Elvis do?"
    }
  ]

What do we know About Love?

By Erkki Izzara

Our job is to make people love stuff. The main tools we use are intuition and humour. The way we organise ourselves to do the job is through layers of creative teams and directors. The higher we are in the food chain, the smaller the chances we meet the people we're trying to charm. So, how can we claim that we know anything about their love?

I met a real person, an actual consumer, for the first time in 2008. The night before, the thought started creeping upon me. For the first time in years, I was nervous for professional reasons – less confident than before meeting any CEO. Getting to sleep was harder than before any first date.

I would meet a student girl at her home. I only knew one thing about her: she couldn't afford the product we were working for. She was picked because she was a fan. Would I really be able to talk with her about ideas and professional views? Would it be a waste of time? Or, would ad-talk make me look like an idiot? It'd probably be an embarrassment to everyone.

Meeting people, discussing ideas with them, and observing them in their own environment is what designers call design ethnography. We at 358 implemented it into advertising work. We called it co-creation. We weren't the first ones to use the word but, to my knowledge, our real-life office-wide experiment of bringing ad making and product making together was a first.

Art Directors and Copywriters share the title of "Creatives", but the way to make advertising is so established that the C-word is hardly the best one to describe it. Why did we want to challenge, and eventually change, the way we work? We wanted to understand what people really think about the companies we worked for. Research gives you answers to the questions you ask but a chat can give you something you don't know you need to know.

Many creative minds get to ideas through discussing. If you do that only by staring at the sneaker soles of your partner, you're missing an opportunity. Talking to recruited consumers at their own homes can make your head spin in just the right way. Loads of ideas start pouring out and you need to hurry-hurry-hurry to write them down.

The result could be all kinds of ideas – both traditional advertising ideas and unconventional things that could be interpreted as advertising: an app, a festival, new packaging, a service, or even a tweak to the product itself. Our first motto at 358 was "anything that helps people like a company is advertising".

Our second motto was a little more empathic: "We help people and companies to like each other." The bit that made the real difference was "each other". No love catches fire as fast as an ad man's love to the product that he's assigned to work with.

But do we love the people who're supposed to love the product?

We have to adapt our love to them to make them love us back. Most of us are convinced that our own sense of humour is the best (ad men seem to be even more convinced than others). Those who are right get pretty far. But if you can adjust your humour to the target group... you're considered a sell-out! And that's scary. An ad man should never have a recognisable style. If you do, you can only hope the clients who really need your style will find their way to you. If not, you'll be neck-deep together with architects and other style-nazis – sooner or later you're alone defending your own aesthetics.

Talking about ideas with people outside advertising serves both as inspiration and a reality-check. It helped me avoid several stupidities. For example, I might have suggested printing pictures of money on the floor of a supermarket for a campaign. Co-creation made me understand the customers would have felt intimidated.

After the chats with the consumers, we distilled insights from all the quotes and ideas in "synthesis sessions". They often led to solid and understandable common sense strategies. A CEO of a bank once said: "These are just like my own thoughts but written better".

When we reach out to people for help, inspiration and ideas, it doesn't mean we're handing over the steering wheel. Both agencies and companies still need strong decision makers. Informed decision making just makes more sense. Especially when it comes to love affairs. Why give tulips to someone who likes lilies?

In this case, love is not just a two-way thing. It's a threesome between people buying the products, marketers and product makers.

To understand product making, imagine a diagram. I've borrowed it from the guys we hired from IDEO. Can you see the classic three circles that all overlap each other? A successful product needs to be a) technically feasible, b) financially viable and c) desirable!

These days, everybody is so aware of financial realities that we can skip viability for now. Technical feasibility is traditionally the job of R&D guys and engineers. Desirability is often left to marketers alone.

Once, a Marketing Director briefed me by showing a comic strip that said: "Now, do the trick called marketing!" He basically outsourced desirability.

Designers think about both desirability and feasibility. Sometimes they are also great marketers, but more often not. Regardless of how good they are, they should always be involved.

Together the whole gang should go to meet the people who use their products. We gathered the troops to understand where the music business is going to sell beer. We also did it to develop an alternative to beer … and for beef. We explored the category boundaries of a fishing brand while pitching for it. We found out that a design brand was mostly bought as a gift. And we built the whole marketing strategy of an operator around 'recommending' because they had the happiest customers.

What happens during this processed chatter is as important as the outcome. The whole gang gets shared understanding of the consumer; they start to share empathy. What do people need? What do they think about us? Why is that student girl our fan?

Companies are not empathic by nature. They're companies. You need that process and shared principles to become empathic. This leads us to the last motto of the day. "Implementing empathy" was kind of the "Intel inside" slogan for us. Without empathy there is no love.

I ain't Gonna Work on Maggie's Farm no More

By Sam Ball

You have been brainwashed.

As soon as you can walk you are told what to do. Then you are put into school, a place with more rules and regulations. You are told what to wear, when to talk, and when to eat. They clip your wings and prepare you for a solid and respectable job. Has a careers adviser ever advised anyone they should be a stuntman, artist, or rock 'n' roll star?

You make it through the system and you think you're free. The world is your oyster. Then you find out that the brainwashing continues throughout your career, and now it's even worse because you have the added pressures of paying your rent or raising a family. Your bosses and colleagues will persuade you that conformity is the best thing for you to progress your career. Don't rock the boat, keep your head down and work hard and you could make regional manager. They will, over time, brainwash you so that your main motivation is security: "I've got a good job. I don't want to get fired. How will I put food on the table?" This fear will blind you as hundreds of opportunities whoosh by.

I am not painting the picture of some corporate drone. I am talking about the creative industries. Music, architecture, art, theatre, dance, the movie business... I don't claim to be an expert on any of these, but do I know a thing or two about advertising. I can confidently say if you were to visit any advertising agency in the world, you'd think that 80% of people who are working there are simply going through the motions. Their motivation to create new things has been replaced by conformist habits and patterns.

The great brainwashed make the "world go round" but they never really change it. For that we need the troublemakers. The troublemakers aren't smarter than you, they are not luckier, and they are not bestowed with any unique powers. Things don't come easy to them. What separates them from everyone else is they couldn't give a f%^& about the consequences of their actions.

People will want you to be who you already are

It was July 1965 and a nervous Bob Dylan, the greatest folk singer of his generation, was about to walk out onstage and make the biggest statement of his career. To the 20,000 folk purists, Bob was their hero, prophet and mystic poet. It would have rocked them to the core when he plugged in his Fender Stratocaster, cranked up the volume and ripped into an electrified version of Maggie's Farm.

As they stood there and watched they felt betrayed. Their blood boiled and a barrage of boos and jeers followed. Did Dylan give a fuck? No, he kept on playing. This was a man breaking away from the traditional folk label that had been slapped on him. Dylan was breaking away not by picking the lock and sneaking out, but by blowing the bloody doors off. It was no coincidence he chose to open that set and declared his independence with Maggie's Farm, a song that is often interpreted as the oppressive nature of the folk music scene.

In the first verse Dylan sings;
"I have a head full of ideas that are driving me insane,
But it's shame the way she makes me scrub the floor"

How many times have you been driven insane by a client who wants what everyone else is doing, despite starting the project with the now hollow ambition of wanting "the very best ideas you have"?

For all their anti-establishment leanings the people who booed that night wanted their singing talisman to remain the same. They wanted the times not to change but to remain exactly how they were. His fans didn't grasp the fact that he had to keep moving, that he had little respect for the status quo.

Dylan's success didn't come simply because he was a master of words, it came because he wasted no time attempting to gain things like acceptance, attention and praise. Bob Dylan was a rebel. The greatest revolutions in arts, politics, culture or indeed anything for that matter, have been achieved by rebels.

It's ok to be afraid

What's stopping more people acting like Dylan? Because of this constant brainwashing we are becoming slaves to fear. And how does fear manifest itself? Fear stifles our thinking and our actions. It creates indecisiveness that results in stagnation. You procrastinate indefinitely rather than risk failure. Here is the biggest revelation of this chapter, nay, here is the biggest revelation of this book. It is so important that you must read it ten times in a row. Don't cheat. When you come to the end of the chapter, come back and read it another 10 times before moving on.

You can be afraid and confident at the same time.
You can be afraid and confident at the same time.
You can be afraid and confident at the same time.
You can be afraid and confident at the same time.
You can be afraid and confident at the same time.
You can be afraid and confident at the same time.
You can be afraid and confident at the same time.
You can be afraid and confident at the same time.
You can be afraid and confident at the same time.
You can be afraid and confident at the same time.

Mike Tyson, a man who routinely cast his life and soul to the altar, is one of the finest students of the unique duality of confidence and fear.

"When I come out I have supreme confidence. But I'm scared to death. I'm afraid. I'm afraid of everything. I'm afraid of losing. I'm afraid of being humiliated. But I'm confident. The closer I get to the ring the more confident I get. The closer, the more confident. All during training I've been afraid of this man. I think this man might be capable of beating me. I've dreamed of him beating me. For that I've always stayed afraid of him. The closer I get to the ring the more confident I get. Once I'm in the ring I'm a god.

If the toughest motherfucker on the planet can be confident and afraid at the same time, then so can you. Let's not piss around, this revelation should change how most of us behave. If you're not worried, scared or ever so slightly shitting it, chances are you're not trying hard enough. In fact, scrap that. You're part of the problem.

Without confidence you make decisions based on fear. With confidence you make decisions in spite of fear.

If you go through your advertising carrier with confidence and fear I can guarantee you will go further, but more importantly you will have more fun doing it. However, a rebellious attitude will mean you will lose business from time to time, but losing business isn't the worst thing to happen to an agency, it's the manor in which you lose business that's important. Take these two examples:

The first is how my agency lost The Royal Air Force account. We had this fantastic campaign that tugged at the heart and raised the spirits of our young audience in a fresh, contemporary way. It had an awesome end line too 'The best by FAR' the last word being the RAF backwards. You'll never see it, so you will just have to take my word that it was great.

Our client at the COI (the Central Office of Information, a government department that acts as a conduit between agencies and public organisations) kept trying to get us to dumb the idea down, something we were unwilling to do. You see the client knew what they wanted, but we new what they *needed*, so we had to stick to our guns, even if it meant a few frosty meetings. We went to present to the RAF, along with another agency that were showing a couple of alternate ideas. In attendance was our COI client and four representatives from the RAF, real military men, who had seen action, not just pen pushers. Every last one of the RAF guys loved our idea and preferred it over the other two presented. We went to the pub and had a drink to celebrate, thinking we could finally make our campaign. The meeting was on a Friday our COI client sacked us on Monday.

The second example is how we lost the Fosters lager social account. We tried and tried to get them to buy more challenging ideas but with very little success. In hindsight we should have resigned them, but instead we resigned ourselves to the fact we were flogging a dead horse. We simply serviced the client; we made the changes they requested without putting up any real resistance. It was no fun for anyone and sucked the life out of the team, worse of all it created middle of the road work, it wasn't bad in that it was comparable to what their competitors were doing, it was just never going to excite and delight the young male beer drinkers of Britain.

So we toed the line and did what the client requested. Ironically, and inevitably, they put the business up to pitch and that was that. We did have a final hurrah when we resurrected Ex-Chairman Freddy Heineken from the grave. We got old footage of him and got an actor to read a script in a Dutch accent. Freddy told them in no uncertain terms that they had lost their way and were doing it wrong, it was the best and last thing we made for them.

You may think the moral of this story is, your damned if you do and your damned if you don't, but there is a huge difference in the way we lost the two accounts. In the first example we died on our feet, and in the second we lived on knees and eventually died on our knees.

Don't be afraid of losing clients the first way. You will often be faced with the choice to do what is right and what is easy, always choose the former. The biggest advantage is that you will meet clients who are confident and understand that to create successful brands you have to behave differently. This is certainly true in my experience. I would go as far to say that every great ad ever created was done when a confident agency met a confident client.

The majority of people have had their confidence and individualism sucked out of them. They will see you as a misfit or a crazy. Your unconventional ideas will make them freak them out. F%^&'em, do them anyway. Do not vilify the brainwashed, but do not pity them either. Many are content with their lot, but if they start messing with your mind, deal with them swiftly. Shoot them between the eyes, dispose of the corpse, move on and feel no remorse. This is easier to do if you think of them not as humans but as sheep.

If you find yourself mirroring them or echoing their thoughts nip it in the bud. Immerse yourself in the art of the rebels; listen to 'Bringing It All Back Home' or 'Rubber Soul'. Read the books the rebels write, watch the films the rebels make.

Remember that the conformists are not born, they are made. Likewise, the rebels are not born, they are made. It just takes more courage, more confidence, and more hard work to make them. Resist the pressures of conventional success and constantly seek and find new and better ways to do things. Be afraid, be very afraid and then get the fuck off Maggie's farm any way you can.

Creativity:
From Art to Intelligence

By Pierre Odendaal & Steve Clayton

"Creativity" is a term thrown about so loosely these days that to begin this article without defining it would be like taking two steps backwards in a hopscotch death match. The Oxford English Dictionary describes creativity as "relating to or involving the use of imagination or original ideas in order to create something". In other words, they don't know either.

But who could blame them?

Creativity can be anything from the fancy footwork of a football player outsmarting his opponent, to a mother cunningly persuading her child to eat that last Brussels sprout. Never mind Jackson Pollock splattering paint all over huge canvases and creating the question of "…but is it art?".

The definition of creativity will remain a long-standing debate. Our context in this discussion is advertising and this is where we will focus.

In our industry "creativity" refers to problem solving. It's the art of finding a lateral solution to a linear problem. The only time that anyone will pay somebody else to do a job is when they can't do it themselves, generally through a lack of know-how. They have a linear problem and, as linear people have no solution, this is where our skills add value. When poor quality cars were flooding the market back in the day, you can bet that it wasn't a Volkswagen engineer that titled a beetle ad 'Lemon'.

In an industry that's been around for over a century, it's understandable that the interpretation of creativity and our understanding of it has changed. That said, the last 20 years or so have been somewhat radical. Society as a whole, whether young or old, acquired a comprehension for the advertising message. People began to ask "why?" instead of "where can I get it?", and they didn't just start showing interest in the products, but the corporations that made them. "What are the ethics of the company?", "Do they contribute to the community?", "Is their manufacturing process green?" these are some of the questions being asked today that strongly influence purchase decisions.

Communication that was good looking was no longer good enough. The consumer expected a value offering. And so we began to see the transition from "art" to "intelligence". The point where creatives had to start selling more and "making pretty" less. We had to include a new approach to messaging where transparency was key. We could no longer pull the wool over people's eyes, a sound, intelligent argument would be required if people were to take interest in our message, and with the internet at everybody's fingertips the public are quick to call out any claims that aren't accurate.

Think back.

Think back to before J. Walter Thompson merged a media house with a graphic design studio to create what we now call an advertising agency.

In fact, think back to before there was such a thing as a graphic design studio or even a media house.

Our industry began through competition, when a fishmonger put up a sign to suggest that his fish was better than that of the guy opposite him.

Later on, a car was reliable. "It got you from A to B", a soap was presumably going to make you clean, a cereal would fill you up in the morning and a shoe would protect your feet as you went about your daily business.

From the beginning to this day, when you read this piece, and into tomorrow when you wake up, there has been a consistent equation:

There's a **client** • who has a **product** • that needs to be pushed into a certain **environment** • so an **ad agency** is employed • to come up with an **approach** • that through specific **channels** • will yield **results**.

So, not so long ago it was pretty simple. If there were two enterprises offering the same product, the one that won was the one that better seduced the people. Since the products were pretty much the same it came down to art.

This is the art of attraction: visually stimulating and verbally convincing.

Imagine standing on the pavement opposite two restaurants and trying to decide which one to go to. You would go to the one that looked like it had the most ambiance. In advertising we know it as "visual appeal".

Back then, if you could just get the attention of the consumers they were sold.

Clients appreciated that while they could make "shoes" for example, other people, creative people, could make ads. Everyone had a field of expertise and the lines were never crossed.

For decades the formula remained the same.

The agencies would convince the public that they needed certain things, new things, things that they had never heard of. The public would lap up the communication and follow the "Instruction to Purchase", and the clients would blindly put their trust and money in the hands of the agencies.

Briefs were simple, products had one offering, consumers had one requirement and if the two fitted together there was profit.

At this point creativity was defined by prettiness and believability.

So if that's "art" then what's this "intelligence" theory?

After all, agencies and the creative minds within them are still applying themselves to the moving of product...

Remember the "lateral solution to a linear problem"? Well, that's where things have changed. These days it's very much about "Less art. More business".

Contemporary advertising dictates that what on Friday was the top side of a coin is on Monday the bottom, and if you weren't paying attention over the weekend you missed the edge. Think about it. While you sleep and dream up the next "big idea", someone somewhere else may be beating you to the punch. It only takes one time zone for someone else to do it first.

For example, consider cars. In the current car market "A" is irrelevant. All cars will get to "B". Today, it is a matter of how safely and comfortably and what features one car has versus another.

Soaps are about skin rejuvenation on a molecular level, breakfast cereals don't just fill you up but infuse you with every vitamin under the sun and "for a limited time only" come with a smile. Shoes tell you if you're fat and your friends are all over your Facebook page telling you what to do about it.

At the end of the day, the first rule of brand building is "consistency". The consumer thinks, "I'm intrigued by the new one but I trust the old one."

Pretty much all advertising before the late 80s / early 90s had been a steady evolution of communication structures that were born out of the industrial revolution.

Then the media consumption bucket began to overflow. An overwhelmed public switched-off to advertising messages and an underwhelmed client began paying closer attention to the *bang* that they were getting from their agency *buck*.

Never before had an individual been bombarded with so many sales pitches, with such high frequency.

We're talking about people who during the 15-minute walk from the bus stop to the office would normally greet 15 familiar faces. They didn't know the faces but they were familiar, and since everyone was going through the same daily motions, there was a sense of familiarity.

Suddenly the distraction of, "New, New, New! Buy me now! If you don't have one of these you're a…" infiltrated their lives. It built up and up and then, as a psychological defence, they all turned off.

Today's creatives were born out of this renaissance.
Where the modern consumer's question is not "is it new?" or "is it beautiful?" but "does it work?" and more to the point "how does it work for me?".

Our clients are educated marketers who judge us on the returns on their investments. The products are competitive on a scientific level. The once accepting environment is sceptical at best and morphs daily, based on popular opinion. The ad agency seeks to perfect time travel in an attempt to stay ahead of the environment. The approach is often more about innovation and its potential than the message, and with that the channels blur, creating an ever-shrinking soapbox from which to make our plea.

More and more the "media department" is breathing new ideas into old briefs. Good creative work is not about the clever headline anymore but about how the overarching idea is applied. Innovation. It stems from technological advances and is generally introduced into any advertising agency through the media department.

With constant advances in our communication devices and the platforms that we use on them it seems like there's a new way to get a message out every week. It's a race between the current and the next best thing and as marketers it's up to us to stay in front.

The good news is that one thing remains the same – the results.
If we aren't getting them, we won't exist.

Welcome the "Strategy department". They've always been there but only recently been given permission to participate in the *"Creative Process"*. Who's kidding who? If there was ever to be a hybrid it would be these two areas of expertise.

As egos are forced aside, the most efficient processes and the most successful results have been generated through this union.

Where once advertising creatives would sell their work based on beauty and poetry, we are now measured by our business acumen and strategic prowess. We can no longer sit in the corner daydreaming, while media schedules and demographics are discussed only to stand up with a good-looking layout.

We need to answer questions. Not about colours but about population consumption, emotions and spend. We need to know what's being said about our brand on Facebook and ensure that the tweets are positive.

Remember the "lateral"?

Everything that we do as creative people is still art. The difference is the measure.

It's about that ability to walk into a boardroom filled with very serious people wearing very serious suits and say, "have you ever thought of this…?"

"This" won't be a layout. It won't be a radio script. And it won't be a web page.

It will be a business solution, an intelligent creative solution, a solution that nobody who can comprehend a pie chart would have come up with. And for just one second all your tattoos will be ignored.

We physically produce things of beauty, but when we're around the boardroom table, or being reviewed on some global Excel spread sheet, it always comes down to ticking boxes. And getting that right is intelligent artistry.

Albert Einstein said, "Creativity is intelligence having fun". You'd be pretty stupid to argue with him.

Emotional Intelligence: Balancing Data and Creativity

By Ben Cooper

Where does creativity exist when everything becomes automated and targeted? Are we in danger of stifling outcomes with predictions based on our prior interactions?

In Spike Jonze's Her (2013), the protagonist Theodore Twombly, an introverted writer and gamer on the verge of divorce, purchases the first artificial intelligent operating system, OS1, to literally run his life. During setup, the operating system – named Samantha – takes on a personality that then grows through their interactions and experiences and the 'OS's' hunger for knowledge. As Samantha becomes increasingly attentive, she and Twombly begin to fall for each other. Despite the fact that Samantha does not have a body, they come up with ways of evolving their relationship into one that feels fulfilling in all facets of the human sense.

Charlie Brooker's TV series Black Mirror pushes similar technological hypotheses into darker terrain. In the episode "Be Right Back," the central character Martha is devastated when her social media addicted partner Ash is killed in a road accident. A friend prescribes her a service that allows people to communicate with deceased loved ones by using their online contributions and interactions to help with grieving. Brooker's idea is that software can build a "you" based on all your emails, texts, Facebook posts and Tweets. What's of interest to this story is the singularly optimistic nature of online posts – we only share the good stuff. As a consequence, the programmatic version of the deceased Ash is not equipped to deal with Martha's grief.

Both stories present an exploration of human need and interaction, but also an exploration of our relationship with the technological interface. Just look around you and see the faces of family, friends and colleagues illuminated by the screens of all manner of devices. A new breed of co-dependence, whether it's an insatiable appetite for knowledge, a desire for game world immersion or the vicarious pleasure of observing friends through their curated posts.

The way we engage with devices and computers has evolved. Touch interfaces and voice recognition are commonplace. Usability is increasingly intuitive. Our inputs are changing, from identity with fingerprint scanning and face recognition, to nuances in speech intonation. These increasingly detailed fragments of familiarity (let's call it 'user capture') will ultimately produce data that's never been collected at scale before.

Taken to extremes, this approaches the 1950's notion of the "singularity" and "intelligence explosion," espoused by mathematician and author of The Computer and the Brain, John von Neumann. By this, he was referring to the expansion of a device's cognitive abilities to the point at which they surpasses that of any human.

It sounds like the stuff of science fiction. Yet the retailing giant Target uses customer tracking technology to identify key life moments based on complementary product purchases. Their statistical genius has created a formula to identify when a woman is likely to be pregnant from 25 products purchased together, for example. This then triggers the delivery of targeted coupons. And the imaginings of Jonze and Brooker are only fractionally ahead of Amazon's suggested products and recently patented "anticipatory shipping", a feature using their truckloads of customer data to predict what product you'll purchase next. For Amazon, this will cut down delivery times and put them ahead of their real world competitors. For customers, it serves as a reality check as to how well computers might know us.

Similarly, Google is busily amassing not only Big Data but "truly massive data… from the minutiae of our lives." Google Now takes your world of 'Google' and presents back to you on a neat little card the most likely thing you'll do next: a card for the weather, a card for traffic on your route to work, a card for your next meeting, the footy scores and a reminder of a friend's birthday. There's no doubt that brilliant service design keeps you coming back for more, in the way that a real world barista who knows your name and order will see you coming back each day.

However, such acuity can be kind of Aspergic – like Martha's new "companion", it does not always allow for the emotional nuances of human situation. In the case of Target, for example, the system in one case identified a teen pregnancy before the woman's parents did (the teen's father found coupons in the family mailbox for cots and baby clothes) – insert "whoops" emoticon here! This caused some confused and heated debate between the woman's father and the store, and even more discussion at home afterwards.

So herein lies the challenge: it's true that pattern based predictions can be helpful. Data affords us an incredible insight into users and their behaviours. But we're in danger of limiting the future by the actions of the past. More importantly, we're in danger of cramping our creative style.

Creativity, by the nature of the word, involves a level of originality and surprise. It not only plays on what has come before (ideas, texts, genres, interpretations) but seeks new ground. It is not only the track beaten down behind but the rocks, crags and waterfalls ahead too. Creativity, the good stuff, takes us further than we've known.

Anita Elberse is a Harvard Professor whose book *Blockbusters: Hit-making, Risk-taking, and the Big Business of Entertainment* investigates the strategy of blockbusters in entertainment. After analysing a decade of data she clearly identifies a formula by which movie execs are minimising risk and maximising return. They go with what's known, in terms of both the story and the cast. This means sequels and book adaptations (read: demonstrated audiences) in plentiful amounts. 2015 is rather telling with *The Avengers*

Sequel, Batman vs Superman, Independence Day 2, Jurassic Park 4, Star Wars VII and *Terminator 5.* But is there a danger that the formula will simply wear out?

In advertising, the answer is yes – and with digital data, as with box office, these failures are self-evident. In a cluttered and savvy media world, lacklustre messages fail to convert, to attract, to engage, and this activity (or lack of) can be easily tracked.

In the case of programmatic paid media, advertisers have the ability to chase users around the web until they succumb to a funnel of conversion and then purchase. But however optimised that experience is – from the specifics of button colours, to exhaustive multi-variant testing – the ad's effectiveness will wear out with exposure. They will simply stop being noticed.

We know that putting the user first ensures the experience works better. Now with native advertising (ad content overtly fused with the user's experience), advertisers have to think about their messages as branded content of specific use or entertainment to the user. In the case of editorial native advertising – you might think BuzzFeed, but know that *The New York Times* et al have offerings too – the publisher plays creative partner with the brand and they work together to create content that is mutually beneficial for both the reader and the brand.

Mini, for example, partnered with BuzzFeed to drive its 'Not Normal' brand positioning; a partnership made in heaven due to the BuzzFeed audience's hunger for the bizarre and abnormal. A dozen articles celebrated "Not Normal" via fashion oddities to environmental phenomena. This content alliance allowed Mini to expand the positioning of its brand messaging and bring their range of unique cars into focus.

In the case of social native advertising – think sponsored Facebook posts and promoted Tweets – the page or profile owner needs to be clear on what value their brand brings to their followers and not veer from that purpose. More telling in this instance is the reactions to the content – was it referred, commented upon, liked etc. Actions validate the content and give the advertiser a unique perspective on where their storytelling efforts should go. It also gives them permission to scale via sponsored media to replicate the endorsement that social uniquely gives.

Oreo's 'Daily Twist' campaign is a good example of the US cookie brand knowing what they stand for and where to fit into social. One hundred ads in 100 days turned trending news stories into visual treats. The already topical stories had an audience from the outset; Oreo simply repurposed them with their twist, then sponsored the content so their creative became news in its own right. Of the hundred posts, the most famous, 'Dunk in the Dark', seized the moment when the Super Bowl broadcast blacked-out: the created image was shared on Twitter and Facebook more than 20,000 times and was estimated to reach five times the number of people who tuned in to watch the game. A planned approach meant Oreo concentrated its efforts on relevancy, reach and timeliness with an outcome that everyone talked about.

It's evident that programmatic media can be relevant, but it lacks soul and context, whereupon native formats are reigniting creativity from both the brands and the publishers to engage with audiences in more interesting ways. Native also affords referral and is more embedded into the social psyche of the web. I predict that programmatic media will be the death of what can be only described as traditional online advertising, or The Banner Ad. Yes, a powerful partner, but misused it turns into a creepy stalker.

On the one hand, it's like painting by numbers; on the other, Jackson Pollock. Is there a happy middle?

Data isn't necessarily devoid of emotion. It can be creative in solving problems and, in some cases, even revealing great beauty.

In the United Kingdom, the Greater London Authority (GLA) has created The London Datastore, launched in 2010 by the Mayor of London, Boris Johnson. It's a free and open platform that gives citizens access to public sector data. It's a smart move in citizen empowerment as the GLA appreciates that raw data often doesn't tell you anything – it's not until it has been presented in a meaningful way that unforeseen outcomes can arise. They are encouraging technical talent to transform rows of text and numbers into apps, websites or mobile products which people can actually find useful.

The GLA initiative has already given birth to some interesting projects: from the fun and educational London Jigsaw App, where users get to show how well they know London by rebuilding it one piece at a time; to helping Londoners commute via the City Mapper, which not only helps them navigate public transport via access to 'Transport for London' data, but prompts them to consider walking or cycling by showing how many calories they'd burn. Being open with their data has allowed London to rally its technically savvy citizens to create tools and services that improve the lives of many. Open data in the context of cities has amazing opportunity to create understanding around societal problems and potential solutions. By cross referencing data on crime, geography, education, demographics, ethnicity etc. governments and citizens can start to understand the patterns that lead to problems.

Where data begins to approximate art is in the hands of artists like Aaron Koblin and Jonathan Harris, whose timeless examples give a unique perspective of the world via data. In Koblin's early work Flight Patterns, North America is reinterpreted with captured flight data. With no reference, the continent takes on a new form via the air traffic of its inhabitants. Harris's We Feel Fine observes humans in another way, by exploring emotion of the published kind. The software harvests sentences containing the phrase "I feel" or "I am feeling" from newly posted blog entries (note: this was before Twitter and Facebook). It then displays them in a compelling interactive experience which it invites you to lose hours exploring. In another observation "I Want You To Want Me," an installation commissioned by MOMA in New York, Harris explores the search for love and self in the world of online dating. The installation chronicles the world's long-term relationship with romance, across all ages, genders, and sexualities, using real data collected from dating sites every few hours. It feels to me that these sensitive and thought-provoking pieces shone a light on the possibilities of connecting with audiences in radically different ways. Yet are now silenced by targeting technologies that chase you around the web. Can a balance be struck?

Vocativ, the global social news network, uses data-mining software that was targeted as a tool for law enforcement and government agencies. The software, OpenMind, accesses the "deep web" which standard search engines overlook. Content like spreadsheets and Word documents and dynamic pages. Vocativ claim they can use the deep web, in combination with monitoring social media, to find news stories other agencies can't.

What makes Vocativ's approach to the newsroom unique is the pairing of journalists and data analysts to produce stories. The technology helps discovery and investigation, then journalists and analysts curate and create stories. This is a smart balance that respects the craft of persuasive writing, yet uses the brawn of data mining to go beyond the surface of the web.

In my own work we deployed social web spiders to index and identify specific audiences and their behaviour with content. The aim was to identify what engages them most so we could build better content experiences. The audience was C-Level decision makers within the Information Technology space. This audience is information hungry and frequent social channels to glean the latest opinion and news on their area. By using directory listings we were able to identify the top companies, via LinkedIn the key decision makers, then matched their profiles to Twitter and other social profiles. From there we were able to build a unique topic dictionary that was tailored to this audience's interests, then use it to highlight how they behaved with industry content; news, white papers and video case studies. Knowing what worked the best allowed us to tailor our own content efforts and, most importantly, measure it once it was released to this select audience. We were able to see who and what influenced them and create opportunities to expand stories and, ultimately, connect to drive sales.

It feels that we are at the intersection of change, whereupon push advertising lacks a role in our online experiences. We naturally look for referred media first, something that's validated by real people, ideally our friends.

We're never going to refer a well targeted banner ad that happens to know I'm in the market for a new coat. We won't even celebrate the search engine optimised website we found as its likely geared for search bots, not human eyes. We will, however, refer friends to a remarkable film or story. We'll encourage followers to download an App we can't live without or visit a site that's interaction design is compelling. We'll share information that's helped us solve a problem or tackle a task we knew nothing about. We will even applaud a service that took the time to look after our needs and go the extra mile. Experience is everything and if you're having a good one, you'll likely shout about it.

So the data we create knows a lot about us. Sometimes more than we do. But we must all find a balance where what it tells us is not the rules but the opportunity to create, to connect. Creativity remains as important as ever to provoke reaction and interaction. We need to find that sweet spot where a hyperlinked virtual and (with connected homes and wearable devices) now physical world can actually help our stories and information connect. It's true that companies and brands will be enticing us to share more of our behavioural data for benefits.

Ironically, in *Her*, it was Twombly who was stuck in a formula, and it took a machine – albeit one with the seductive voice of Scarlett Johansson – to teach him how to "live". By stepping away from his devices, rejoining the humans and learning to risk again.

The takeout of this is not necessarily just a philosophical one, however. The "formula" in which advertising often finds itself stuck is one of structure and process. If programmatic advertising is the lot of media companies and emotional storytelling that of creative, what is needed is in fact better communication practices between the two. As media companies begin to forge creative capabilities and creative companies become more media savvy, we edge towards the brave new world of an agency capable of a holistic approach with laser accuracy and intuition. The irony is that this is where we came from, albeit when media was simpler before industry fragmentation and we became, by some degree of necessity, specialised. But now we need to return, head and heart joined, and ready to take a risk.

Creative Talent Means Nothing if Your Boss is a Moron

By Dave Birss

I spent most of my advertising career as a freelancer.

Not an inbetween-jobs-and-desperate-to-pick-up-work-from-whoever-calls-me freelancer. No Siree! I was a proper don't-offer-me-a-job-I'm-not-interested-in-being-on-your-stinking-payroll freelancer.

It was a great life.

Unless there was a recession.

Over the years I ended up working in lots of different creative departments run by lots of different Creative Directors. I was always amazed at how creativity flourished in some companies and withered in others. So I started to take notes, just in case I ended up running a department myself one day.

I was fascinated at the different management styles of Creative Directors. They ranged from passionate, creative geniuses to unpredictable, explosive coke-heads. Some of them liked to give the good briefs to the whole department while others quietly hoarded them in an effort to hold onto the glory.

And the amazing thing was that their behaviour defined the quality of the work far more than the level of talent within their department.

A few years ago I decided to take a break from advertising. My commitment-phobic personality meant that I couldn't even stick to one industry, never mind one job. I took everything I'd learned about building a creative culture and I offered it to businesses. That's how I pay the rent now. And I scratch my creative itch in other ways that don't require a logo in the bottom right corner.

So I want to share with you a dozen things I learned about growing creativity in any business - along with some input from some truly legendary Creative Directors. Feel free to stick a fluorescent Post It note on this page and casually leave the book on your Creative Director's desk.

1. Recognise the good work

I'm not talking about the ability to tell good ideas from crappy ones. Let's take that as read. I'm talking about giving recognition to the people who came up with the ideas in the first place. And that recognition should be public and congratulatory. Giving creative people credit is more motivating than giving them a cash bonus. And it makes all the other idea-people want to try harder so they can get the recognition next time.

"A great CD will always convince you you're onto something good. A great CD will make you feel like you're a genius – and this job could be the one that makes you." Alan Young, St Luke's

2. Keep it accountable

I once worked with a terrible Creative Director who used to brief the entire department on any big opportunity that came in. As a result, hardly anyone did any work on it. He'd then make some bland idea-soup out of the half-hearted scraps he got. And thereby lose every decent opportunity that came his way. It's much better to keep your team small. So small that there's nowhere to hide and your reputation is on the line if you don't deliver.

"The perfect Creative Director will spend her time focusing less on the kerning in a poster and more on how to get the right people to collide powerfully." Nils Leonard, Grey

3. Inspire the department

Inspiration is such an important ingredient in creative leadership. The boss should be showing examples of the kind of idea they want people to produce. They should be pointing people towards the interesting stuff that might spark an idea. And they should have enough charisma and passion to get people excited about what they're doing, even when it seems a bit tedious. This is one ability I've seen declining at a frightening rate in recent years.

"You are there to inspire others and get them to do their best. You need to be able to listen more than you talk. Understand it's a business but that you can be playful within it." Patrick Collister, Google

4. Prove you can do it

I once heard it said that a good Creative Director is someone you can trust to crack the brief if you can't. There's something in that. If you're managing a team of creative people, you should probably have more experience and ability than they do. Just as you'd expect the manager of a McDonald's to be pretty good at flipping burgers themselves. It's probably a good idea to show off your skills from time to time to prove the point. Just not all the time.

"In my opinion, CDs should only write in a crisis to make sure the teams are getting as many opportunities as possible. A great CD will rip up their own work in order to promote the ideas from people in their department." Alan Young, St Luke's

5. Share the opportunities

This point balances off the last one. Only a bad leader keeps the good briefs for themselves. That shows that they put their own priorities above the rest of the department. Or - just as bad - shows that they don't trust the rest of the department to produce good enough work. Regardless of the reason, it's pretty destructive for morale.

"What makes a terrible Creative Director? EGO (in my opinion). Masses of confidence and inspirational qualities yes, but ego no. I know there are a lot of

successful CDs out there that have biggies. I think they can f*** off, personally."
Laura Jordan-Bambach, Mr President

6. Free people from their desks

Forcing people to work creatively at their desk is a waste of time. Office desks are designed for executing rather than thinking. If people feel the pressure to look productive, they go to their computers and start doing stuff. Or even worse, they start watching YouTube videos in the vain hope that it'll give them some inspiration. Just getting out of the office - or moving to a different part of the office - is enough to change people's perspective on a problem. Everyone has a mobile phone these days, so you can still keep in touch with them. Liberating people from their desks is the simplest way to liberate their minds from the obvious.

"People want to have a more fulfilling life. They don't necessarily want to go into an office every day. They don't necessarily want to keep doing that same job day in, day out. We have to think about more flexible structures." Sir John Hegarty, BBH

7. Give clear feedback

There's nothing worse for a creative person than vague feedback. The job of a Creative Director is to offer direction to their creatives. It's better to have a wrong opinion than a vague, indecisive one. At least a bad decision to kill a good idea gives you somewhere to move on from. Saying "there could be something in that idea - explore it a bit more" is usually a waste of everyone's time. If you want people to develop an idea, tell people exactly what's wrong with it, what needs to be addressed and what you want them to come back to you with.

"A good CD is one who points you in the right direction and gives you the courage to take risks. A bad CD is one who snaffles the best briefs for himself." Jeff Stark, ex-Saatchi & Saatchi

8. Defend your staff

Creative ideas are often brutally torn apart by the shirt and tie brigade. They don't care about the talent and passion that led to the ideas. So they throw around criticism that would knock the stuffing out of the creatives. A good creative leader will protect their staff from these harmful barbs, because encouragement nourishes the creative soul far more than criticism ever will.

"A great CD won't have a department. They will have a crew. An understanding that goes beyond the culture of an agency. And they will maintain and create the rarest entity in our game, trust." Nils Leonard, Grey

9. Remove the obstacles
The measure of a great creative leader is the output of their department. The better the work they produce, the better you've done your job. There's more chance of them doing something brilliant if you take away the crap that's preventing it. Stuff like politics, pointless meetings, unrealistic deadlines and bad briefs. Go round the department every morning and ask what's getting in the way of them doing something jaw-dropping. Then deal with it for them. That gives them no excuse for not doing something astounding. And they'll love you for it.

"The perfect creative director presumes that her people are talented and want to contribute. And accepts that, without meaning to, the company, the process and even herself are stifling the work and its ability to be brilliant in some way." Nils Leonard, Grey

10. Hire people who scare you
David Ogilvy once said "If each of us hires people who are smaller than we are, we shall become a company of dwarfs. But if each of us hires people who are bigger than we are, we shall become a company of giants." A good leader should be looking to curate a department of frighteningly talented people and making sure they have everything they need to do the best work they can.

"I always liked what Kenny Dalglish said when he was player-manager of Liverpool. On Match of the Day they asked him how he was making the transition from being one of their greatest players to managing a team. Dalglish said 'I'll know I've got the team right when I can't get on it.' For me that's a

great creative director. It's your job to get the department to do better work than you could do yourself." Dave Trott, The Gate

11. Don't assume the client is an idiot

Creating an us-and-them division is never going to lead to anything good. It just makes everyone's job more difficult and leads to compromised work. The client isn't there to crap on your creative genius, they're there to make sure your ideas are going to help them achieve their business objectives. That's not a bad thing. A good creative leader will gain the confidence of their bill-paying clients, giving them more freedom to do effective, ground-breaking work.

"Talk to clients. It's the only way to find out how they tick. It's the best way to build trust. And trust lets you make the work that you want to make." Tim Clegg, Saatchi & Saatchi X

12. Keep learning

Lead by example. No one is ever too senior to learn something new. Be curious about everything. Learn all you can about the business. Research your clients and get to know about their industries. Read up on new technology. Find out about the latest thinking in psychology and human behaviour. And let your staff know that you expect the same from them. Create a learning environment and your department will never stagnate.

"A great CD wont just set the agenda on the work, they will give the agency a true north. And will give not only the creatives a purpose, but make everyone who brings great things to bear a chance to shine." Nils Leonard, Grey

If you work in a creative department, these points should help you work out if it's any good - and if your Creative Director is the kind of person you really want to work for.

If you found this book on your desk with a fluorescent Post It note marking this chapter, good luck.

Ideas Are Gifts,
Not Possessions

By Bridget Jung

"You will never win fame and fortune unless you invent big ideas. It takes a big idea to attract the attention of consumers and get them to buy your product. Unless your advertising contains a big idea, it will pass like a ship in the night. I doubt if more than one campaign in a hundred contains a big idea." David Ogilvy

From the scotch soaked, cigarette smoke perfumed days of the 50's to the Mac Book littered millennial offices of today, creatives have always chased the fabled **big idea.** Its pursuit has made careers and destroyed them, won pitches and lost them, forged international allegiances and inspired the fiercest interagency rivalries.

In this chapter, I'll be exploring the way in which coming up with a big idea has changed, what they look like today and where they could take us tomorrow.

Lets start with the traditional creative team. It was Bill Bernbach who first put Art Directors and Copywriters together to form a creative team. He believed two heads were better than one when it came to advertising. Back then big ideas lived as either TV, print or outdoor advertising. Their aim was to literally interrupt, to stop people in their tracks. Bernbach felt that blurring the lines between words and pictures, gave more depth to the creative concept. It was an idea that soon caught on and teams of 2 fast became the standard practice.

Fast-forward to 2014 and successful teams are made up of more than 2 people. Most likely it's a dynamic group of experts embracing all aspects of ideation, creative technology, experience design, art direction, story telling and production.

The Google re:brief project dramatises this organisational shift perfectly (http://bit.ly/1j9nLRj). They asked how the iconic TV spot "Hilltop" for Coke would live and play out in today's media landscape.

The original *Hilltop* Art Director, Harvey Gabor, worked with a multidisciplinary team to reimagine what the big idea would look like today. The team turned the sweet metaphor (and melody) 'I'd like to buy the world a Coke' into a reality.

The 2012 interpretation of *Hilltop* resulted in display banner ads that could connect people to Coke machines on the other side of the world. By clicking on the banner ad, the person could literally buy (someone in) the world a Coke.

This highlights the first fundamental difference in how we execute ideas today compared with 1971: we used to simply *say* a message, now we *do* the message. The big idea remains the same, however it's no longer something that a conceptual team simply hands off for execution. Execution and ideation are interdependent.

I believe the second shift we are seeing is that we are no longer limited to metaphors. We can do more than just fake it with impressive CGI or incredible storytelling. Mercedes invisible car (http://youtu.be/Y1l2xaZN5Rk) is a great example of our ability to actually create the magic of advertising, for real. Some smart technology, a whole lot of LEDs and some clever camera work made it possible to really make the car invisible to the public. Invisibility was the metaphor to support the claim that this car had zero impact on the environment. The stunt was filmed and went on to become one of the most successful viral ads we've seen. It also can be held responsible for the flurry of stunts that have swamped YouTube since then.

This upfront role of technology in the creative process provides us with some of the biggest creative opportunities today. Sir John Hegarty sums it up well *"Creativity challenges technology; technology inspires creativity"*.

It's no surprise that this new role for technology dramatically challenges the definition of what the creative team is and does.

I'd argue that digital creatives have evolved in a collaborative creative process and work environment because they have always had to hack solutions. (You're only as good as your programmer.)

The very nature of digital has always meant that the execution is not an afterthought but instead it's the process. Hacking solutions has become second nature with the incredible explosion of platforms, devices, social networks and technologies that influence our creative playground. Ideas need to be shared, built upon, stretched, challenged, supported and made better through collaboration. It's why this chapter is called 'Ideas are gifts, not possessions'. It was something that my old friend and mentor, Mark Beeching, taught me a long time ago and, I feel, it only keeps getting more and more relevant.

Collaboration and co-creation is the new source of creativity. It requires confidence (not ego) to give your idea away to someone else - whether that's another agency, partner or even your consumers. Interestingly, strategic planners have always had to give ideas away to creative. It appears that we must now do the same. It's no longer about controlling or policing the idea in a matching luggage approach. It's about giving it away and enjoying the ways in which it'll come back and, delight and surprise you.

When trying to understand successful collaborative models it's interesting to look at the Film industry for inspiration. It's perhaps the most dominant creative industry in the 21st century. It's always been a collaborative industry. It's hard to say who or what is responsible for (or the owner) of a great film: Director? Scriptwriter? Actors? Producer? Photographic Director? The great story, which was based on a great novel?

None of these roles or factors is single-handedly responsible for the success of the final product. It's a cumulative effect. Although what's interesting to highlight is that everyone can win an Oscar for their particular contribution. So it's no surprise, that the Oscar for best film is always the one with the most individual Oscars.

The Cannes Lions Festival is the equivalent of the advertising industry's Oscars. And in line with evolution of creativity, its awards are also evolving. In 2005, in recognition of the new integrated approach emerging in advertising, the festival first introduced the Titanium category. This rewarded campaigns that excelled across a range of media channels. Subsequently, this grew into Titanium & Integrated in 2007. Then, last year, both Jury Presidents felt a need to clarify (and maybe justify) what each of these categories meant.

Today's Cannes Lions recipients are winning big, across categories. *Dumb ways to Die* makes this point well, cleaned up in 2013 with 5 Grand Prix, 18 Gold Lions, 3 Silver Lions, and 2 Bronze Lions across pretty much every category – making it the most awarded advertising campaign in history to date.

Dumb Ways to Die beat serious competition in each category too. It won not because it was a big idea that had been adapted to different channels giving a coherent and consistent campaign. But because it was a simple, powerful idea that lived in different ways, creating value and earning attention across different touch points.

The flip side of the new post-digital playground bringing a world of opportunity is the new challenge it also presents. Things are only getting more and more complex. We have never asked so much from an idea as we do today.

Ironically, I believe that as the briefs are become more complex, the ideas need to become simpler. But these are simple, powerful ideas that can live in complex ecosystems, across channels, in real-time, that always create value and earn attention for the consumer.

Another big winner from Cannes in 2013 was *The Beauty Inside* by Intel and Toshiba (http://youtu.be/qyMQIMeSCVY). It took home 3 Grand Prix, 2 Gold, 5 Silver, 2 Bronze, and that's in addition to 9 shortlisted entries. It's perhaps the most perfect idea I've ever come across so far. In my opinion, what makes this brilliant, is that it's a perfect idea for Intel and only Intel.

A lot of the advertising we see today is category specific. You can swap in and out brand names and it still works as a campaign because you're selling cars, luxury, chocolate bars or whatever the category may be, but in the end it's not necessarily brand specific. *The Beauty Inside* has succeeded where so many agencies and brands have failed: giving the idea away to the consumer. It's ruined UGC for us all, making other attempts seem cheap and meaningless. A fantastic script and faultless storytelling gave anyone the chance to play the lead character of Alex in this social film. But it was done in a way that made sense for the brand and the user, ultimately resulting in incredible participative storytelling done with great talent and incredible passion.

I find it interesting that what would have once been considered as a 'web series' now can take home the coveted Film Grand Prix at Cannes Lions (in addition to Cyber and Branded Content).

The comparison between the advertising industry and film industry is interesting given that *The Beauty Inside* is perhaps the first 'ad' to beat regular programming and take home an Emmy Award for Outstanding New Approach to a daytime series.

Which brings me to my final example. This big idea was the elephant in the room at the Cannes in 2013. Red Bull Stratos is perhaps the **biggest idea** we have ever seen in advertising and yet it was not entered in any advertising festival. (No doubt it would have radically changed Cannes and any other advertising festival if it had been).

The Stratos team was composed of *"world-leading experts in medicine, science and engineering, including a former NASA crew surgeon, record-breaking aviators, and designers of some of the most innovative aircraft ever produced"* (http://www.redbullstratos.com/the-team).

As we look towards the future we'll no doubt see this type of approach more and more. Successful advertising will be built on powerful organising ideas that live over time (and in real-time), across channels with a programmatic logic. Felix Baumgartner's infamous space jump clearly demonstrates the shift from saying to doing. It shows us how brands can create magic for real. And most importantly, it's an interesting example of how this new breed of collaborative creativity can redefine what advertising is, does and inspires.

#givesyouwings

CULTURE

We Love Digital

By Mark Anderson

Like, I give a shit

We humans are needy. From birth to the grave we spend our time wanting – wanting food, wanting friends, wanting her, wanting him, wanting *that* car, wanting *that* life... the list goes on.

Psychologically, we are pretty screwed up. We have a hunger for approval that turns us from timid individuals into the bloke up the front, screaming for attention.

We pour our lives into devices – sharing ourselves between 'friends' and 'followers'; refining our likes and dislikes, and contributing substantially to a growth in online cat videos. But is this version of ourselves really us? Or is it just what we think people want to see?

Are we are giving too much away too easily in our search for acceptance, without fully understanding the consequences? When nothing is owned then nothing is cherished and everything, eventually, becomes valueless.

And what about the brands we work for? How can we, as creatives, help them navigate this continually changing landscape and measure the value of their efforts? An army of followers just isn't enough. Can we keep pace? Should we bother? And if we do, what form should it take?

Always on... Standby

The digital world is evolving at an unprecedented rate, software developers create apps we didn't know we needed, hardware comes to market before a market exists for it. Consumerism has moved on.

The brainiacs have answered all the problems we faced in managing our social lives, and we now supposedly have the tools to enrich our life by ourselves – staying informed and online is easier than ever.

In a world where we are bombarded with information, the technology created to save us time is actually taking it up. The question is whether this makes a difference – would we find something to fill our time either way?

The content of choice tends to be disposable. It's the video you watch once and then never again, the app you download for free stuff that you go on to delete straight away, a sound bite of news that just scratches the surface. In a disposable world, there is less value in the things we consume – with an increase in volume we decrease the amount of emotion or rational engagement we can give any particular thing.

To go a bit further we could ask whether social media is killing advertising? Maybe that's a tad brash, but are we spreading the content we have too thinly on overly extended budgets, just to tick all the boxes at a planning level?

We don't need to tick every box. An agency should have the remit (or the balls) to stand up, have an opinion and not be timid. A client should have faith in their agency – if they haven't then they are working with the wrong agency. Together they should work out a strategy that is unique to them and their values, defining the creative and using the channels that are best fit for purpose. Instead of just throwing mud at the wall and seeing what sticks, we should have the confidence and the knowledge to know that the platform we are choosing is right. Otherwise we risk devaluing the conversation and wasting the time, money and effort invested.

This is where it's our responsibility to create meaning and build relationships with our brand's consumers – creating communications that are more responsible, balanced, and focused. Every day you see brands or agencies get it wrong — VISA at the 2012 Olympics for instance. But when it goes right it ticks so many boxes on so many levels – as with Dove's Beauty campaign. And the payoff is more than any KPI set within a brief. To understand the audience is key, to understand people is more so.

The boundaries are blurring between the things we do and the things we share – a difference that was once quite obvious, but now our on- and offline lives are merging into one. As such we have begun to confuse what is work and what is play, what is social and what is professional. The balance we all craved just a few short years ago is slowly turning to mush.

In my opinion there hasn't really been a division of time at all. For the majority of people there isn't, and has never been, a separate identity dependent on locale or activity. Yes there may be subtle differences, but our hard-wired character will always be the base from which all interactions are born. We just live... and muddle our way through. Trying to be as socially accepted as possible in any given circumstance – be it work or play. The difference now is in the tools available to us - it has become too easy to broadcast every waking thought.

In China, the Internet has emerged as such an uncontrollable force that there are camps dedicated to curing children of their Internet addiction. Where social media draws huge numbers, and 24-hour Internet clubs keep the population stuck to their screens – if there ever was a division in time, then it has truly been shattered.

That's not to say the Internet is bad, but I believe our online future needs an 'off' button, or at least a standby. A social Faraday cage, where temptation to post, tweet or upload is contained. Where valuable time is spent doing something altogether different. Then we could share the shit out of that. At least that might be of interest to people.

Digital definitely has this power – it can reform the way we work and live. It can inspire people to do more, and to discover worlds they never knew existed, to *be* more. This power is no more evident than in the way it has inspired political change. From the lead up to Obama's election in the US, to the voice of the people living the Arab Spring. People of all ages are sharing opinions and creating visibility on things that actually mean something to them – and online has became the hub of these discussions. Digital is changing the political balance of countries, it has the power to do good. This is how brands should use the digital platform.

A culture of over-sharing

Every single day I hear people say, "Today I'm giving up Facebook", "Twitter is just full of shit" and, "Flickr used to be good".

I think we need to learn how to become better curators of our lives. To be able to recognise the valuable, and to create an opinion – be it spoken, image or word. Eating a burger or taking a dump is not interesting. Making complete idiots famous for being idiots has no benefit to the greater good of the world. Warhol once said that everyone would be famous for 15 minutes – maybe instead we should make that 15 seconds… and the rest is just gravy.

The conflict comes when we try to be all things to all people – it's exhausting. People want effortless content – we don't want to commit ourselves to an idea and we don't want the hassle of judging what we post before we post it.

Yet if we feel the need to pander for recognition or adoration – to be wanted and loved… Then we should probably say something that people want to listen to.

So, I want people to care. And if they do care, to show it in the right way. To hold value in the words they believe in. To have a standpoint by which they are rooted, and welcome the opportunity for discussion.

Twitter is a brilliant place for people to share and discuss great opinions. But look at the top followed Twitter accounts – the people we choose to follow are not pioneers or revolutionaries, they are pop stars and reality TV icons. And yes, this isn't new. It's been happening on every medium since media began – TV, magazines, but what does that say about us? A butterfly flutters past and our attention is won over...

With the dawn of digital we have been privileged to experience the perfect platforms for shared thought. As creatives our role is to help brands be more responsible in their communications. For brands to create things of value that touch the hearts and minds of users and inspire them to engage. It's not all about volume. It's about quality. It's about being smart.

Personally, I have had enough. I would like to see the age of constantly disposable content come to an end. Let us make a pledge, that together and with our clients, we stop promoting bullshit five minute Branded fun, but instead define a sustained commitment to something of value to the Brand, something that reflects its values and beliefs. Brands now have the opportunity like never before to say what they want, to whoever they want. It is time for to stop wasting this opportunity. It is time to take a risk.

Erm... I said that!?

The things we choose to share are often unconsciously shaped by our peers, and then absorbed by the media we use to share them on – our ideas go on to lead their own lives, be it for good or for evil.

We press send and we wave goodbye to our content. Losing control of where it appears, who sees it, and even what it ends up saying. Much like Chinese whispers, the little details change – but are we, and should we still be, responsible for something once it has left our keyboard?

A great example of this is the trade-off between sharing a story and it becoming news. With his jokey message to the Metro about a fabric conditioner stain shaped just like Jesus, Dave Gorman made the news in a whole host of different publications. But the further a story goes, the more things change – what was originally said can be taken out of context, or in places rewritten altogether.

As agencies we talk about creating narratives that consumers can enjoy, participate in and share. But there is more to a great strategy than this. To allow ownership to be transferred to the people we create it for. We have opened our creations to a collaborative environment – so is now the time to let go?

The value of a story shifts. Its meaning, and its backstory lost. But it can gain something new – a lifespan. People will judge it and share it based on their opinion – and so a message can spread incredibly quickly. The digital world gives life to many new ideas, as well as playing a part in destroying many others. It is a great platform from which to judge public opinion, but also from which to raise awareness amongst an audience that can be hard to reach.

If brands can learn to harness this power and be truly comfortable in allowing a conversation to take its own form, and be happy to ride the wave wherever it takes them — rather than trying to control a single message across all media — then we have taken one small step into true communications. To 'get out of the story' and start being the story.

Great examples of where brands have taken a back seat and handed over to the end user have resulted in Footlocker bringing us 'Sneakerpedia' – a global resource for all sneaker freaks to share their love. Footlocker enabled the platform, the rest was left to us. And Red Bull's Music Academy – a platform for global musicians. Their finely honed strategies to align with cultures, groups or activities means that Red Bull are never seen as fake. They commit, their message is clear and the result is that their advocates are true to the brand.

The final countdown

So, as consumers we are needy. We live through our devices, favouring easy and disposable content, but this content is not strong enough to form attitudes and change behaviour – neither is it personal enough to create true empathy and engagement. We are truly on our first few footsteps into a brave new world. We will stumble, fall and pick ourselves up. To carry on in the knowledge that we are better for it.

And as advertisers or marketeers it is our responsibility to help brands create communications that mean more. Smarter, less intrusive, more considered content, which will allow for more intelligent relationships between client and consumer.

People desire meaningful relationships – smarter communications with meaningful content, not superficial likes and approval. They need a substantial brand meal rather than an endless diet of junky ad snacks.

And it is our job to deliver...

300 Year Old Philosophy Powered by the Internet

By Julian Cole

The 300 year old school of thought of Libertarianism is seeing a renaissance thanks to the internet. If you have read anything about Edward Snowden, Wikileaks, Bitcoin, Uber, AirBNB, PayPal, 3-D printed guns or Silk Road you have probably had some exposure to ideals of libertarianism. These radical libertarian ideals have found some traction in permeating pop culture in the last couple of years thanks to a number of projects facilitated by the internet.

Libertarianism has been around since the 1700s. It is an idea of holding personal liberty above all else. That the government hold too much power and it should be limited, at the very extreme end contends that the government should not even exist.

In America, this has translated into an actual political party, the Libertarian Party. They are classified as fiscally conservative/socially liberal. Fiscally conservative refers to the idea of free markets; they're looking for less intervention from the government. Socially liberal being that individuals should be able to say and do whatever they like. However, as a political party they have not seen much success, they have received less than 1% of the vote in the last 50 years in America and most people do not understand what they stand for. It was not until the Internet that they were able to start showing the benefits of their ideals.

The earliest trace of applying Libertarianism values to the internet can be traced back to an email mail list in 1992 called the 'Cypherpunks'. It comprised employees of high-tech companies and well known computer scientist researchers of the day. The group was interested in Cryptography, the study of how to preserve the privacy of online communication from third parties, namely governments and businesses. Founding member Eric Hughes wrote the Cypherpunk Manifesto, "Privacy is necessary for an open society in the electronic age. ... We cannot expect governments, corporations, or other large, faceless organisations to grant us privacy ... We must defend our own privacy if we expect to have any. ... Cypherpunks write code. We know that someone has to write software to defend privacy, and ... we're going to write it." The Cypherpunks gained popularity when they lobbied the Clinton administration against violations of privacy. Clinton tried to introduce the policy initiative called Clipper Chip, a chipset for secure voice communication, it would give the government the opportunity to read your internet traffic when authorised by law. They went on to create a number of successful programs including off-the-record messaging which allowed for encrypted conversations over MSN, and PGP an open source email encryption service.

Where the early Libertarians were interested in the freedom of individuals in regards to online activity, it was one of the original members Julian Assange who had the realisation to use the cryptography to show a different side of the debate. He realised that there were no safe ways for individuals to be whistleblowers about their governments abuse of power. Cryptography allowed for privacy of messages between individuals but it also allowed an opportunity to keep these individual safe. Julian created the site Wikileaks for whistleblowers around the world.

One of the proponents of Libertarianism is skepticism in the government, that if the government is given the chance they will do the worst that is possible. Creating Wikileaks added wood to the fire in terms of a person's skepticism towards their own government. Overnight he had started to sow the seed of doubt in people's minds. This led to a number of whistleblowers coming forward as they felt comfortable that they could get their story out there anonymously, with leaks relating to the abuse of power by the government in regards to Guantanamo Bay; the Afghanistan War; corruption in Kenya; illegal airstrikes in Afghanistan and Iraq War logs. All examples of the abuse of power by the government.

One of the key whistleblowers that Julian inspired was Edward Snowden. In 2013, Snowden hit at the heart of the social liberties debate when he revealed that the US government were listening to their own people. What the cypherpunks had originally feared had come true and it was impossible to miss this story. Libertarians and the general public saw this as a gross injustice and the skepticism of the government increased.

It was not just the scepticism over the power that the government had in terms of monitoring its population that was a concern for Libertarians, it was also related to commerce. Libertarians believe that the government should not be in charge of their population's currency. The first instance of this was in 1998 with PayPal. Libertarian and founder of the company Peter Theil's vision for the company was 'to create a new world currency, free from all government control and dilution — the end of monetary sovereignty, as it were.' However PayPal ended up being government regulated when it was sold to Ebay. This set the stage for Bitcoin, a cryptocurrency that was free from government regulation.

Bitcoins got their early success thanks to another Libertarian online venture, The Silk Road. Ross Ulbricht was convicted in 2013 as being the mastermind behind the Silk Road, which has commonly been referred to as the Amazon for buying drugs. The site was a libertarian nirvana in Ulbricht's eyes: "Silk Road was founded on libertarian principles ... The same principles that have allowed Silk Road to flourish can and do work anywhere human beings come together. The only difference is that the State is unable to get its thieving murderous mitts on it."

It has both the fiscally conservative approach of the government not being involved and the social liberal element where people could buy anything they wanted. The site's customers were a small base of dealers and buyers, although they got to experience a libertarian marketplace. The currency that made this all possible was Bitcoin. A currency that allowed for transactions to be anonymous in the same way that money can't be tracked offline. The value of Bitcoin comes from the fact that there are a finite amount and no governing body can produce any more.

Both Bitcoin and The Silk Road have provided the general public with real life examples of what the Libertarian values are. They have won over a number of fans with examples of what can happen when the government are not in control of the your choices and currency.

It is not just happening on the fringes of the internet anymore, Libertarianism is gaining popularity in Silicon Valley as well. Libertarians also believe that the government should not be in control of services - this should be left to the people and the disruptive economy, one of the latest movements in Silicon Valley, is disrupting many government regulated institutions with a new wave of start-ups. Investor Chris Dixon got straight to the point of what they are trying to fix - 'regulations that truly protect the public interest are necessary. But many regulations are created by incumbents to protect their market position.'

Uber is currently the poster child of this new generation of disruptive start-ups. The mobile application connects cab drivers with passengers via a mobile app. Mike Arrington, founder of TechCrunch, who has been very enthusiastic about the company since its launch in 2010, claimed 'let's help break the back of the taxi medallion evil empire.' City taxi services are one of the most regulated bodies in a city.

Uber have provided a model to other starts up to challenge government organisations. Uber didn't try and work through the red tape of government utility regulatory bodies. They scaled fast and got a number of loyal fans on board and, by the time they got into legal trouble, they used social media to mobilise their fans and lobby government over antiquated laws that no longer made sense. In DC and San Francisco, Uber fought legislation and got old laws overturned in their favour, thanks to their vocal fans.

It is not just Uber vs. the taxi industry, there are a number of other high profile start ups that are taking on government regulation. Peer-to-peer home rental start up AirBnB recently got 235,000 people to sign their petition to legalise AirBnB in New York City, much to the dismay of the government regulated housing board.

The internet has been an amazing opportunity for a 300 year old radical philosophy to help permeate pop culture and show why their point of view makes sense. Through the internet they were able to show why the population need to decrease the power of the government at all opportunities. Through Wikileaks and Edward Snowden they were able to show the governments abuse of power when it came to freedom of communication. Through Bitcoins and Silk Road they were able to give you a choice of currency that was not controlled by a government and a freedom of choice. Then through this new school of start ups that are disruptive to government, they were able to give you an option to services that were only ever offered through government regulated services.

New Creativity for the New Culture

By Vladimir Ćosić

The third millennium brought with it an era of eclectic creativity, opening an enormous window of opportunity for both creators and consumers. Thanks to digital media, almost every person on the planet has the possibility of creating content that could theoretically be seen by everyone.

Because of this, the boundaries between art and advertising that were once clearly defined have almost disappeared. Yes, the boundaries have become blurred since the days when Andy Warhol's Campbell soup can resembling packaging was quickly adopted as a true work of art, or perhaps even earlier - the first time that a ruler had the idea to have his surreal portrait done in order to promote his own government among the minions (which instantly transformed his personality into a brand). And, yes, brands like Coca-Cola, Nike, Adidas and Puma (and many others) for decades played an important and undeniable role in the (sub)culture.

But never in history has advertising had the task of achieving artistic value in its basic postulates. On the other hand, art probably always had a tendency towards commercialism: no matter how the artist "just wanted to express" himself, his artwork does not exist if it's not shared with the audience; in addition, artists have to eat to live, and food costs money.

One of probably the biggest turning points in the history of the relationship between advertising and art (or more broadly between "commercial" and "personal") happens at this very moment, mostly because of the new means of mass communication that can't be ignored.

Amidst this uncertainty, a new phenomenon is shaping up. It's called "fast evolution." It is of greater proportion and a more powerful meaning than ever before when advertising, art and creativity in general are concerned. The media in the traditional sense no longer exist – literally every action of any brand or individual via the Internet and social networks has become accessible to everyone. The outcome is a dramatic change in the directing of campaign budgets, and the whole area of media planning has become a field of creative expression as much as the campaign idea itself. The production has changed as well. Many campaigns consist of a powerful message only; some of the videos made by mobile phones are way more (virally) popular than TV commercials made with enormous budgets.

Focus groups and other recently popular forms of testing the public opinion are substituted with "in vivo" tests on social networks, which are now by far easier, faster, cheaper and more flexible than any other available method. A campaign that doesn't go 'viral', doesn't exist. "Commercials" are no longer just commercials. They "aren't exactly advertising, but are very interesting", they "look like commercials, but I don't know what they are" and "I don't know if it is some artistic act or a commercial". They are now better known as "branded content", which is essentially art sponsored by the brands, art with the purpose of product sale or a commercial in a new, artistic disguise. Increasing numbers of brands are setting goals and missions which, beside sales, aim for ideals of a better world. Artists are turning to advertising methods in their work, so it comes as no surprise that it is hard to differentiate between advertising and art. Questions like "Is Banksy's work a campaign or art?", "Is Pharell's new album a commercial?", "Is Dove's last campaign just a psychological experiment?" are irrelevant. The boundaries between science, art and advertising are so porous that they are nearly non-existent. Brands have become modern patrons of art, scientists have become artists, advertisers have become scientists, and the artists got employed in the agencies where they are creating what they would naturally create at some other place. The influence of advertising on our digital culture has increased to the extent that it's on equal terms, or even above, art.

You are not convinced? Ultra famous Pharell's music hit "Happy" has been seen eighty million times at this point. For the comparison, the multi Cannes Grand Prix Award winner "Dumb Ways to Die" has about seventy-five million views. The number of such examples is endless. Let us remember that just a few years ago we were switching TV channels whenever we see a commercial, while pop stars were worshiped to idolatry. Someone may say that the number of views on Youtube is not a relevant way to measure impact on people's lives. If you think this way, I personally believe that you are greatly mistaken. If you do not believe me, take a closer look at what teenagers are clicking on the internet and contemplate for a moment how it affects their behaviour and the development of their personality. Or wait for them to grow up and see what will be the final result. These are not dark premonitions or visions of the future, but only attempt to draw attention to a phenomenon that largely occurs every day, at the level of the Beatles influence on our parents or grandparents. For those who need more in-depth argument, I suggest you look at any serious strategic analysis of results of specific campaigns (enter "Cannes winner case study" in the Youtube search engine, for example) and you will find out in a very tangible way how the campaign affected (changed) the behaviour of people.

Don't kid yourself; advertising today has tremendous influence on our lives. As a matter of fact, it always had, just that the "quality" of the influence is different – advertisers are not only selling us the products, we are also buying into the ideas, aesthetics and higher aims served by the brands, same as we do with art. Popular culture is almost unimaginable without it. Having all of this in mind, the best campaigns of today are those that share characteristics of any other form of art: emotional potential, craftsmanship of the form inseparable from the essence, and the power of the idea to change the world for the better. All brands that don't realise this and don't find their place in these new circumstances are destined for mediocrity, and will soon lose the attention and the trust of their audience. Now, do we really want all brands to be culturally famous agents of change? And even if we did, is this realistic? Well, as in everything, some brands will have more success than the others; but, what we can be sure is that brands with an ambition that is larger than just selling us the product are the ones that will have our attention.

Simultaneously, some artists practicing non-commercial, sometimes even autistic art forms are either doomed to oblivion, or else rapidly becoming more commercial, and in achieving this goal, the artists are ready to use well-tried advertising means, and even to give up on the idea to be more popular among the target audience.

And this is how the boundaries between those two worlds are rapidly disappearing. Inside this vacuum, a completely new kind of creativity is rising. The word "creativity" that in the end of the last millennium became so devoid of meaning that it became an unpleasant sounding cliché, now achieves a completely new dimension, equally meaningful as ever in the human aspect, with an influence probably bigger than ever. The most exciting ideas are born on the places where science, technology, and creativity meet. The best of them are extremely relevant for people (whether we call them art lovers or consumers), changing their lives for the better in a very tangible way.

Combining truly human insights, ideas and goals with extremely smart advertising and scientific methods, *"new kind of creativity"* has the best of both worlds (advertising/art), and the possibilities that lay ahead are boundless. Creativity is becoming something new, undefined and very broad; it is becoming a field where creative human beings are using scientific, artistic and communicational tools of all kinds, merging and combining them in a meaningful way to have greater impact than ever before.

Although it's hard to say how things will look ten years from now (to be honest it's hard to say even what will be happening in next year), it's pretty clear that era ahead of us will be exciting – at least for the artists and brands who embrace the change and have something meaningful to say to the world.

Stuffocation and its Impact on Brands

By James Wallman

Probably the most important question you'll ever ask yourself is this: how should you, and the rest of society, live in order to be happy?
As you're reading this, though, chances are you're asking yourself something a lot less philosophical, something like: how can you market your clients' goods so that people buy more of them?

Fair enough. I doubt you're reading this book for advice on how you, or anyone else, should live. Don't dismiss the first question out of hand yet, though, because the two are intimately connected. By that, I mean that if you know where people are looking for happiness – and status and identity and meaning as key ingredients of that – you'll have a much better idea of how you can sell to them.

There was a time, of course, when people looked for status, identity, meaning, and happiness in material goods. That time was called the 20th century, when the possibilities of mass production and the magic of mass media combined to create a materialistic value system that believed more was better, and greed was good.

And the system worked. First, it hauled billions of people out of poverty. Next, it provided them, and us, with central heating, indoor toilets, colour TVs, Ataris, Barbies, BMXs, Louboutin shoes and a myriad of other consumer knick-knacks. It was the best idea of the 20th century, taking society from scarcity, which had been the condition of 99% of humans since the dawn of time, to abundance. Lucky us.

But then something happened. Or, rather, lots of things did. And then, not only did materialism not look so shiny and great anymore, but all those things added up to what I think is the defining problem of our generation, a problem I call *Stuffocation*.

Stuffocation is about how we have enough, and how we've had enough of stuff. Don't take my word for it, though: take the "Have you had enough of stuff?" quiz at the end of this chapter. And consider the Center on the Everyday Lives of Families (CELF) study, the most extensive piece of research ever conducted on how ordinary people are living.

After more than a decade of research, the team of anthropologists, ethnographers, and psychologists concluded, as the final report states, that we are living in "the most materially rich society in global history, with light-years more possessions per average family than any preceding society", that we are at a point of "material saturation", that we are coping with "extraordinary clutter", and that we, as individuals and as a society, are facing a "clutter crisis".

So, why is *Stuffocation* happening, and why now? If you ask a different expert, you'll get a different answer. An environmentalist will tell you it's because we're worried about landfill, carbon footprint, climate change. A philosopher, like Alain de Botton, say, might tell you it's the status anxiety that comes with meritocracy and materialistic consumption. A psychologist, like Oliver James, might say all this stuff is giving us affluenza, that mass production and mass consumption is causing mass depression. A political scientist, like Ron Inglehart at the University of Michigan, for instance, might tell you that, as we now live in a stable society with enough food to eat and a guaranteed roof over our heads, we've climbed up Maslow's hierarchy of needs and become post-materialist. A demographer might tell you it's because of the rise of the global middle class – making resources still more scarce and costly – and urbanisation – when people choose to live in cities rather than the countryside, they are trading space for experience.

And a technologist might agree with all the others, but point out that the shift away from materialism is simply because we can: why have a second car when you can use Zipcar? Why fill your carry on with books when you can take a Kindle?

And what do I, a seasoned trend forecaster, think?

When I write these reasons down and consider the list, two thoughts strike me.

The first is: what about Facebook? Social media is not only changing how we communicate, it is changing how we present ourselves and signify status. In the 20th century, you could indicate your status with the Breitling watch on your wrist, the Prada handbag on your arm, or the Louis Vuitton wallet you use to pay. But, unless you made a point of telling them, no-one would know that, last weekend, you had been to a concert, Secret Cinema, a pop-up restaurant, or that you played golf on the roof of Selfridges. Social media has turned that 20th century truth on its head.

Now, only a relative few will see your car or your handbag. But with all your friends and followers on Twitter, Instagram, and Facebook, many more will know that you are watching the sunset from your riad's rooftop in Marrakech, or on a chairlift in Chamonix, or about to run the New York marathon, or see the Stones in concert, or you're at TEDxHoP or SXSW. That means experiences are now more visible, more tangible, more valuable, and more likely than material goods to contribute to your status.

The second is that these factors are not minor blips that are here this year, gone the next. All of the factors causing *Stuffocation* – the stable upbringing, the stress of stuff, the environment, the rise of the middle class, the move to cities, the rise in costs, the switch to digital, and the rise of social media – are the result of observable, observed, long-term trends. Taken singly, each of these would have an effect on the world like a wave surging and crashing against a sea wall. Since all are arriving at the same time, they are massing into a greater, weightier tsunami-size wave, creating a perfect storm for today's materialist culture. That is why, now, and for the foreseeable future, so many of us are disillusioned with material goods and materialism, and feeling *Stuffocation*.

So, as our fundamental values, attitudes, and behaviours are changing, what can you and your brand do about it?

The simple answer is: focus on selling experience rather than stuff. I don't mean ditch anything that's tangible. We are still flesh and blood. We still need and want and use and use up material things. But we want less material clutter, less waste, less monotonous, commoditised stuff. And we will still want status.

"People still want to keep up with the Joneses," says Jim Gilmore, who, with Joe Pine has been promoting the experience economy since the late 1990s. "Before, they wanted goods that were shinier, faster, more powerful. And they still want to keep up in the experience economy. But now they want things that are different – more durable, say, or more egalitarian, or more participatory."

This is useful, but better still, in my opinion, is in a statement Gilmore and Pine made in *The Experience Economy*: that you should try to make every engagement your audience has with your brand touch them "on an emotional, physical, intellectual, or even spiritual level".

There are some doing that, I think, and, at the same time, addressing the problems of, and taking advantage of the opportunities inherent in, *Stuffocation*. For example: Bompas & Parr, Patagonia's Common Threads Initiative, Puma's Clever Little Shopper, and, of course, Apple.

Have you been to a Bompas & Parr event? Each one, like crazy golf on the roof of Selfridges or dinner at the Andaz Hotel, is designed to not only give you a visceral experience, it's designed to share. "Everyone is an autobiographer nowadays, it's like everyone is actively writing their own biography all the time," says Bompas. "So stories are becoming even more important. In the '80s, people wanted a fast car. Now they want a good story to tell."

In its Common Threads Initiative with eBay, the outdoor brand Patagonia asked people, as the company's founder, Yvon Chouinard said, "to not buy something if they don't need it". This is a radical, revolutionary statement. It is the antithesis of the "more is better" idea of materialism. Yet it is the sort of thing that makes sense in a world feeling *Stuffocation*.

Puma created a bag that, rather than add to the clutter in your home, or the guilt you get when you throw it out, just disappears. Put the brand's Clever Little Shopper bag in hot water for three minutes and it harmlessly dissolves, so you can pour it safely down the plug.

Apple has become the world's leading brand because of its ruthless focus on experience. It makes everything pleasant, from the stores, to the moment you open the box. "Not only do the guys at Apple make sure their products are products people love to use," says Joe Pine. "They even think about the packaging, about the 'box opening experience', so even that is unique and engaging."

You can mine each of these examples for ideas. But a still better place to look for inspiration, I think, is in that fundamental human question, the question that Aristotle asked in the Nicomachean Ethics almost two and a half thousand years ago: how should you, and the rest of society, live in order to be happy?

In the 20th century, as we progressed from scarcity to abundance, the answer was materialism. Then, people found happiness, status, identity, and meaning in material things. Now, instead, in this time of abundance and so much stuff we are feeling *Stuffocation*, the answer is what I call "experientialism". Now, feeling *Stuffocation*, people are finding happiness, status, identity, and meaning in experiences. If you, and the brands you work for, can help them find those things, through experiences rather than stuff, you are more likely to connect with them, and sell to them.

Have you had enough of stuff?

1. In your home generally, do you ever worry about the mess and that things aren't in the right place?
2. Is there a part of you that wishes there was a "clutter fairy" who would clean it all away, work out what you really need, and get rid of the rest?
3. When someone you live with brings something home, is your typical response "but where are we going to keep it"?
4. In your bedroom now, if you wanted to hang a new dress or shirt in your wardrobe, would you have to heave the stuff that's already there left and right to make a gap, and jump in with the new thing, because if you weren't quick enough that gap would close up?
5. Do you have clothes you haven't worn for more than a year or, even, never worn?
6. When you open a drawer, do clothes pop out like they're trying to get some air?
7. In your kitchen, when you put something away in the cupboards, do you have to push and pull and poke, to fit the thing in your hand around all the other stuff that's already there?
8. Even when the kitchen looks clean and tidy, like a picture in an interiors magazine, are all those cupboard doors camouflage for the bedlam behind?
9. If you have a garage, is it packed so full with junk that there's not enough room to house the number of cars it was designed for?
10. Think back to a time someone gave you something in the last year. Perhaps it was at Christmas, when Auntie Doreen and Uncle Peter held out a gift-wrapped box. Maybe it was your birthday, when your mother really shouldn't have, but did, and handed over something, she said, was just the perfect thing for you. Was your gut reaction ever to think "not more stuff"?

If you answered "yes" to *any* of these questions, you, like millions of others, are feeling *Stuffocation*. Join the conversation by tweeting your score, and look for #stuffocation on Twitter.

Ads Send Out More Than the Clients' Message

By Carl W. Jones

As creatives we are trained to take a problem and solve it using advertising tools and techniques. Messages are designed to sell a product or service, and we do not necessarily consider the consequences that a branded message has on society. We focus on an ad's creation, its cumulative effect, and rarely pay attention to how advertising reflects what is considered 'normal' within society.

The following examples are ads created during the 'golden age of advertising' by the Madmen working on Madison Avenue in the 1960's. The advertising messages created for American brands, by transnational advertising agencies based in New York, reflect a society that permitted violence towards women, white superiority, and stereotypes of female inadequacies, all presented through a patronizing male point of view.

Doyle Dane Bernbach's (DDB) long running advertising campaign for *Volkswagen* launched a German car in post-war America. One magazine ad used a typical 1960's male condescension where "women are soft and gentle but they hit things" with the car, to pitch car parts as "easy to replace... and cheap". (1)

In an ad for *Kenwood* mixers, the headline stated, "The chef does everything but cook - that's what wives are for!" (2). This message clearly re-enforced the perception that a woman's place is in the kitchen. A campaign for

Leggs brand men's pants went further, portraying a woman as a trophy being stepped on by a man who stated "it's nice to have a girl around the house." (3)

American society saw these advertising messages as cultural reflections of the times, and the creatives who came up with the ads had no reservations with showing women as inferior to men.

Ads for household brands in the early 20th century also used perceived racial differences to emphasis a product's benefit: a little white girl asks a black child "Why doesn't your mama wash you with fairy soap?". The body language of the two children reflects the awkwardness of the conversation while emphasizing the white child's superior role in the encounter. (4)

Consumers saw these branded advertising messages and accepted them as reflections of contemporary society, just as slavery was at one time accepted as "normal". In these more enlightened times, we now know that those norms are wrong and deeply insulting.

Creatives and clients need to question more than the creative idea when evaluating branded advertising; they need to look at the symbols used in the message and ask: does the ad demean a person or group to make a brand appear superior?" If the answer is yes, then they need to go back to the drawing board and start again.

So how are we doing now? Surely we have moved on? Let's look at some examples. How might the following branded messages be interpreted looking back from the future?

A controversial 2013 American trans-media "anti-rape" campaign seemed to blame women for getting raped, instead of the men who violated them. It showed a woman in a bathroom stall with sexy underwear down around her legs – and the headline "she couldn't say no". This ad blamed the victim for the rape suggesting that because she drank, the woman provoked the assault. The ad targets the "violated as opposed to the violator" by suggesting the falsehood that if a woman drinks, then she is "asking for it" (5). Again, creatives and clients need to consider all angles and interpretations of the advertising message when exposing it to a larger public and realize how more than just the brand message is coming across.

Numerous McDonald's TV ads from various agencies around the world have used cultural and racial stereotypes to sell themed hamburgers. The agency for McDonalds Germany fell back on a racial stereotype of reflecting the Mexican as a mustachioed male wearing a sombrero and poncho to sell a TexMex themed burger (6). When a Mexican burger was released in Australia in 2010, the same cartoon stereotype of a mustached male wearing a sombrero was appropriated. (7) This conventional image was also used in advertising created in London for the UK release of a Mexican hamburger. (8) On a simplistic level this characterization may appear funny to Australians, the British and Germans, however, one must question whether it would it be acceptable to use Jewish or African American stereotypes. Mexicans travelling the world do not appreciate being demeaned by these images. Apart from Mariachis, the only people seen wearing sombreros are the "gringo" tourists at the Mexican airports.

This is not to say that Mexico is a country free from controversy in advertising. In a long-running image campaign for a national, family-owned department store, 'insights' that reinforced racist and classist attitudes were appropriated to sell luxury goods. Billboards placed in major urban centers presented Caucasian females wearing designer gowns. What is not shown is what caused the controversy. Mexico's population is made up of 15% indigenous peoples, 80% are mixed European and indigenous blood called mestizo, with the residual 5% being Caucasian. Looking at the *Palacio de Hiero* advertising, a question arises: why is 95% of the population not reflected in the advertising? (9) Presumably, the majority of consumers would want to see themselves reflected in ads. European, Canadian and US advertising certainly use models that reflect the majority of their peoples, so why not Mexico? As creatives we need to realize what we do not put in an advertising message can have as much power as what we do put in.

In a 2013 General Motors (GM) campaign, racial stereotypes were used in a commercial that was aired globally on TV and the Internet. A 1938 song, "Oriental Swing" that featured the lyrics "now, in the land of Fu Manchu, the girls all now do the Suzie-Q... Ching, ching, chop-suey, swing some more!" The ad also made fun of how geisha girls can't say "r" and say "Amelicans" instead of "Americans." (10) The ad was quickly taken down after an outcry in the press. The client and agency responded with the usual bland statement of "we are sorry" and "will revise our approval process."

Also in 2013, the well-respected social commentator Dr. Boyce Watkins wrote "Mountain Dew Releases Arguably the Most Racist Commercial in History". (11) In his blog, Watkins explained how the soft drink manufacturer used racist stereotypes in a TV commercial where the "suspects" are all black, and the "good guys" are mostly white.

In this Internet connected, multicultural world, we should think twice before using a racial stereotype to sell a brand. We should recognize that the whole world has the potential to see any digital communication. As creators of advertising, we need to realize that when we create messages we are also re-enforcing standards and attitudes that we (and society) perceive to be correct. Looking back at the early 21st century from the future it would appear that advertisers repeatedly used racial and gender stereotypes to position brands

Stereotypes of female body shape in beauty magazines and advertising, have recently come under attack in the mass media. However, women are not the only ones affected by unrealistic body images, presented in the communication industry; teenage males also experience body dissatisfaction. A documentary released in 2014 called "The mask you live in" questions men's unobtainable roles and expectations in society. These views were re-enforced through advertising messaging distributed through the mass media. Since the 1980's there has been an increase in the use of overly muscular men in advertising, from Calvin Klein's 80's billboards (12) to the current posters for Abercrombie and Fitch. (13) This imagery has a negative effect on the self-esteem of young males who obsessively focus on trying to obtain large muscles and six packs. This thought disorder has been called "Bigorexia".

Advertising would also have us believe that the stereotype of a "real man" is defined by the beer or whisky he drinks. Just examine the advertising messages targeting men during sports events: men cannot cry; don't do house work; can't touch each other; have large muscles and six-packs; and stare sexually at women. These ads make it appear that there is only one way to be a man, to fit into western society. A future retrospective look at advertising from the early 21st century might suggests that if you do not match the implied codes of masculinity shown in advertising, then you aren't really a man.

Advertising broadcast in any media, communicates more than just the client's strategy. It also sends out covert messages about societies norms: class structure; race; politics; sexual attitudes; what is permitted and what isn't. This is especially true when the same stereotype is repeated in many different branded messages. There may be a hilarious TV commercial, made funnier by using racial stereotypes but the ad functions by abusing somebody. As makers of advertising communication we should exercise social responsibility. We need to realize that, when creating messages, we also reinforce standards and attitudes that we (and contemporary society) perceive to be correct. In the future, some of these messages will be judged as demeaning or simply wrong.

I am not saying that using stereotypes or featuring insights is wrong, but as generators of advertising messages, we need to be aware of the power that our 'cumulative' messages have; reinforcing negative stereotypes and perceived social norms. All Mexicans do not wear sombreros, men can cry, and women do not asked to be raped.

Advertising messaging can broadcast a positive, branded communication, that can reverse negative, and gender stereotypes. In a well-known campaign, the ideal 'female body' as traditionally presented in advertising was effectively challenged by *Dove*. (14) Ogilvy's *real beauty* movement challenged the beauty and fashion marketers on the way they portrayed women with unrealistic stereotypes. In part, due to this effort, the female target market is now aware of retouched ads. "As soon as they see one, major luxury brands are publicly challenged for retouching famous actresses beyond recognition in their advertising, and 17-year-old girls are demanding that the glossy magazines they read feature more real girls in their pages. *Dove's* campaign worked."

This ground breaking movement is an example of how a brand can be socially aware, and broadcast a message that confronts media generated stereotypes. The global, multimedia communication had the power to raise awareness, and changed the way women see themselves, as well as meeting client sales expectations.

So fellow creatives, let's apply our talent & knowledge to move advertising forward, and remember: Ads in any medium send out more than just the client's message.

Ad References

1. Agency. DDB. Headline: Sooner or later, your wife will drive home one of the best reasons for owning a Volkswagen. Year: 1960's. http://www.automopedia.org/2009/06/26/10-most-offensive-car-ads/ (accessed on May 11 2014)
2. Kenwood. Headline: The chef does everything but cook-that's what wives are for!. Year: 1960's. http://www.boredpanda.com/vintage-ads/?image_id=vintage-ads-that-would-be-banned-today-10.jpg (accessed on May 11 2014)
3. Leggs. Headline: It's nice to have a girl around the house. Year: 1960's. http://www.boredpanda.com/vintage-ads/?image_id=vintage-ads-that-would-be-banned-today-18.jpg
4. Fairy soap. Client: Palmolive. Headline: "Why doesn't your mama wash you with Fairy soap?". Year: late 19th or early 20th century. http://www.boredpanda.com/vintage-ads/?image_id=vintage-ads-that-would-be-banned-today-2.jpg (accessed on May 11 2014)

5. Rape. Headline: She couldn't say no. Year: 2013. http://www. businessinsider.com/anti-rape-psas-that-blame-the-victim-2013-3 (accessed on May 11 2014)

6. McDonald's Germany. Agency: Leo Burnett. Year: 2013 http:// www.youtube.com/watch?v=z1eeEYRXpCE (accessed on May 11 2014).

7. McDonald's Australia. Agency: Leo Burnett. Year: 2010. https://www. youtube.com/watch?feature=player_embedded&v=uhqCQQYibkA (accessed on May 11 2014).

8. McDonald's U.K. Agency: Leo Burnett. Year:2012 https://www. youtube.com/watch?v=1BH4fbZOqEE (accessed on May 11 2014).

9. Palacio. Agency:TBWA Teran. Year: 2001. http://www.myt.org. mx/tolerancia.php (accessed on May 11 2014).

10. General.Motors. Year: 2013 . Client: Chevy traxx. http://www. nydailynews.com/autos/ching-chong-chop-suey-gm-pulls-racist-ad-article-1.1332381 (accessed on May 11 2014)

11. Mountain Dew. Year: 2013. Client: PepsiCo. http://www. yourblackworld.net/2013/04/black-news/mountain-dew-releases-arguably-the-most-racist-commercial-in-history/ (accessed on May 11 2014).

12. Abercrombie. Photographer: Bruce Weber. http://www. abercrombie.com http://www.thedrum.com/news/2013/06/17/ abercrombie-fitch-faces-list-backlash-after-ceos-only-cool-kids-comments-are (accessed on May 11 2014).

13. Dove. Agency: Ogilvy Toronto. Year: 2006. Client: Unilever. Case study video: http://www.dandad.org/en/dove-evolution/ (accessed on May 11 2014). Case study report: The Dove AdMakeover: Unlocking the Social Power of the Dove Brand. Jay Chiat Strategic Excellence Awards Issue: Gold, 2012 Case study Warc.com

14. Calvin. Agency: In house. Year:1982. Photographer: Bruce Weber. http://www.corbisimages.com/stock-photo/rights-managed/ BE058155/calvin-klein-underwear-advertisement-on-billboard (accessed on May 11 2014).

EDUCATION

We Are Young, So Let's Set The World on Fire

By Marc Lewis

Education is not the filling of a pail, but the lighting of a fire.
William Yeats

There is in every village a torch - the teacher; and a fire extinguisher: the priest.
Victor Hugo

Just as Britain is a patchwork of villages from John o'Groats in the north to Land's End in the south, Britain Plc. is also a patchwork of villages. I work in a village called Advertising, as do many readers of this book. If you are a reader from the UK then we probably know each other and have possibly broken bread together. My wife works in a village called Occupational Psychology, which is quite a bit smaller than the village of Advertising; you can fit the entire population into one of those generic conference hotels.

In every village, the most important asset is its people. This is why it is so important to develop the skills, knowledge and general wellbeing of people. When villagers flourish, so too does the village. There are two ways to motivate people to learn and act in ways that are beneficial to our society; we can light the fire of curiosity, hunger for self-development and camaraderie, or we can impose systems and rules that prescribe the knowledge that needs to be acquired and the behaviour that is expected. The first way is the way of the torch and the second is the way of the fire extinguisher.

Would you rather be remembered as a torch or as a fire extinguisher? Both have their uses, but I hope that you picked the former. If you picked the latter then this chapter is probably wasted on you and it is unlikely to provide any value. This chapter is for aspiring torches and explains how we can burn brighter, for longer. This chapter is for those who want to shine brightly and for those who want to share their flame with others, so that their village glows from wall-to-wall.

Before I begin, I should share a disclaimer; I run the School of Communication Arts in London. I have developed an extremely unorthodox learning model through which my forty students learn from a network of over six hundred mentors. I shall take a moment to explain how this works for the benefit of the school, our students and mentors before I share my wildest dreams with you.

Traditionally, education is provided as a transaction between a teacher, who usually stands at the front of the classroom; and students, who are all simultaneously listening to that teacher. Knowledge mostly flows one-way and the success of a cohort is directly linked to the abilities of the teacher. Many teachers are fantastic. Many teachers are not. So traditional education is a bit of a lottery.

My classroom is designed to look like an agency's creative department. Teachers only stand at the front for an hour or so each day. They spend the rest of their time in school having meaningful conversations with small groups of students. This is where the magic happens, where flames are lit.

I employ a core team of seven permanent part-time teachers, all of whom are working within the industry when they are not in school. We endeavour to welcome half a dozen mentors to the school each day and we describe someone as a mentor if they visit the school at least once a year. They come from across advertising, film, fashion, music, technology and other creative industries.

Mentors sit with groups of students and chat about whatever they want to chat about. The conversation will often start with the students' latest projects but usually meanders unpredictably. They might discuss a film, a book or some art that inspired them in some way. They might talk about a project that the mentor is working on back at their company, using it as a reference to help shape the students' understanding of their project. They might talk about whatever is in the news.

In our school, the transaction of knowledge between teachers/mentors and the students is two-way because conversation flows freely. Students benefit greatly because they are learning from experienced practitioners who have a wealth of experience, but mentors also benefit in a number of ways.

We invite mentors to complete a short survey after they spend time in school and the first question we ask is, '*On a scale from 1 to 7, where 1 is a complete waste of time and 7 is the best possible use of your time, how do you rate your time in school today?*' - the most common answer is 6 and the second most common answer is 7.

The second question in the survey asks mentors what they gained from their time in school. Here are some of their answers;

- It makes me excited about the industry
- I loved being energised by a group of excited, enthusiastic young creatives
- Helping people; feeling that their work (and hopefully their future) would be a little better for my input
- The energy and the enthusiasm is so infectious
- It was so inspiring
- It sounds trite, but coming to the school always reminds me how many people helped me when I was starting out, and how much I owe them. So being able to help such brilliantly talented students is a source of genuine joy for me.

Companies benefit when their employees spend time mentoring at the school because they return energised and proud to work in their industry, and because they become better at developing talent within their workplace. It has been reported that mentoring improves retention rates and productivity. The mentor/mentee relationship is, quite literally, a win-win.

Companies also benefit because their employees take on an unofficial role of talent scout. Most of our students will eventually be employed by the agencies that their mentors work for. So mentoring becomes a cost-effective recruitment strategy as well as a powerful tool for improving the wellbeing and productivity of employees.

In my wildest dreams, the model of learning that we have developed at the School of Communication Arts will become the standard for vocational learning. Our school is owned by the advertising industry and our focus is on preparing talent to enter the industry. But our model could (and should) be adapted to other vocations such as architecture, engineering, fashion, landscape design and even teaching. In fact there are over 200 subjects covered by degree programmes that would benefit from a model where the majority of learning happened between a wide network of mentors and mentees.

For this to happen, an industry needs to come together and recognise that it is a village. When this happens, it will quickly discover that it is home to plenty of torches. These torches simply need a place to light new fires and a framework to make sure those new fires don't run dangerously wild.

Until very recently, I struggled to find a succinct way of explaining just how important the role of mentor is in vocational learning. I was in China a few weeks ago and a wise old man told me an idiom that left me breathless because it encapsulates the value created when a village comes together to share responsibility for preparing the next generation of talent: Once you teach someone, you are their teacher for life.

When you spend time mentoring in a school like ours, you won't just be lighting a torch. You will be lighting an eternal flame and you will be remembered forever. People who have been mentored are much more likely to become mentors. This is virtuous, viral marketing. With that in mind, why would anyone ever want to be remembered as a fire extinguisher?

Do you want to become a mentor? Here are a few places that would welcome you with open arms;

1. School of Communication Arts (www.schoolcommunicationarts. com/mentors)

   The leading ad school, based in central London and home to 40 students, one third of whom benefit from industry-funded scholarships, and a network of 700+ mentors.

2. Young Creative Council (www.youngcreativecouncil.com)

   A group of advertising creatives that aim to inspire across disciplines. They run workshops, talks, portfolio nights and socials.

3. Horses Mouth (www.horsesmouth.co.uk)

   The social network for informal mentoring, where anyone can give and anyone can gain. There are mentors from a wide number of industries waiting to help, and more are always welcome.

4. She Says (www.weareshesays.com)

   The only global creative network for women. She Says provides free mentorship and events to women in creative and marketing businesses.

5. The Prince's Youth Business International (http://www. youthbusiness.org/)

   Youth Business International helps young people to start and grow their own business and create employment. They are a global network of independent non-profit initiatives operating in over 40 countries.

Cultivating a Creative Culture

by James Kirk & Jon Barnes

Recently, a 7 year old boy bravely decided to get involved in some very serious affairs. He took the initiative to create something that the world's biggest nuclear powers have been desperately trying to perfect since 1997. This could be the biggest arms race since the cold war. It's the most sensitive document since the leaked U.S. Embassy Cables of 2010. Oliver has developed the planet's only instruction manual for a Nimbus 2000 broomstick.

For him, this was no laughing matter, a bad job could mean this scientific breakthrough would get into the hands of Slytherin graduates around the globe. Outside of school, he worked tirelessly, making sure the manual was clear, concise, and full of the kind of pastel illustrations and iconography that only an idiot wouldn't understand. This *Dummy's Guide To Creating The World's Most Awesomest Nimbus 2000 Broomstick*, is a result of hours of labour, love, and insatiable studying. It is the brainchild of a creative genius who would stopped at nothing to ensure Gryffindor's brand guidelines were followed to the letter. So how could a young child come to create the most revolutionary invention since the World Wide Web? The answer isn't a simple one, it isn't a particular skill set that has allowed Oliver to create this, but a mindset.

Oliver is always creating, always feeding his curiosity and most importantly, always learning. Whilst the creative industries love to obsess over creative genii, the purpose of this chapter isn't to put this little boy on a creative pedestal. Instead, we'd like to propose that creativity is something precious we lose over time because of the systems that constrain us. Oliver is an image of the creative spirit we are all born with, that few hold onto and that our industry must focus on nurturing. However, before we go into the attributes we believe creative businesses need to nurture, we'd like to start by providing a better idea of how this young child made something so pioneering as a Nimbus 2000 manual.

Oliver loves Dr. Who, and for Christmas he received a real Sonic Screwdriver, with which he's been on many intergalactic missions through time and space. This once took him back to medieval times where, dressed as a knight, he slayed the nastiest dragon the land had ever seen. When Oliver isn't travelling through time and space he's busy being a goalkeeper, and recently his team won their first ever game. You see, his team isn't really that good, but we're not sure Oliver knows that. He still throws himself in 100%, mimicking everything he's seen on TV watching the Premier League with his Dad.

Oliver just does what he loves, and he loves lots of things. His parents give him the freedom to be creative, try new things within a safe environment and keep expanding his knowledge and interests, for the mind of a child isn't yet bound by silos and systems, and nor should ours be. We believe the notion of a learning organisation is still too rare, and through this chapter we would like to suggest that our industry needs to focus on fostering cultures where people can re-learn four key traits often forgotten from childhood. These are adaptability, curiosity, empathy and fearlessness. We'd like to put forward the thought that companies must embrace a learning philosophy in order for people to take on the same behaviours we display before going through a copy & paste, industrialised educational system.

This shift from industrialisation, towards a knowledge economy and a service society is creating a faster moving cycle of change than ever before. This demands creative businesses to be adaptable and curious enough to find new solutions to problems. In a world where change is the only constant, adaptability is our evolutionary prerogative, particularly in industries that are looking to shape the future. This means that, much like Oliver, we need to ensure our skill sets and interests are broad, that our approach is holistic and that we are forever students. Turning our hands from one hobby and craft to another, like a child switches between presents on Christmas day. It is no longer enough to embrace one skill, in a digital age versatility trumps vocation and this spirit is indicative of a culture of learning.

This ability to adapt is the consequence of restless curiosity. Curiosity to explore, to play, to try new things, meet new people and to see the world through the eyes of a child. Always amazed, always fresh and always new. There is little room for cynicism and prejudice in a business that needs to find inspiration from the lives of others in order to solve their problems. Curiosity for us isn't just something that gets switched on or off, it follows you home, it is the driver behind most of your conversations and it is a way of life which allows us to stay young, flexible and endlessly passionate. To quote Leo Burnett: "Curiosity about life in all of its aspects... is still the secret of great creative people."

The main difference between a child and an adult however, isn't simply the diverse sources from which they gain inspiration, but the fearless commitment they put into living their passions. As we grow older, we fill our mind with barriers and find reasons not to do things. This isn't the case with children whose minds know no limits and for whom what can and can't be made is a difficult concept to grasp. It's this fearlessness that allows them to make great things without inhibitions. An example of this is the stop motion iPad film Oliver made recently using mainly LEGO characters. Most adults would spend time thinking 'how are we going to achieve this?', or 'is this possible?', 'won't this go wrong?', whereas children just do it. They jump in without thinking too hard and long about the if's and the buts. In Dan Pink's TED talk entitled 'The Truth About What Really Motivates Us', he states his belief that mastery is a key human motivator and this is something that young children pursue with far more fervour than adults. A child will work for hours trying to make the best Lego car they can, whereas most adults would give up quickly. Fearlessness is a key attribute to adopt in an industry where 'rapid prototyping' is the new buzzword.

An important shift we'd like to draw attention to is a move in the last couple of decades towards 'human centred design'. As we finally come to the logical conclusion that we should design things for people, the ability to understand what people think, feel, need and want is a critical skill to have. This is illustrated wonderfully in the acting and role playing that children enjoy so much. The moment a child puts on a costume, they become their character as if they were method actors, and nothing can take them out of this. Whether playing the role of a knight, Ben 10, or a big scary monster, this allows them to imagine worlds that don't yet exist and understand people they have never met. The same attribute we'd hope to see in any good service designer or creative, the ability to put yourself in somebody else's shoes. Anybody up for agency drama school?

It seems that the attributes needed for the creative industry to thrive are there in most people when we are young. As Ken Robinson famously said though, 'School Kills Creativity', and this is such a shame as school can often make it difficult for us to follow individual passions, foster curiosity and ultimately, make things: the kind of skills we should be nurturing our whole lives. Having experienced both traditional education and a progressive learning philosophy like Hyper Island, we feel strongly that businesses must create environments where people learn by doing, share knowledge, have personal freedom to challenge norms, and fundamentally, learn to learn. In this context it becomes possible for people to develop as adaptable, curious, empathetic and creative human beings.

Since the issues with traditional education are widespread, it is no surprise that businesses are picking their talent from these forward thinking learning approaches and searching for people with an unquenchable thirst for new experiences and a desire to learn as long as they live. As Hyper Island alumni, we certainly feel that the learning experiences and tools we gained have allowed us to carry on growing in order to adapt to a changing world. For a creative company to really thrive and create the best work they can, a good talent recruitment policy isn't enough, it is a learning culture that is needed. A culture which encourages people to develop passions, try new tools, stretch and learn every single day. A learning organisation liberates, challenges, nurtures and gives room for people to grow and adapt as their industry shifts shapes with the times, and this is the essence of a philosophy that will allow a creative business to always be at the forefront of creativity.

As for Oliver, his 'Dummy's Guide To Creating The World's Most Awesomest Nimbus 2000 Broomstick' probably won't be an international bestseller anytime soon. He doesn't really care though, he's got a new hobby now, making iPad stop motion films. Unlike in business, creativity has no objective for a child, it is just a process to express and explore curiosity. The test for Oliver's parents is to help him to continue with his hobbies and keep daring to venture outside of a factory-like system which leaves no room for diversity. The test for businesses is to move on from structures which result in homogenous thinking and towards learning cultures which allow minds to wander, and individuals to discover new approaches and learn from each other. So in the current climate where creativity is our most precious economic resource, maybe businesses should think of expanding the popular saying 'education starts at home' to 'education starts at work'.

Transformers
(or The Madam and The Belle)

By Anders Sjöstedt

1

Swedish message.

Back in 2009, a pioneering digital media school in Sweden thought it seemed like a good idea to offer its knowledge and methodology in a more concentrated form to businesses and professionals.

Hyper Island is the name of the school, and at its core lies in the fostering of collaborative minds. In early 2010 we set up shop for our executive offering among the hipsters on the Lower East Side in New York. In the US, as well as abroad, my colleagues and I witnessed panicking ad agencies and concerned brands, all trying to figure out how to handle a new, increasingly digital world.

Since then, we've worked with all the major network agencies on the planet. Their challenges were all similar; a separate digital department, led by a recruited free-thinking tech guru, had been set up to explore these new opportunities, often alienating the rest of the organisation, labelling these old guys "traditional" (and thus, of course, making them more so). The set-up invariably created the feeling on each side that they were largely ignored by those in power and that the other side was getting all the serious attention.

The preferred solutions with most of these ad agencies were similar too; some kind of quick-fix that didn't disturb regular business and required minimal involvement from the very busy leadership. This is of course a peculiar approach to a challenge that everyone admitted is disrupting an entire industry; especially when we're dealing with companies that want their clients to let them move up the strategic value chain.

We also began working with global consumer brands, and found their approach to digital development (well, any development) quite different. There seemed to be no illusion of a shortcut or any tendency towards a fire/hire solution. Decisions were slow, but once they happened they were integrated, and leadership was heavily involved.

The approach of the ad agencies meant that we saw a lot of initial interest and investment, but very little follow-up and limited positive effects. The brands had the opposite journey; small initial investment that slowly grew, committed follow-up from both leadership and HR, dedicated strategies and slow but substantial effects.

Why such a difference in approach to the same challenge?

2
What drives change.

When working with these agencies and brands, we based our work on a belief - a chain of beliefs - that the increasing use of **technology** causes more change and **complexity**, creating a world where one person can't have most of the answers and where there are **no absolute truths**, leading to a greater need for constant **exploration** and true **collaboration** between diverse people, requiring skills to successfully build strong **group dynamics** and communication, demanding that we both as individuals and organisations build stronger **self-awareness** of our strengths and challenges, to repeatedly be able to drive **transformation**.

TECHNOLOGY >
COMPLEXITY >
NO ABSOLUTE TRUTHS >
EXPLORATION >
COLLABORATION >
GROUP DYNAMICS >
SELF-AWARENESS >
TRANSFORMATION >

We also decided to believe that very few organisations or adult individuals can handle this challenge without support. Any transformational journey gets easier with the help of an external partner who is both challenging you and helping you discover what it is that holds you back, as well as pointing towards what can lead your forward.

Five years and hundreds of interventions later, I still have the same belief, and it's probably stronger than ever. I've met many leaders who say they prefer to hold off on major strategic decisions till it all "settles a bit".

That is not a very good strategy. Change will never again be this slow.

3
Why change sucks.

One of the inspirational speakers I've often invited, the barefoot and swearing Irish gentleman Mark Comerford, sometimes asks his audience: "Which ones of you like change? Raise your hand!" Depending on the setting, between half and two-thirds of the group raise their hands. He then walks up to one of those who has a hand raised and says: "So you like change? Well take off all your clothes and give me all your money."

Nobody likes change; we just like the kind of change that we ourselves prescribe. Anyone claiming anything else is a liar.

One could say that there's always been change, that things have never stayed the same. *We've dealt with it in the past, so what's different now?* The simple answer is: everything.

Until recently, we all lived in a world that did change, but slowly enough for us to be able to build our individual wisdom in a linear growth, gathering experience and insight that gave us seniority and gravitas, until we retired and passed away.

[birth]
UNCONSCIOUS INCOMPETENCE >
CONSCIOUS INCOMPETENCE >
UNCONSCIOUS COMPETENCE >
CONSCIOUS COMPETENCE >
[death]

Now, that linear journey of competence has become cyclic, and the wheel keeps spinning faster as increasing innovation makes change more frequent and more extensive. The stages are the same, but most of us are in several parallel cycles, on different levels, at the same time. With technology disrupting all industries and changing the lifestyles of every human being, the journey towards *consciously competent* is still relevant, but only when we see it as part of a constant re-birth. In a fast-changing world, relaxing into conscious competence immediately makes us unconsciously incompetent.

For most of us, we're slowly coming to terms with a life where we'll have to try to learn something new about stuff we know absolutely nothing about. This is challenging, but only truly uncomfortable if we try to resist it. Yes, we sometimes reminisce about simpler times and dream of running a small hotel somewhere exotic. Some of us begin new lives as chefs or yoga instructors, professions that still offer some linearity and have the benefits of allowing people to find comfort in their *conscious competence*. But for the rest of us, we better enjoy feeling clueless and find our own ways of continuously wising up.

Finding out how you like to learn new things, and applying this consciously to your challenges, is the only way you can pull it off. It's also the only way that any company can succeed – brand or agency.

4
Fear.

I meet many people who feel that the digital and technological development is too fast and too vast for them. "There are so many new things I don't know anything about that I don't know where to start, so I just shut down." If you're not feeling this yourself, you probably have a client or a family member that uses this as their protective mantra.

So how can we help – or be helped?

In discussions, I sometimes use the example of a well-stocked magazine store. When you walk in, the walls are covered with hundreds of titles. Most of them you've never heard of and you don't know what they are about. Does this make you panic and pull out? No, of course not. You go to your familiar sections and titles. If you have some time to spare and feel a little curious, you might decide to also buy a new interesting title from your regular section. If something new is happening in your life, maybe you're getting married or you're buying a boat, you could find yourself venturing over to other unknown sections, thumbing through unfamiliar editions. No fear, right?

Anyone can be helped to approach new technology and digital offerings in the same way. Start with what you feel familiar with, expand from there and venture over to areas where you experience a need or an interest. Like the magazine store, browsing is free and there are plenty of people around to give you good advice. Even better, much of what you find is free (or almost), and it usually fits in your pocket.

We all survive because we have a respect for the unknown and prefer proven solutions. When a linear development has led us to a *conscious competence* within a field or a profession (like an experienced, successful leader of a big corporation), it is naturally very uncomfortable for us to deal with the *conscious incompetence*. So, as professionals, we let others deal with the new stuff, hire twenty-somethings to tweet for us or purchase a digital start-up (who, by the time you understand what they do, have already passed their prime and are usually overpriced).

As all this new stuff is seriously disrupting all our markets and industries, delegating without insight probably isn't the best option. If you don't know what questions to ask, and if you don't know what answers to challenge, you cannot win.

5
Agencies and change.

The agency approach to change is simple:

- Get a quick, generic understanding of the challenge.
- Find the fix and hire it (and, if needed, fire someone to balance the cost).
- If you can't hire it, buy it.

It's based on the belief that talent and creativity is a limited natural resource, there to be tapped, often fragile and perishable. You mine the quarry till it's empty, then you find a new hole to dig. The revolving-door strategy is helped along by increasingly flexible employment laws in most countries, allowing us to see human resource as disposable cogs in the machinery. That most agencies are based in attractive metropolitan areas also strengthens this behaviour. There's always someone new, bright and shiny that you can lure in through the front door.

The view of the career timeline shared by most leaders in the advertising industry – that you should change jobs every three years or so, to show that you're on the move – adds another problem. If you know you're leaving soon, you build a place that you won't mind leaving.

With leadership perpetually overwhelmed from pitching (a business practice that no other industry except architects would be dumb enough to apply) or handling client emergencies, and a weak HR department dedicated to hiring and firing, the mind-space available for innovative, structural solutions to disruptive challenges can be fit into a matchbox. This in turn attract clients who operate in a similar way; career-driven, attention seeking, short-term focused and disloyal.

All agencies I meet complain that their clients "don't get it", that they ask for creative approaches but never actually give any leeway to innovative ideas. It's a mistake to think that the problem – and the solution – can be found outside the agency. Any client relationship is like parenting; you lead by example. They won't do what you say; they will do what you do. If you listen, really listen, they will begin to do the same. If you show that you're both brave and vulnerable, well, you get the drift.

The pitch habit perverts the relationship between agency and client. It teaches the client that they can, and should be, superior and demanding (and slightly erratic, keeping everybody on their toes) to get any decent results. It strengthens the belief inside the agency that they will only be liked when they are all dressed up, brilliant and convincing; never when they admit insecurities and invite to open dialogue. This dynamic will keep any agency in constant emergency mode, unable to give sufficient attention to solid long-term excellence and adaptivity.

Agencies that want to work constructively with disruption, transformation and change must do it together with others; and first of all with their clients. Begin with trusting that whatever confusion and stress you feel, they most certainly feel it too. If your pitch didn't build openness, trust and transparency, make sure that the client knows that the first thing you do in your collaboration is to de-pitch. You can't hurry trust*, but you can make sure it starts to grow.

When I ask an agency employee to explain why their favourite account is the favourite, it always boils down to the quality of the trust and the openness of the collaboration. Why make it so rare?

* Thank you Susa Pop in Berlin. "Vertrauen kann man nicht beschleunigen."

6
Brands and change.

If agencies have their own challenges when dealing with disruption and change, so do brands. If agencies struggle with true transformation because they're *on* speed, I see that brands often stumble due to the lack of it.

The extent to which an *if it ain't broke, don't fix it* approach is successful depends completely on the definition of *broke*, and I have still to meet a brand that is very specific about it.

Brands in general have a lot going for them. One blessing in disguise is that many are headquartered in not-quite-globally-attractive locations. A revolving-door practice to talent and excellence simply won't work in Älmhult or Bentonville; you have to hire right, train them well and make sure they stay.

Another strength is their HR departments. While this function is understaffed in most agencies (and usually focused on hiring), training and development of staff in most corporations is often a well-calibrated investment, especially among consumer brands. As a rule, brands that focus on the development of their employees, like IKEA, have at least ten times as many HR-focused employees as a typical network agency. This means that brands have access to a skilled and professional unit to both develop, and drive, strategic transformation within the organisation – not because it's a nice thing to do, but because it pays off. (Research from Center For American Progress shows that the full cost of replacing a senior employee in an advanced position can be as much as two annual salaries.)

This focus may attract professionals looking for a stronger purpose and more long-term commitments, but it also fosters a culture where you're encouraged to stay in a role until you have created a substantial and sustainable impact – something that always takes more than three years to accomplish.

Still, within a brand organisation, there is often dire need for alternative viewpoints, innovative solutions and removal of habitual roadblocks (strengths that I find within many good agencies). Brands themselves lament this, but still find it hard to invite the alternative viewpoint, because the cherished loyalty and commitment makes outsiders untrustworthy, even dangerous. *They don't understand us.* The freelancers and the constantly changing work force that can make agencies so dynamic and action-oriented aren't there to open up the minds. Collaboration exists, but it lacks challenge and diversity*.

When I ask a brand representative to describe a good agency partnership, it strangely enough always about deep understanding of needs and respect of each other's strengths (yes, the quality of the trust and the openness of the collaboration). It sounds like there should be mutual interest.

* My friend Max Samuels labels it The Consideration Game. "Don't call me on my shit and I won't call you on yours."

7
So.

In comparison to agencies, brands in general have a more coherent – and therefore more successful – attitude towards change. Here are some interesting differences in behaviour that I have observed over the years, when supporting brands and agencies to handle transformation.

<u>Brand</u>	<u>Agency</u>
"Welcome, we're all waiting for you. Coffee?"	"Wait here, they're all late."
"I'm with our clients today, so let's speak tomorrow."	"I need to cancel, my client is calling."
"Our agency doesn't understand what we need."	"Our client doesn't like what we do."

"We need to change, we're losing clients."

"Let's postpone this change talk, we're losing clients."

"Here's the team that will be working with you."

"They're all in a meeting, can I take a message?"

"If this approach works, we'll roll it out."

"There was some good initial excitement, but it all kind of fizzled out."

I believe that the main difference allowing a brand to take a structured, pro-active approach on how to deal with a transforming world is how clients are viewed. For a brand, the business HAS clients. For an agency, the business IS clients.

This means that the business of the brand – if handled correctly – is constantly evolving to attract and retain the right amount and type of clients. The client is important, but the focus is on building the right business to get there.

When the business IS the client – as is the case with most agencies – this perspective gets lost. Strategic development, structural improvements and strengthening of your assets is something that's discussed at occasional leadership summits, only to be quickly abandoned and forgotten when the next pitch or client emergency unexpectedly (sic!) appears the next day. In terms of the second oldest occupation in the world: The brand thinks like the madam, hosting the relationship and building the assets to maximise the attraction. The agency, with all its energy directed towards pleasing the next client, has the mindset of the, well, you get where I'm going.

Our only answer to the challenge of speed and change is improved collaboration. Not just passing the buck, but actual co-working where we help each other exceed and succeed, and where *everyone* is seen as a potential partner. Both agencies and brands struggle with collaboration, but their strengths and weaknesses are reversed, making them – at least in theory – ideal partners.

Collaboration requires trust. Trust is built on honesty. And with honesty, someone has to start, take the leap. Any agency waiting for their client to take that step will probably wait a long time. The very thing that many brands need is to learn to trust the outsider. Agencies often do that very well.

8
Two letters.

Dear agency,

I love your cool office and your receptionist is really pretty. I would also love if you could see that you are creating everything you experience. You get inconsistency because you are inconsistent and you're not fully trusted because you don't trust yourself (that sometimes boastful approach is just an overcoat to keep you warm). I wish you would believe that you can use all that amazing talent to be a transformative force who truly builds solid growth, both for yourself and for your clients. Don't get distracted by the calls for instant gratification (be it that of your ego or your client's). Persistence is the only fix that works.

Dear brand,

I'm glad I finally found your office; I was on the wrong side of the highway. Your coffee is not very good, but the way you always prepare so well for our meetings makes me all warm and fuzzy. My only wish is that you take yourself and your business a little less seriously. If you want innovation, you must take time to play, and make it the core of your company. Be generous when you share insight and problems with your partners. Find ways to explore in diverse teams and launch small. Teach your teams how to operate below the corporate radar. Iterate constantly, learn as you go, use proof-of-concept to build support and snowball every success. Without deviation from the norm, progress is not possible.* And be nice to your agency, they mean well.

Sincerely,

Anders Sjöstedt

* Thank you, Frank Zappa.

How to Punch Procrastination in the Face

By Jake Attree & Laura Jordan Bambach

Procrastination is a three-legged acid devil that needs an exorcism.

That's not an overreaction. We all yearn for being able to actually sit down and get on with whatever we're supposed to be doing. As creative people who are measured on the quality of their ideas, on time and in budget, it can be daunting. The blank page. The empty screen. F%^&. We wonder how we're ever going to get started, and get magical. We wonder how to reach that energised state where something "pops" and it all falls into place. Call it "being focused," call it "getting in the zone," but there's a man with a very unpronounceable name who calls it "Flow."

It's the feeling of being completely engaged in what we're doing. We feel incredibly in tune, free of any kind of distraction so we can just be in that magic state of mind where the ideas come easily, time does weird things and the work almost feels like it's discovering itself.

For a moment, we feel like we're creatively weightless.

You might have had an experience with Flow, or not. Either way, here's a collection of thoughts on why and how we're able to get to this kind of mindset, and how eventually, we might learn to be able to control it.

In the 60s, Mihaly Csikszentmihalyi (Flow's dad) became interested in the creative process of a few of his artist friends. As they'd sit and paint, he'd observe, noticing that they could go for days at a time without really eating, drinking or sleeping. They were so engrossed in their work that their minds had a strange power over their bodies.

He was so impressed by what he saw, that he's spent the rest of his life studying what happens when human beings go beyond generic concentration and into the "optimum state of mental operation."

There are recurrent themes in how people describe the feeling too.

A chess player will talk about their experience very similarly to a racing driver. No matter what we're doing, our brains behave in the same way in order to maintain the focus.

They find a kind of sweet spot.

Oz Mohammed is an MA Maths and Teach First graduate.

"I guess I know when I'm in the zone because I start to see all the connections on the board. Between all the scribbles of equations here and there I start to see how they tie into each other. How I can manipulate them to get to where I need to get, whether that place be known or unknown at the time of doing it.

It's very literally like looking at an undone puzzle, at first I'll familiarise myself with what parts are where and how I'd use them, this mathematically normally involves playing around with the equations to see how they tick, then I can start to play with them. Sometimes it's rubbish and I don't get anywhere, other times I'll get into the zone and from there it's just automatic. But not automatic in the sense that I'll do it without thinking, but more in the sense that it becomes the clear way forward. It's searching for an answer in a way that you know is progress, rather than throwing a rock down a hole and hoping it makes a noise. I still have to concentrate on staying on the path and heading towards where I'm trying to go.

It feels great when I'm there, it can be beautiful. In a lot of cases, it can give more of a clear understanding of some natural phenomenon than words possibly could. Being in the zone I guess is the feeling that you can speak the language fluently."

Andy Sandoz is Creative Partner at Work Club

"I get as close to the real problem as possible.
Then I look away.
It's like a lens on the world.
Everything I see is a possible solution, everything is a metaphor.
Some of them stick."

A while ago a photographer called Robbie Cooper did a great project called Immersion where he took portraits of people as they were gaming.

If you've got a console, you might not be aware that you pull ridiculous faces when you play it, which is exactly what you'll see if you check out the Immersion photos.

There's a good reason behind the furrowed brows and poking tongues. Gaming is one of the best examples of how Flow works. As we start playing a new game, we're not likely to be that good, so the developers start us off in the shallow end, then as we get better, the game gets suitably harder.

Flow exists in a place where our skills match the challenge we're facing.

The same goes for the drivers, the knitters, the writers and the whoevers; as long as we know enough to carry out the task, we allow ourselves the chance to achieve optimum levels of focus.

But there's a fine balance. If we're doing something which is too difficult for us, then we become anxious. Or if our skills are beyond the challenge, we get bored.

This is exactly why Flow is more achievable if we're doing something we enjoy. We can grow with our passion and the better we get at it, the more we can do with it. Hence why people working within the creative industry are more likely to have these experiences.

A brilliant designer will most likely have been interested in design all their life. So when their day-to-day mostly involves designing things, it's no wonder they can relate to occasionally being in an amazing place mentally where they're free from distraction.

Simon Jefferis is a designer and musician.

"For me, it's less about the space I'm working in and more about who's in that space with me. Certainly at uni when we'd be sitting around talented people who are quite like-minded it was very easy to move stuff forward because you'd have the right people around to help your train of thought.

An environment isn't about where I am, it's who I'm with. I could be up on a roof, but if I'm with my friends who I work well with, I can come up with loads of exciting thoughts. Same way that if I'm in the studio with a bunch of people, it's just very helpful."

If you're doing something you love, even if it's just for an hour a week, there's a good chance you've had an experience with Flow without really knowing it. Next time you're there, pay attention the process that's lead up to that moment. If we know our best working environments, we can recreate that level of focus more easily.

Dennis Christensen is Associate Creative Director at Dare.

"A good run down regents canal followed by a large chicken curry with rice and peas gets my juices flowing every time."

Dave Birss is MD of GetAdditive.com.

"I don't think I've ever come up with a good idea while sitting at an office desk. (Some would argue that I've never come up with a good idea at all.) Working in the same old environment leads to the same old approaches.

I find the best places to work are coffee shops, pubs, airport departure lounges, trains and museums. These places seem to have the right balance of uninterrupted me-time and inspiring distractions. If my thinking gets stuck in a rut, I just need to look up and see a fat bloke across the aisle picking his nose. That'll take my thinking somewhere different.

I vary the way I work depending on the task. If I'm coming up with ideas, I scribble in my notebook. If I'm writing, I use a basic text editor on my iPad. And if I'm designing, I use my notebook and Mac together. If one method isn't working for me, I'll move to another.

I also separate my inspiration time from my idea-generation time. I believe that combining them leads to derivative work.

And sometimes a wee glass of whisky is all that's needed to free the ideas. I find that stress can stop the ideas from flowing - and a dram of the good stuff loosens me up enough to get things moving again."

Dave Bedwood is Creative Partner at Lean Mean Fighting Machine

"Erm, I wish I knew exactly then I could recreate it at will.

I'd say a few things have emerged over the years without conscious effort - I've sort of come to notice them.

I always use pen and paper. But it's always a moleskin pad. And it's always my Mont Blanc pen. Sounds wanky, but having the right instruments gets my mind in the right place. I can't start any other way.

I work anywhere but the office. And I tend to stare into space until my mind goes empty. Getting bored is painful but necessary. I then do something else.

I then literally chain myself to the computer and write, doesn't matter the quality, one rule is I can't stop. In that sense, at that stage, I force the flow. It sort of feels like getting a dirty felt tip pen, and constantly scrubbing it until eventually its original clear colour runs again."

Sam Ball is Creative Partner at Lean Mean Fighting Machine

"It takes a little time to get into the flow, but there are techniques you can use to get you there faster. Before I start work I may listen to a John Lennon interview, or watch Ali wax lyrical before a big fight. What they say rarely has anything to do with the immediate task at hand, nevertheless, it gets you in the right frame of mind in which to tackle the task. Listening to them builds your confidence, everyone needs a little pep talk from time to time. Start your work fired up and you will get into the flow much quicker."

Dip Mistry is a Creative at Dare

"Research. Drink a quart of whiskey. Research. Read a plethora of blogs you have no interest in. Research. Haggle at a car-boot sale. Research. Hangout with old people you may never see again. Research. Smoke a phat one. Research. Have 2 or a 100 personal projects on the go. Research. Remember everything you hear, see, smell and taste. Research. Forget everything you hear, see, smell and taste. Research. DO more life. Do more research. And if you're lucky, you may find your 'flow'. Now where was I...Research."

We should work on praising ourselves better too. The more we beat ourselves up, the more we'll associate what we enjoy doing with negative feelings - and that'll make us want to do it less and less.

And don't censor the work. When Hemingway said 'write drunk, edit sober', apart from encouraging booze he also meant that the 'doing' comes first. Don't focus on what other people might think. You can end up hating the work just because you think someone else will. It's the reason that old-school creatives did a lot of their work in the pub, we've all heard about it, but those days are long gone.

So how about applying it to group work? There are lots of people talking about their individual experiences, but not much about how Flow works in teams.

That's mainly because isn't common for people to be able to work at that level together. Everyone in the room has to be in the zone by themselves if there's any chance of a group getting there together, and the more people that are involved in something, the higher the chances are that not everyone is going to be on that level.

Some people find it easier to work by themselves and feedback into a group. Others, if they've been working together long enough, are more comfortable in a team situation. Confidence plays a huge part in group dynamics. Holding something back can stifle the creative process, and this has a direct effect on the team. We feel like we're being judged, they feel like we're holding something back.

One way for teams to work more effectively together is to develop trust through practicing feedback. More often than not, it's easier to say you trust a colleague rather than actually demonstrating to them that you do. When everyone's confident that thoughts and ideas won't meet any kind of judgement, a team can progress in working better together.

You can practice feedback by taking a few minutes out of your day to reflect on what's happened, then writing on a post-it what you think each of your team members did well, and what they could've done better.

In fast-paced agencies its sometimes hard to take the time to reflect, and can be uncomfortable to feedback, but it works. And in the long run it gets everyone where they need to get to faster.

The same can be said for:

Establishing the key goal together.
Trying to blend egos so you all take credit (and blame).
Listening (properly).

These things are tough to introduce into agency culture, but allow whole teams, rather than just individuals, to get into the Flow, and create great work.

There are always going to be things we don't want to do. Things outside of our passions that we just want to get done so we can move on. Flow doesn't come anywhere near those. It's not a quick fix for chores.

But it is less illusive than you first imagine for tackling the fun stuff. It requires both intense focus and a looseness of thought that helps connect one thing to another in a new way. It likes inspiration from elsewhere and thrives on ritual. It loves drink, walks and John Lennon. It sometimes even has a voice – ever woken up with the Eureka moment screaming loud in your ear? Or heard an internal voice start an idea that you had to stop everything to catch, as if it's a ghost whispering in your ear?

And like us, it prefers to be around what we love. It's reserved for those rare moments when everything just goes right. When a thing feels like it's creating itself. When it's 2AM in the morning in pitch jail and everyone is working as one. It's the most powerful, and wonderful feeling a creative person can have. That's when the three-legged acid devils get a fist in the face from Mr. Csikszentmihalyi. And us.

INNOVATION

Role of Innovation Within Advertising

By Daniele Fiandaca

As conundrums go, the one currently occupying adland could be of life-or-death proportion. Defining the role of innovation within advertising is occupying the great and good of the sector, and rightly so because it's pivotal to future-proofing what we do, and how. It is something many and diverse agencies – including Albion, AMV BBDO, BBH, Billington Cartmell, DigitasLBi, Karmarama, McCann, PHD and VCCP, to name just a few, are currently preoccupied with, not least because all have hired innovation officers over the past three years or so.

In the UK alone, there must be more than 50 agencies that have added into the usual mix a specifically innovation-led title, usually at senior level. It's an increase that is matching, and arguably trumping, the introduction of such roles within client companies.

So what's driving this relatively recent fixation?

Surely innovation should be at the heart of advertising and creativity? It was certainly central in the world of digital advertising. In the formative years of digital, which coincided with my first 5 years in the sector, I can't remember a time when we weren't innovating. It was core to survival – the industry was moving so fast that you constantly had to find new and better ways of solving problems. And this is probably the reason that most of us who have grown up in digital have found it so difficult to distinguish between creativity and innovation.

Yet there is a distinct and palpable difference, most interestingly summed up by Theodore Levitt, a Professor at Harvard Business School. As he puts it: 'Creativity is thinking up new things. Innovation is doing new things.' It's certainly a simple and clear definition. But like many such demarcations, the reality is far from straightforward, and in the wonderful world of communications we're now always finding and activating new ways to deliver interesting experiences to our audience.

To get a clearer idea of the factors that have driven the rise of innovation – and why I believe it's such a key component of what we need to deliver as an industry – we need to look beyond the face value of the here and now. We need to look at the context of the market we now operate in. And never have we been in a market in which change has been so rapid.

As Ray Kurzweil, director of engineering at Google observes: *"We're entering an age of acceleration. The models underlying society at every level, which are largely based on a linear model of change, are going to have to be redefined. Because of the explosive power of exponential growth, the 21st century will be equivalent to 20,000 years of progress at today's rate of progress; organisations have to be able to redefine themselves at a faster and faster pace."*

It's that pace of change, combined with the pressure to redefine, which is having significant impact on our clients' businesses. Put another way, change is now a do-or-die business imperative. If you need proof, consider the fact that an incredible seventy percent of the companies that were on the Fortune 1000 list a mere ten years ago have now vanished – unable to adapt to change.

So businesses need help, especially in navigating the communications landscape. The challenge faced by the specialists – the communications agencies – is that clients aren't necessarily willing to pay for this help. Alex Jenkins, editor of Contagious Magazine, sums it up nicely when he recalls a client telling him: "I didn't want to pay for my agencies to experiment and innovate as much as I needed them to." This clearly presents challenges for agencies, especially in a time when margins are being constantly threatened and the pressure to deliver ongoing fees from clients is just increasing.

This is one of the reasons that the role of innovation has gained currency – it's a direct response in recognition of the fact that there needs to be time allocated to looking at clients' businesses in a different way. Anders goes even further in his chapter earlier in the book when he advocates the need for agencies to help clients actually adapt at a business level, rather than just a communications level.

From where I'm sitting, it's also the biggest challenge we're facing. Innovation is so wide in its scope it is unclear exactly what we need to be delivering for clients.

When I asked my peers for their definition of innovation, the general consensus funneled down to doing something new to solve a client's problems. There were some variations including: 'Innovation to me is about change and transformation'; 'being brave enough to do something different'; and 'entrepreneurial response to change'.

But assuming we define innovation as finding new and better ways to solve client's problems (and it is worth noting that innovation and technology are not synonymous – old media and old products can be used to solve problems in new and better ways), the next step begs the question of which problems? And how? And do we need to limit what we do to clients' problems?

Eight years ago, BBH set up Zag to create and develop new brands, which it will license or sell to third parties in return for a share of ongoing sales revenues. Other agencies, such as Droga 5, have since dabbled with similar models, while most recently, shops such as Mother and Wieden & Kennedy Portland have launched their own tech accelerators to get closer to the tech community. This is something that is also close to clients' hearts. Jeremy Bassett, strategy and new ventures director at Unilever recently commented at the launch of the IPA's Adapt programme that "partnering tech start-ups will be how we pioneer the future of marketing".

It is here that I would like to provide my view on the opportunity innovation brings to the industry. I concur with Professor Andrew Hargadon, Director of UC Davis Child Institute for Innovation and Entrepreneurship when he comments "Thomas Edison, Henry Ford and, now, their modern counterparts were capable of creating one breakthrough after another because they built innovation strategies around recombining existing technologies rather than inventing new ones." In a similar way, I believe that by adding a layer of creativity to new and existing communications technologies, namely by innovating, we can help solve client problems.

So what does innovation in advertising actually look like? I had hoped that the introduction of an innovation category at Cannes Lions in 2013 would give us all a steer. It was an exciting recognition of the integral role of innovation in advertising. Now though, I'm wondering whether it ultimately only served to confuse the landscape even further. Rather than celebrate innovation within the advertising space, it awarded innovation within a product design sense in 2013 (e.g. a two-sided phone and a credit card which incorporated a digital display) while 2014 seemed to be more focused around technology rather than innovation (e.g. a kinetic façade and connected signs, tennis rackets and headsets).

At least 2013's Grand Prix winner by our good friends at Barbarian Group sat perfectly within the comms space – an open source software tool for professional creative coding which provides a platform for developing physical installations, mobile apps, music visualisers, screen-savers and completely new categories of projects. It is a great example of the ad industry not just reacting to, but actually leading tech innovation. And by making it open, the agency is part of the ecosystem, something I touch on later.

Cannes also brought some other great examples of innovation through the Converse Hack a Chuck competition, which we actually ran as Creative Social in 2013, to find interesting ways to hack a Chuck, in turn creating content to launch Converse's Google+ page. Entries included turning a Chuck into a Wah-Wah pedal, LED Chucks, Chucks with Drone support, Chucks which turn your dance moves into bespoke images and of course, our own entry from Cheil, a skateboard which is unlocked using a pair of Chucks and then monitors your location, distance travelled and your key tricks (using an accelerometer).

Other recent examples include MRY's collaboration with Spotify to create Placelists, a location based jukebox which allows you to connect with the people you love, through the music you love, in the places you love; IKEA's Klippbok iPad App by the Monkeys, which essentially brings the flat-pack furniture king's showroom to your front room; and the Facebook app by Tool that works out who to avoid if you want to stay healthy - or, if you already have the flu, who to blame. And, of course, Pereira O'Dell's Inside films for Intel and Toshiba that merge social media and movies, and have produced three "social films" so far, including the multi-award winner The Beauty Inside.

Obviously innovation does not necessarily have to be driven by technology; one of my favourite examples of this in 2013 was the Coke cans that you could split into two. Another example I loved (as did Dave Bedwood) was Paddy Power's hijacking of the Ryder Cup by sky-writing tweets.

Given the round-up above, it's fair to say that innovation in advertising in its truest and most exciting sense is alive and thriving. So what are the challenges that the advertising industry faces in delivering innovation?

Surveying my peers, more than 60% said that the biggest barrier to success is time and money. Many are lucky in that they have dedicated innovation team members. But even then, most heads of innovation have to grapple with a secondary role that has clear revenue attached.

The fact is the return from innovation is still unproven, mainly because it cannot sometimes be directly charged to the client. In any case, at its most successful, it should have an impact on the whole agency and subsequently, its output.

However I have found that there need to be some core pillars for innovation to be successful:

Determine senior responsibility: I am not advocating that all agencies have to have a head of innovation, but they need to have someone at board level with responsibility for it so that it fits clearly into the overall business plan (hence being supported by the overall management team). Where agencies do hire someone though, it must be clear that hiring them is not enough – there has to be a commitment from the wider senior team that cultural change is likely to be needed and this change is likely to be perpetual.

Innovation must not operate in a silo: Part of the role of the innovation team has to be to ensure that everyone in the agency has the opportunity to be innovative and that innovation is baked into the overall process. Any briefs tackled should be in collaboration with other members of the team, especially creative and tech. As Alistair Campbell, Creative Director at Guardian Labs comments: "One of the biggest challenges is persuading everyone that it's their job to innovate. No-one is going to do it for them." The way agencies achieve this may differ. At Cheil we did this by creating a wider team who have responsibility for innovation and allocating time aside. At DigitasLBi they have a lab within the agency. When they believe there is a big innovation opportunity, they brief the creative technologists from the lab at the start of the process, alongside the creative team and production. Ideation and execution are interdependent.

Strong planning department: I still find that the best ideas come from matching a human insight with technology to solve a client problem. While a large proportion of those in a senior innovation role actually come from a strategy background, they still need a good team of planners to ensure that they are finding true human insights, which is very different from a proposition. The strength of the Tesco Homeplus subway virtual store, which won the Media Grand Prix at Cannes in 2011, was that it tapped into a cultural human truth. Koreans are the second most hard working nation in the world, and in giving them the opportunity to shop while waiting for the tube, they were given one of the things most precious to them: time.

Provide time for innovation: We all know Google famously lets its team spend 20 per cent of its time on new things, as does 3M (in case you're interested, this is how Post-It notes came about). I understand that in an agency environment this can be tough, but the best way to innovate is to provide time to think outside tight deadlines.

Set an R&D budget: Agencies keep on advocating to clients that they put some budget aside for research and development, so we need to do the same. At Cheil we invested in a 3D printer, Arduino training, and kit and prototypes for new products. Using these technologies helped us sell in the NX Rover campaign to Samsung, where we built a robot to allow people to remotely take amazing photos from their computer from inspiring places around the world, as well as opening up other new opportunities with clients.

Become part of the ecosystem: Not only do we as individuals need to invest in testing new platforms (in order to swim, you need to get in the water) but you also need to do the same at an agency level. This may mean actually launching your own product, but this might be more with the intention of 'learning' to make your product better for clients, as opposed to aiming for the next big money maker. A good example of this is Little Printer from Berg, which Mark Cridge described as "their own probe - put out there as an agency learning tool."

Expand your network: Tied in with the above is finding new relationships and partnerships to help deliver innovation. A good example of this is Leanmeanfightingmachine's partnership with Queen Mary University of London. The agency works with Queen Mary's media and arts technology Ph.D. programme, which has a mission to produce post-graduates who combine world-class technical and creative skills and who have a unique vision of how digital technology transforms creative possibilities and social economies. They sponsor students and get them to tackle briefs and challenges we set them. LivesOn, a product that allows you to tweet from your afterlife, came from this collaboration.

Provide the right culture: While responsibility might reside with someone senior, for an agency to be truly innovative, it needs to permeate throughout the agency. This can only happen if you have the right culture. Tom Uglow, creative director of Google Labs, describes innovation as a combination of exploration and experimentation, which equates to play, which equals fun. So if you are not having fun, you will never be able to innovate. In addition I believe one of the key challenges for agencies in the next 2-3 years is going to be the ability to constantly adapt to change. This means creating a culture of agility, one in which we are constantly challenging the way we work, sometimes using different processes to solve different problems. This is going to also require a different type of talent which is why at Cheil we focused on hiring what we called 'curious mutants'; and

Deliver clear KPIs: This is essential. It provides focus as well as determining the parameters of success. These KPIs will be a mixture of revenue, new business, awards, reputation and developing IP.

Irrespective of the above, there is one thing that every agency needs to be truly innovative. And that is a brave client. As PJ Pereira says: "Corporations like to talk themselves out of brilliance." Fortunately there are quite a few brave clients out there. Hopefully, some will read this book and maybe even pass it on, as perhaps you, dear reader, should too. Because I believe that however you define innovation, offering it to brave clients is going to represent the best opportunity for our industry going-forward. And this will ultimately mean that agencies need to invest in the future (in terms of talent, dedicated time and budget), deliver new structures and processes that make them truly agile, and deliver new services which will help clients adapt to this new future. If we focus on what advertising has historically done well, which is help connect brands to people, then I think the future is bright and innovative.

ALL BALLS. SOME BRAINS. Keeping Innovation From Becoming the New Irrelevant Art in Advertising.

By Anders Gustafsson

"Listen... nobody's got a f***ing clue."
These words were whispered to me at this posh little member's only club in London's Notting Hill area (perhaps just an "ok hotel bar" to the posh people populating this neighbourhood, but to me the place was rad). The whisperer was a well known agency CEO at an equally known global agency. According to him, these winged words about advertising in general were once spoken by one of the famous Saatchi brothers. I know very little about them I must admit (apart from the agencies and that awkward strangling pic with the TV chef) but the quote stuck.

I find there's a very liberating touch to these sorts of Uber-universal truths when told by a leader in your industry. And having just talked myself that day at London's Saatchi Gallery in front of a crowd of creativity and technology enthusiasts – I certainly felt like I could relate. It wasn't really that I doubted my marketing ideas and insights about (in this case) social media. It was more the notion of what brought me there in the first place. Me? Speak at a fancy tech conference in London? Are you high? Clearly nobody's got a clue. I'm in!

EMBRACING YOUR AREA OF INCOMPETENCE

Innovation is a word that's being thrown around a lot in advertising right now. The same way "big idea", "halo effect" or "game changer" was just a while back. We're hopelessly addicted to trendy naming in our industry. We thrive on whatever's the new way of saying the same old thing. You'd think we'd be the only ones immune to it but instead we just keep getting high on our own supply.

It's ok. It's fun. And there's nothing wrong with having a little fun. But behind the buzz - we're still in *the business of making and make believe.* And what was once the art of making campaign products driven by lifestyle photography in the 1980's – is now called making interactive tools and applications driven by social storytelling in the 2010's. But the art of making is still a creative process based on the same basic brain wiring: *Think. Try. Repeat.*

I've found it to be a lot about daring to explore the unknown. Almost like a sports psychology strategy, and in my case one that works for both personal development and running creative projects at an ad agency. Simply, embracing this notion of initially not fully understanding how to solve something and keeping at it instead of finding ways of killing it (out of fear). To boldly step into your area of incompetence. Here you'll find new inspiration and with it - opportunity to innovate at the true meaning of the word.

It's not really about the latest technology either. *It's how you use that technology in the context of an already programmed human social behaviour.*

It's that moment when you look at a new phone, application, social channel, piece of software or even a plain bus stop down the street and go *"Hey you guys, wouldn't it be awesome if you could actually _____ simply by _____ this thing here? I bet people would love that. I know I would."*

Now, the importance of having nice people around you when you start embracing your area of incompetence cannot be understated. Whether it's an open minded and sharing creative team, curious producers, excited developers or one of those freakishly smart planners. It has to be "no dicks allowed". Any agency today with a somewhat healthy creative culture is perfectly able to figure out how to assemble the right minds to make innovation come to life – whether it's by including the people with the right answers to begin with or by quickly delegating things to the most suitable individual in the room. Just. No. Dicks.

The other trick is to always move forward. When I was working for Alex Bogusky – and this was at a time when he was still very much involved in things at CP+B, we had this rule saying we were never allowed to say "No". Just to figure it out or find the alternatives and move forward. It was called "to keep the momentum" and to be "delusionally optimistic" about things. And it went for everyone. Creatives, account people, producers and business affairs (especially business affairs, actually).

I still think that's brilliant in all its naïve simplicity. There's literally a hundred ways an idea can get killed before it sees the light of day. Whether it's budget, timing, testing, client, competitors, natural disasters or politics. Why try so hard to kill it ourselves before it even gets there? (Unless of course the idea sucks to begin with. But that's another chapter.)

Just try it. Put a bunch of assertive, smart individuals in a room to explore their area of incompetence with the simple rule not to kill. You'll be amazed what they will come up with. And how far any group of people can push something if they really put their minds to it. If nothing else, they will love their job that day.

DIRECTOR OF INNOVATION. QUE?

In 2010 I moved to San Francisco and started working for Rich Silverstein and Jeff Goodby.

I was used to running the Scandinavian Airlines account (as the name implies - a big account by Scandinavian standards) and had successfully helped in building an amazing team in Europe producing literally hundreds of print ads, banners, interactive experiments, radio and TV spots every year. We reached awareness goals and won awards. Good times. The move to the US shouldn't be that difficult, right? Wrong. North America truly is "a whole 'nother beast". Skipping the most basic things here like the difference in size and the unavoidable politics that comes with it, just the overwhelming dominance of TV is fascinating.

"Ok. Cool. Where's the script?"

I quickly realised I needed to make a choice. To join the 101 super talented young writers wanting nothing else but to write the next funny TV spot… or to focus on whatever's not TV. On whatever's different.

Enter the Director of Innovation.

It made perfect sense. Find the opportunities to do something that's not TV across all clients. Don't get me wrong here. I'm extremely proud of the TV work I've done in the US and going on production is always a lot of fun. You stay at nice hotels, meet nice people and get to hang out with celebrities. (Some of them nice.) But my passion was still trying to make things people had never seen before.

I know what you're thinking… shouldn't the Creative Director be in charge of the innovation? Isn't innovation sort of our job/whole purpose to begin with? Of course it is! But every agency is different and everyone has to figure out what works best for them. Big agencies still need specialists. And while Special Teams might not represent the most desirable positions in the NFL – you're not gonna make the playoffs without a good kicker. Besides, everyone is always looking for a timeless solution, but you know what – when navigating a company there is no timeless. Only now. Agencies and the people who populate them have to live in the now and act from that. Try new things. Explore. At the end of the day, what title goes on your business card is irrelevant anyway. At least to people I know. Thank God.

The point being, whatever measures your agency is taking to inspire innovation in advertising using the latest technology, changing titles or not, just always make sure proper authority is **1.given** and **2.clearly communicated** internally. I cannot stress this enough. Otherwise you will just waste a lot of precious meeting time having a former Creative Director explaining to account people that she/he is not really "in charge of the banners". And hope everyone gets it in time for client introductions. Sad face.

ROBOBRO

The other option is of course what we've all come to know as the "Hybrid Creative Director". The interdisciplinary creative.

A 'Robobro'.

(Some years ago I randomly stumbled upon this picture of Robocop in a pink frat style bro-polo and it just felt like the perfect manifestation of the new Creative Director.)

50% new cool technology. 50% same old human behavior. 100% in sync with pop culture. All in an awesome Paul Verhoeven meets John Hughes kind of way.

Metaphors aside, the real Robobros and Robosistas in advertising will likely manifest themselves in a less colourful and more natural manner. And they will most likely be more successful by not being a one-man-show. Teams are a lot better in general I've noticed.

So perhaps instead of searching for that unicorn hybrid, it's time to pair up the traditionally merited Creative Director AD/Copy with an interactive more tech savvy Creative Director AD/Copy counterpart? This is probably the best (and certainly the quickest) way agencies can kickstart being more successful at innovating across the board in advertising right now.

INNOVATION AS IRRELEVANT ART IN ADVERTISING

It used to be that art directors and designers were accused of confusing their own art with ads. Today the same thing goes for developers and innovation. It's not their fault really. They probably ended up working for an ad agency for the same simple reason artists once did. The paycheck. (Possibly the people, and most likely the hope of getting your ideas published in some way, shape or form.) And that's fine. But in advertising we make things that help a message or brand come alive and add value to consumers when solving an existing marketing problem. And whether you're a Creative Director, Director of Innovation or Master of The F***ing Universe we still have to make sure we're relevant.

Innovation without a brief is called *having a business idea* and as much as I love inventing random cool shit – why would I turn it into a crummy commercial? We're not the next Facebook folks. We're selling beer, cars and insurances. We're making people aware of a new apple juice. Making them like an old forgotten body-wash brand again.

You are not Luke Skywalker my friend, you're Boba Fett. A gun for hire. Suck it up or become a startup.

INNOVATION AS RELEVANT ADVERTISING

When it comes to inventing something never seen before there's obviously no recipe. But there are different angles from where we can approach the creative process in how to use technology to innovate in advertising. So, in an attempt to get more tangible - I'd say it boils down to a few things that have seemed to repeat themselves a lot over the past decade.

1. New sexy technology.
2. Relevant context.
3. Same* human behaviour.

Here's the trick: Successful innovation for big brands always finds a way to innovate and still work on broad platforms. It manages to identify and adapt to the human behaviour within that platform. Preferably doing so by demystifying the technology (hence the broad).

"Well, duh!?"

Fair enough, but this has not really been doable up until just recently. Or even worse, even when it's been doable it's not been done! Think about it. (And if you're in advertising, I'm sure you're more than familiar with the background to all of this.)

For the longest time, interactive advertising was using technology to chase "first downs" instead at looking at human behaviour and relevance on a broader scale. I know, because I was doing it too. The first Facebook photo gallery app idea before even all my (real) friends were on Facebook. The first contextual Spotify idea before Spotify was global. The first... /insert new technology here/ ...idea. You get it. And as long as they kept handing us pencils, lions and pens for it, why stop, right?

In our defence, it wasn't our fault Facebook wasn't publicly traded or Spotify wasn't available in the US yet. The relevance was there, the innovation was there, simply not in the sense of the established broad platforms we've got today. (Let's just say back then no broadcast producer was making millions just showing Internet sensations on TV.) Still, we saw it coming and we were not gonna be held back.

But this eagerness to chase first downs and getting rewarded for it is exactly what eventually led to the rhetorical battle in the ad community putting "Storytelling" against "Digital".

Excuse the short derail here, but if there's still even a shred of doubt: There is no such thing as "digital" any longer and there's not been for quite a while. There's only life. Everything from your telephone, car stereo or airplane ticket, to your TV menu or ATM is already in the timeless shape of digital. What can make it innovative on the other hand - is realising the interactive potential of a specific format and how you allow consumers to interact with it. And storytelling has never been the opposite of interaction, has it?

The thing is: any story can be translated into something interactive. Something a little less expected. Something little bit more innovative. Now, if it *should* is another question. That still depends on the brief and ultimately, the problem at hand.

Beyond the old "digital" label lies the immense global marketing power of existing and now widely populated platforms. YouTube, Twitter, Google Maps, Yelp, Craigslist, Facebook, Google Hangouts, Shazam and Pandora/Spotify are not what they initially were. They're all grown up. And interactive advertising has been forced to grow up alongside them.

It means that relevance in innovation can now operate within huge, populated channels and with the speed of early adaptors - since the threshold for audiences to enter newer digital platforms has been severely lowered. It's finally true mass communication.

No more first downs. (Except by the Oakland Raiders. Sadly, they are few and far apart. Go Raiders.)

A new exciting technology like instant messaging or social media can definitely change human behaviour – but the behaviour within that platform will then find its target, its "norm" and stay that way. Like the way we use texting compared to emailing, or how we communicate on FB compared to Skype. This becomes the context. The framework for how you come up with relevant advertising ideas, if you will. The tech innovation might present a whole new set of rules, but technology can't tame our human behaviour. It's like the dinosaurs in Jurassic Park. Us humans will always do what feels most natural and what makes the most sense. With or without logic. Just look at what happened with Google+.

INNOVATION IN CREATIVE TEAMS

As a Creative Director you can't just give feedback – you need to properly structure and lead the creative process. Map things out. Inspire. The same goes for innovation in the creative process.

Keeping it tangible here, I use what I call "buckets". (You know, paper notes on a wall. Or in your head.)

These are basically a handful of relevant territories where we can start exploring new ideas in tech innovation together. Each bucket can hold 5,

10 or 100 ideas. A bucket can be called "mobile", "in-store", "social" or "OOH". Or perhaps it can be called "video content ideas", "packaging", "stunt/event" or even "product development".

The product, brief and the problem at hand naturally set the number and type of buckets. Usually a working handle or existing tagline affect what goes on the wall. Then, what's most relevant/effective usually determines what stays. The buckets worth keeping are what eventually make it into the deck - and the best ideas in each bucket get presented to the client. Easy, right?

In this process a lot usually get structured by the traditional creative flow/team. The lines and the handles that feel right usually are. (i.e. creative talent at work.) But from my experience there are two other types of knowledge that add tremendous value and should be included throughout this process:

1. Planners
2. Developers

(Depending on titles at your agency the planner might be a strategist, or the developer perhaps an interactive producer) – but what you want out of it is really:

1. Someone sticking with it from a purely strategic standpoint.
2. Someone coming at it early on from a strict tech standpoint.

Not to mention the value of simply having two more brains with a slightly different perspective. The key is to get everyone onboard early, and more importantly, at the same time. That way you avoid having to do things twice and it's also the special sauce for the group dynamic. Team structures can be hard to mix up even just a little bit. Trust me I know.

Actually, I know it to the point where it has led me to believe one of the biggest problems of our time is the territorial pissings of spoiled creative teams. The fearful, over-protecting of ideas that slowly kills all the good energy and fun in the room. It's a disease and one that usually ends up defining the true difference between a creative and a Creative Director. It can divide departments and complicate necessary change.

Every agency is different - but from my experience the best way to deal with chemistry/people/team related problems like this is just to be very inclusive, transparent and available from the start. Make sure the creatives feel comfortable and in charge of things. Make sure the developers feel valuable and listened to. Get stuff on iCal and make sure everyone gets the invitation.

Open doors. Lead the way.

INNOVATION 2014...

I never worry too much about the future. I never try to predict what's next because trying to be in the now is hard enough. The world is just getting more and more full of things to interact with. Whether it's new social platforms, games, art blogs, wristbands that measure the calories in your poop, a trending breed of dog, drones that print Metallica's next concert on the moon in 3D, or simply the fact that three generations are now crossing over on Facebook – there's enough innovation, tension, truth and plain shit out there to create new stories for any brand already.

A million little things are going to change advertising this year, but I believe that within three specific platforms certain things will change in 2014 based on growth and a normalising human behaviour. Namely: Social, Mobile and Physical.

...IN SOCIAL: "THE DAWN OF THE PARENTS"

In 2013, social media once again proved to us how interactive platforms have become mass communication. (Not talking about the hype or the Facebook IPO, just the width.)

That day at London's fancy Saatchi Gallery I remember comparing Facebook to the dog hatch scene in "Dawn of the Dead". (If you've for some reason missed the past decade's crazy zombie trend – I'm talking about the 2004 remake of George Romero's classic with the same title.) The scene when the survivors on the roof of the mall discover another survivor on a roof across the parking lot. The lot is flooded with zombies so they send a dog over with supplies. When the guy opens the dog hatch to let the dog in he keeps it open a split second too long and the zombies grab ahold of it, quickly swarm the building and eat him.

Just like the summer of 2008, right? The summer we all truly experienced the dead returning back to life. When every high school flirt, college buddy or kindergartener you ever knew added you on Facebook.

And now, just when you've figured out the language and social code to successfully maintain that social relationship (perhaps how to keep your distance) – another social attack is imminent: It's The Dawn of The Parents. I'm not talking about the pictures of newborn babies clogging up your feed. I'm talking about the social Armageddon that is watching your own parents help themselves to your social life online, without a manual. Getting access to every picture ever posted of you holding a beer or singing karaoke. Adding friends from your friends-list that you don't even remember adding in the first place. And that dreadful feeling when your dear mom is using your nickname from when you were 4 years old to comment on a random pictured you're tagged in, blissfully oblivious about the fact that this is not a private message to her son, it's a broadcast message to everyone her son ever knew. Talk about technology demystified. It's the dog hatch all over again.

Suddenly the balance between tonality and being relevant has never felt more important. Of course, this opens up for innovation in stealth settings, great insights for creative ideas and new truths following the change of social behaviour. But all that aside, the best advice I ever read on social was "Be yourself and don't do anything stupid."

...IN MOBILE: "INNOVATION IN LIMITATIONS"

Our mobile behaviour has reached the point where we need help from ourselves. With every 10 new apps celebrating the potential of being 100% available, all the time, there's suddenly a need for 1 contextually smart app, blocking, rerouting or weeding out that very same possibility. Whether you're in traffic, on vacation, at the gym or on a flight to Phoenix, mobile sanitation will hopefully help us take back and focus on what's really important in life. Fear of missing out (FOMO) has become the norm in our lives so fast it's suddenly an abundant territory where brands can act as relevant remedies.

The digital hoarding extension of FOMO is just so ironic when you think about it. It's slowly making sure that we are in fact missing out on every single first hand magical moment. From sunsets to weddings, field goals to puppies. Pretty soon we've got everything on file and nothing in our heads.

I'm not saying it's not super awesome that mobile has allowed the interactive extension of any physical thing. The next couple of years we will definitely see every connectable household device get connected to our iPhone. Locks, thermostats, espresso machines, alarm clocks, you name it.

But in 2014, more than before, the challenge for agencies will be to limit our desire to make brands even more mobile. Is this really relevant? Is this really useful? Is this really, truly adding value? These are the questions we will have to ask each other a lot more often. The brands that can keep doing things just to show off innovation will still exist, but the risk of simply becoming the new irrelevant art is getting higher with every new app in the store.

...IN PHYSICAL: "SOMETHING TO LEAN ON"

Our increasing need for nostalgic security blankets should not be underestimated. I'm sure there's a flood of essays already out there, or currently being researched, just on the topic of books, vinyl records and how they relate to our basic emotional need for "things". I would simply argue it's finally gotten to the point where it's a broad consumer truth and not just a hipster trend.

What fascinates me is the gap between logic and love in the matter. I know I've got access to every Iron Maiden album ever recorded 24/7 through the music cloud service of my choice but still I really, really want to buy "Somewhere in Time" on vinyl again. Why is that? It makes no sense whatsoever! (Buying it on vinyl again I mean, not buying this specific album, it will always be my all time favourite Maiden album.)

From a strict marketing standpoint it means that we are possibly going to see a lot more stories supporting *cognitive dissonance* – creating and adding arguments to justify buying things that innovations in technology supposedly have replaced already.

In the case of my Iron Maiden album collection it manifests itself in me saying things like "Taking back the ritual that was once how I used to enjoy music" or "Hearing the album the way it was intended". (For audiophiles I'm sure there's a whole separate range of amazing arguments, leading up to things like Neil Young developing that Pono player and all – but I never cared much for differences in quality impossible to detect with the limited sophistication of the human ear.)

Past nostalgia, in terms of pure product innovation, we're likely to see more new physical objects as part of not only the marketing message and creating a social object for the sake of PR – but also because of the real demand for these "things". Something to touch, smell and put on a desk.

Moby Dick on my iPad is obviously no different from the original hard copy – but a reproduction in the shape of a big, thick saltwater stained beast of a book presented on an oak table in front of an open fireplace just messes with my whole perception of what a true reading experience can, and probably should, be. It becomes something else. Time well spent. A memory. A social bragging right.

And that bragging right could be what drives the whole idea of, in this case, innovation in product design. The human behaviour, not the technology itself.

Oh yeah, and big budget TV has finally found it's way to YouTube. There's no denying the power of sharing great video content any longer. It's forcing producers to think outside of .30/.60/Super Bowl and it's putting the pressure back on creatives, directors and ultimately clients to tell better stories.

A SIDE NOTE

Through Creative Social I've been introduced to some of the most interesting people, artists, buildings, foods, minds and experiences in my life, at some truly unique locations all over the planet. I feel blessed. Not because of the network of somewhat "important peeps" in advertising or the opportunities it has created for me on different levels. I feel blessed simply because of how these people have made me a less ignorant person and more pleasant guy to be around.

I wanted to contribute to this book to feel like I'm giving something back. Hopefully my contribution sparked some new ideas. Or perhaps even inspired you in some way. Maybe it just made you feel better about yourself (whether it's because we think the same way or simply because you've realised you're much smarter than I am). If nothing else, maybe you got a laugh out of it.

And there's nothing wrong with having a little fun.

Skin in the Game.
The Curious Phenomenon of
Agencies and Start Ups.

By James Cooper

You know the story. Every time a start-up IPOs, or is sold for a billion dollars, often to another start up, the advertising industry collectively sighs, "We could have done that". Most people that work in advertising are dreamers. So it's no surprise that many agencies are flirting with the idea of making their own products and companies (let's call them start-ups for this chapter).

This chapter is about the people and agencies that have done just that. Some of them have worked. Many of them have not. In fact most of them have not - but that's actually on par with the most successful start up incubators.

First a little background. Right now I am Head of Creative at a company called Betaworks. We were started in 2007 primarily as a seed investment company for start ups in the social media world. We wrote the first cheque for Tumblr. It was for $50,000. When Tumblr recently sold that $50,000 was worth around about $6m. Not bad, although a lot of other cheques tanked. But we have also built products. Some you will have heard of, Tweetdeck and bit.ly, possibly Chartbeat if you are a publisher. Recently we are building more and investing less. Last year we rebuilt and relaunched Digg and we also exposed the world to Dots - one of the most successful mobile games ever, currently around 20 million downloads.

Before betaworks I was a Digital Creative Director at various agencies, big and small. But I was one of those people that said, 'I could do that'. In 2008 I left my amazing job as Creative Director of Dare in London to be Creative Partner at Another Anomaly - the spin off of Anomaly that was supposed to just work on creating products and IP. It was a start up for start ups! After a year it folded. But Anomaly have had some success in the start-up and IP business. A lip balm called *EOS* that Anomaly helped produce and promote is now the best selling lip balm in the US, outselling established market leaders like Chapstick. I was also part of the team that made *ByLaurenLuke* a make-up product fronted by Lauren Luke, a single mum from the North of England that we found on YouTube. For a time Lauren was very hot. The product was on sale at Sephora, Lauren had a column in the Guardian as well as her own nintendo game. It didn't go on to achieve global success but I learned a lot and it changed Lauren's life for sure. You hear of overnight product and start up sensations but for the most part that is a rarity. These things are very, very hard and take a lot of time effort and money. They are incredibly stressful too. So why on earth would any ad agency want to get into this game?

Since the pesky internet came along it has been increasingly hard for agencies to make money servicing clients the traditional way. The relatively easy profits made on a 30 second spot have disappeared. Technology has also made it easier for clients to shop around and reduce fees. Where once the agencies were in charge, now they have to work harder for less money.

So agencies look to find new ways to make money. In the late 90's, agencies got a hard-on for behaving more like management consultants. Now an agency CFO sees something like Instagram, and even though he knows it's not his agencies core skill, god damn if there isn't that little bit of him too that says, '$1bn. We could do that'. Look at this way. What's the alternative? Another meeting with procurement as they reduce fees yet again?

The other problem any modern agency has is retaining talent. As I said, the best people in the industry are dreamers. We are 'what if' people. We have been trained to ask questions and think creatively. And now you can't open the paper or Facebook without reading about some young upstart making millions for a simple idea they had with a few buddies.

The grass is always greener of course. A lot of us dream of the start up life but are not ready to give up the salary and lifestyle. We want to become *armchair entrepreneurs* as I call it. We want the thrill of the start up with the safety of agency life. So an accelerator program or internal innovation program is, on the face of it, a decent way to keep people engaged and make your agency seem modern. I'll explain why that is usually a massive fail.

Agencies developing their own start-ups.

Droga5.

One of the most successful agencies in the world, Droga5, was an early mover in the start up world. You may remember the online video shopping portal, Honeyshed? Although Droga were clearly the lead in HoneyShed (David Droga was 'partner' and 'creative chief' and people remember it as a Droga thing) it was actually a joint venture between Publicis, Droga5 and production company, Smuggler. The press release said it was home shopping for the digital generation. The elevator pitch was probably more like 'web QVC for hipsters'. Back in 2008 Honeyshed made big news. But soon the idea of a hipster girl trying to persuade you that a puma sneaker (A Droga client back then) was perfect because "You can wear this to the club. You can wear this while you get jiggy. You can wear it just to have a latte" fell flat and after a year of pretty low numbers, never more than 7,000 visitors a month, it was shut down. Were Droga a little too ahead of the game? Back then people were still not that obsessed by online shopping and social media was not that big. There is a part of me that thinks this could actually work now.

Undeterred, Droga continued to put out new products. They scored another PR success with Thunderclap, a social amplification tool that launched in 2012. The tool is a neat way for a person or cause to gather together to be heard. They call it 'a crowdspeaking platform'. Thunderclap is still live but after a good start has struggled to grow. I'll make an educated guess as to why that might be:

In the advertising business we are addicted to the new, the bright, the shiny. And like all addicts we don't think clearly. So, we overestimate the amazingness of something. We get really excited and go the extra mile to make things happen. This can last for a while, a month, two months, maybe even a year. But think about the normal cycle of a campaign. You start a campaign thinking this is going to be the best thing ever. Same for new client relationships. Then the realities set in and if we are very lucky a campaign does well, sells some products, maybe wins some awards but that's a rarity. I think the same thing happens with these agency start ups. Once that enthusiasm wanes and the product doesn't do as well as expected (which is entirely natural) it's very difficult to remain enthused.

Interestingly Thunderclap won Droga5 the Innovation Lion at Cannes in 2013. So while Droga may not have proved themselves as the start-up kings, they are the undisputed masters of Cannes. In 2009 Fallon won for a Twitter client they built in-house called Skimmer. And of course 'Pay with a Tweet' won the Cyber Grand Prix in 2011 for R/GA. Well, sort of - they hired the team that did it. Smart, if just from a PR point of view. Making your own product was *en vogue* and I think we awarded our peers because we thought that if we did, then maybe we would get to work on similar projects.

Mother and why Brainstorms don't work.

David Weiner, the editor of Digg worked at Mother before joining his start up. Mother successfully launched a hot dog business and recently launched an app called Proust - a game where you and a friend place things you like or hate in order. It sounds silly, and it kind of is, but that is why it works. Neither of these products have anything to do with any of their clients. David told me that Mother was good at fostering an environment where if you had an idea it shouldn't be tossed out. What is interesting to me is that there was no official program. The worst thing in the world is when an agency or organisation tries to force innovation into a timeframe.

'Brainstorms don't work', David told me. The notion that 'Thursdays at 2-4' is innovation time is helpful for agency management but never works. Weird stuff happens when you least expect it. And you have to have a hierarchy that accepts that and is willing to act accordingly.

Forced Innovation Fails

On first inspection it's true that it's never been cheaper to make a product. An in-house team can pull together a prototype for an app in a couple of days. But there is a huge difference - a canyon - between a prototype and a successful product. At JWT we had what I would call a 'forced innovation' program called 'Go Grants'. The idea (not mine, I must caveat) was that JWT would give $25,000 to an idea each quarter. On the face of it not a terrible idea and the first session was good fun. The idea that was chosen was pedometer for pets. Now, I had tried to pitch this very idea to Iams when I was at Saatchi a couple of years before. 'Nike + for dogs!' I asked the team if they were sure that no similar product existed and they assured me it did not and they were going to make it. For $25,000! Let's just say that Go Grant disappeared very quickly. But the real point is not the money. The point is that the team got excited and then disheartened because it was a token gesture. No one really checked to see if there were products like this. No one was ever really prepared to spend the money required to make this product. No one ever really believed this was a product the agency would make. Programs like these do more harm than good. They promise everything and deliver nothing. There is no skin in the game.

Teehan + Lax and 37 Signals

Let's look at two more examples from agencies that illustrate the problems and opportunities. Teehan + Lax is a great digital advertising agency. In 2008 one of the designers wanted an easier way to store and find images that he was using for a particular project. Long story short they built a product called Image Spark. By the end of 2012 it had just under 50,000 user accounts. Very successful when you think about it. But in early 2014 they decided to shut it down. John Lax explains:

Clayton Christensen, the father of disruptive innovation, says, *"you can't start a disruptive business from inside an incumbent one."* The incumbent business will always take the resources from the disruptive one.

As soon as Image Spark launched, the people who worked on it (the resources) went right back on to the work that paid the bills.

We are used to short term euphoria in agencies; pitch wins, award wins, even one great meeting - but find it difficult to maintain. Lax continues:

"This is actually what happens with most products. They are rarely complete failures nor are they complete successes. They limp into the world on launch and then the real work starts. The real work of maturing and scaling."

37 signals is another web design agency. You have probably heard of 37 signals not for the client work they do but because they built Basecamp. The story of Basecamp starts out similar to Image Spark - it was an internal idea as a response to an internal problem - file management. But the key difference is that Basecamp was suitable for people outside of the creative industry. Basecamp had scale. This was not the original intention but by 2005 basecamp revenue surpassed web-design revenue, and 37 Signals suddenly worked out that they were a software company.

The story does not end there though. What is interesting is that 37 Signals went on to launch a lot more products Ta-da List (2005), Writeboard (2005), Backpack (2005), Campfire (2006), The Job Board & Gig Board (2006), Highrise (2007), Sortfolio (2009), the all new Basecamp (2012), Know Your Company (2013), and We Work Remotely (2013).

But in early 2014 they decided to scrap all that and just work on Basecamp. In fact they renamed the company to Basecamp. From their website:

"Because we've released so many products over the years, we've become a bit scattered, a bit diluted. Nobody does their best work when they're spread too thin. We certainly don't. We do our best work when we're all focused on one thing."

They are not just putting skin in the game, they became the game.

BBH

BBH has a division called Zag that was set up pretty early in London to look at making products. I have found a huge difference between UK and US agencies with regards to entrepreneurialism. In the UK it's sort of laughed at, possibly because the size of the market is so small. If you get 1% of any market in the US you potentially have a very healthy business.

BBH have not had a breakout hit in terms of making products. Again, it's easy to snigger at this 'failure' but that's just the reality. It is incredibly hard and the odds are stacked against you from day one.

From Agency to Going Solo

One agency person that has flown solo is Noah Brier. Noah was at Naked and Barbarian in New York before leaving to set up Percolate, a New York City-based technology company building the world's first content marketing platform. While in the ad world Noah built a pretty interesting site called Brandtags, which he sold to Solve Media. When I spoke to him he said this was just a great surprise because he had no plans to do anything with the side project and it gave him a little money to help build Percolate. Although Noah was at The Barbarian Group, which has had it's own successes building products - they sold an iTunes visualizer to Apple and made Cinder - he never thought about doing percolate within Barbarian or any other agency. Why is that? Noah told me it's because although on the face of it Percolate is related to the ad business it's still a technical product. Fundamentally, you need the technical chops to build an amazing product and agencies don't have that.

Agencies and Accelerators./ JWT and Techstars.

I set up the first agency deal with the start-up accelerator Techstars in 2011 when I was at JWT NY. Techstars has since done a number of deals in the marketing space. They have one with R/GA and Nike, but let me explain exactly how the deal I signed worked.

We signed a two year deal for $30k. We got a fancy press release and a logo on their site in return for giving them time with eight of the most talented people in our agency. We split into two teams and then saw all the companies that went through Techstars for two years. Companies go through an intense 3 month program where they get a little capital but mostly advice from mentors. They then do a Demo Day where they ask for funding from VC firms. In 2011 maybe half the NY teams had funding before Demo Day, whereas in 2012 most companies were already funded (cue shouts of bubble) and Demo Day was more of a formality. Techstars NY seemed to work a little bit like provenance in Modern Art. Where if Charles Saatchi or Larry Gagosian likes you - then everyone else likes you. Start-ups, very much like modern art, are all in the eye of the beholder. You are buying potential.

We would help with branding and sometimes strategic issues. We would also make connections - a lot of the companies had some sort of media part to the business. If I'm honest I'm not sure how much we helped. On a scale of one to ten, maybe a two? Because it's hard. Really fucking hard to run a business, and really hard for an agency person to say something new and insightful when your previous experience has been selling soap powder, rather than raising money or launching software.

One idea was that we would introduce the start ups to the JWT clients. It's my experience that even though you would think that's a big a draw for clients, it really isn't. My advice on this would be - make sure the organisation and everyone connected to the organisation is genuinely ready.

R/GA and Techstars

R/GA seems to be taking a more long-term approach. They set up an internal accelerator program with the help of TechStars New York to focus on connected devices. This makes sense as R/GA has had some success with Nike Fuelband. The program is housed at the New York agency, with 10 companies given office space and limited access to R/GA resources such as strategists, developers and creatives. R/GA clients are also invited to mentor some of the start-ups. At the end of the program the companies did a demo day at SXSW 2014 in Austin and then another in New York. Both R/GA and TechStars will own a small part of the companies.

Wieden and PIE

Other agencies that are active in this area include Wieden and Kennedy with their incubator program in Portland. The Portland Incubator Experiment, or PIE as it's known, is an ongoing collaboration between the agency and local entrepreneurs. On the site they ask, 'What the hell does an ad agency know about startups'. Bullseye. I personally don't believe that people in agencies have the right background to make that killer point about a startup. But that's not the point. The point is that the very act of getting these people together and giving them a space might be enough of a catalyst to spark something great. PIE has been going for four years and has seen 40 startups go through the ranks. I'll admit I had not heard of any of them - but again that's not the point. We shouldn't judge agency incubators by their ability to produce the next Instagram or Snapchat. Statistically speaking *no-one* is producing the next Instagram or Snapchat.

I spoke with Renny Gleeson from Wieden who helped put the program together. He said it started because there was a lack of technical people in the agency. But there was a great deal of technical talent in Portland. Gleeson wanted to make sure whatever they did had a positive effect on the overall technical community in Portland. So, initially, it just became about giving these guys some space in the agency. After a period of time they began to get access to briefs from the agency. They would help out in a fairly ad hoc way.

"Like any good start up it has evolved" said Renny. From a fairly low key and fluid start, PIE is now more of a program and has built in relationships with Wieden clients such as Coke, Target and Google. The start ups receive mentorship from these clients. Renny sees the program continuing to be fluid but acting as a sandbox as Wieden looks to forge relations with the new kinds of companies that operate in new business paradigms. There is a new generation of companies that will all need great ad agencies. One way to speak their language is to have internal, albeit, not permanent, expertise. That seems smart to me.

Why would start-ups want to work with Agencies?

Steve Cheney is one of the more vocal start-up guys. He was at GroupMe for a long time. He now heads up the New York office of Estimote, a low energy bluetooth 'i-beacon'. He wrote a pretty famous post about why start ups should not talk to agencies. Basically a colossal waste of time. So I spoke with Steve. It wasn't that Steve and GroupMe didn't want to deal with brands, he said. They did hundreds of deals with companies like Nike, Hulu and ESPN but Steve went direct. He felt that most of his agency contact was with 'low level flunkies' tasked with finding hot stuff to make the agency look good, 'no one had any real power to do a deal'. Steve explained, 'Even if this was to educate clients you're going to be one page in a 100 page deck. So fuck that.' Fair enough.

So how about the start ups that go through accelerators? And the accelerators themselves? Why would they want to work with agencies or brands? Well first up, there is the money. TechStars' deal with Nike and more recently Disney are apparently worth millions. So kudos to them. I spoke with David Cohen, the founder of TechStars, about the other advantages beyond money. He said that he gets good mentors and sometimes gets work, like strategy and creative, for free (certainly true with JWT). I asked him if he thought it was a fad. *"I don't think it's a fad - I think even big companies like being close to innovation, and Techstars provides them a quality filter and context to do this." "But"*, he continued, *"I think it will come and go to some extent. Like the hotness of the start-up market itself. The smartest agencies will engage in good times and bad, consistently and reasonably."* And on the subject of whether agencies should develop their own start-ups he was pretty clear: *"Most don't try. The good ones are helping their clients".*

Agencies as Funds?

So would an agency ever fund a start up from scratch? There have been examples of networks investing in start-ups. In June 2006 IPG paid $5 million for a 0.4 percent stake in Facebook. They later sold that holding for approximately $227 million.

One agency has set up a fund in this space, KBS+ in New York. They set up KBS+ Ventures to invest in early stage entrepreneurs focusing on advertising and marketing technologies. Some of the companies they have invested in are SocialFlow (a social targeting and content company we created at Betaworks) and RewindMe, a TechStars New York company that looks at past behaviour in order to give rewards. KBS also wrote a (free) book called *Creative Entrepreneurship* that collects a lot of articles from the key start up players such as Paul Graham, Dave McClure and Fred Wilson. It remains to be seen how the investments will pay off but it seems more like a talent and training play.

Start Ups as Agencies.

Read any article about advertising right now and you will see stuff about native advertising and, inevitably, Buzzfeed is in there somewhere. Whether you have a fondness for listicles or not, there is no doubt that Buzzfeed is taking budgets from agencies. Buzzfeed gives lessons to agencies. As does Tumblr. At betaworks we are starting to work with clients like GE, Samsung, Pepsi and Subway - on a number of very different projects.

If you are a client what's cooler? To work with an agency that has been around for 100 years or a few months? Where do you think you are going to learn the most? A listicle may not be amazing but when tenure is only 18 months you might not be looking to do something amazing. You might be wanting to learn something for the next job.

Conclusions

When Nike + was unveiled all those years ago, it was rightly heralded as a breakthrough piece of work. Agencies no longer merely advertised product, they could make product. That was a dream come true for a lot of us dreamers. We would make our own product and make the most awesome campaign - because *we would be the client*. I think that is where a lot of this comes from. The desire to eliminate the tedious client process that most of us have to deal with. Sadly, as I hope I have shown, it's a lot harder than it looks. Nike + worked because two of the most innovative and cash rich companies in the world wanted to make that happen. This was not an agency initiative - although agencies were needed to complete the story. When you look at the scarcity of other success stories - even within the agencies that have managed to launch products and businesses - it is tempting to say that these things *only* work if you have the resources and philosophy of Nike and Apple.

But this trend is not going away. So should agencies stick to what they are good at, even when it's harder to make money, or should they roll the dice?

My point of view is that it depends entirely what the agencies' motives are. It's fine to just want to dabble, impress some clients and get a press release, as long as everyone involved knows that. There is no pretence.

On the other hand if an agency has a hankering to make the next Instagram, then everything needs to be set in place. A budget. A serious budget. A stand alone team, that probably includes weirdos from outside of adland. No client work, not ever. Even that make or break pitch. And an agency management that stays 100% behind the team no matter how badly they fuck up. If you are managing an agency and have the stomach for that, you're willing to put skin in the game, then Godspeed! – I truly wish you well.

My Neighbour Has a Bicycle

By Ana Andjelic

Innovate or die. It seems like the advertising industry has been living in the shadow of this mantra for the last fifteen years. Long gone are days of advertising as usual, and more adept agencies and clients alike have been in constant reinvention mode, trying to adapt their business to the Fear Factor that consumer behaviour has become.

It all started with nerds sharing code. It continued with people sharing content, ranging from the latest news to the most intimate moments of their lives (just look at Secret. Actually, don't). Now micro-entrepreneurs, who are just like us, are sharing property, possessions, skills and knowledge.

It sounds like an amazing thing. Except that, if you are a brand in the business of *creating* all of those things, it is actually not. It is dangerously close to a pure panic of being squeezed out of business by virtually anyone describing their model as "AirBnB for X." And with good reason.

Total revenues of the collaborative economy sector exceeded $3.5 billion in 2013, with growth going upward of 25 percent, claims Forbes. Rachel Botsman, founder of Collaborative Lab, assures us that the P2P rental market alone is worth $16 billion. The Economist got so smitten that it proclaimed 2013 "The Year of Collaborative Consumption." Mary Meeker, the queen of Internet trends, decided that sharing economy was one of *the* trends for 2012. Some go as far as to predict that collaborative economy as potentially a $110 billion market. US Investors, always keen on being the first to discover and fund the next big thing, turned their watchful eye to developments in the collaborative economy start-up scene. The result is that is more than one third of start-ups with business models revolving around sharing cars, labor, office space, equipment, and pre-owned products received a total of over $2 billion in VC funding. Lyft raised $60 million. Airbnb raised double that amount. Avis bought Zipcar for $120 million. Google funded Uber for $258 million. eBay/Paypal bought Braintree for $800 million.

The numbers are dizzying, and they implicate a very real and powerful economic force. Forget about all that hippie, "join the movement!" talk. We are dealing here with a new business model based on self-interested consumer behaviour. This model is viable, sustainable, and above all, aimed at putting your brand out of business.

Something that at first seemed like a social phenomenon is actually firmly an economic one (further demonstrating that separating the two had never been a good idea). Just like the rest of digital disruptions, it is deeply rooted in human behaviour that got amplified, translated, fortified and turned into a cyborg, half-human half-technical version of itself. The specific behaviour that steadily fuels the collaborative economy is a combination of value-seeking, convenience, instant gratification, quality control, and looking for less mass, more unique, experiences. Using Uber as an example, this means that I, as a consumer, am looking for: a) a transportation option cheaper than Yellow Cab, b) available at the swipe of my application rather than standing at the slushy corner, c) instantly present at the moment I call it (no lingering at the above mentioned slushy corner), d) customer reviews-supported, and e) quite a pleasant, sitting in someone's roomy car instead of smelly cab, experience.

Brands don't provide this. They don't provide this superior experience. They don't even compete on the basis of customer experience. Their go-to market strategies are not customer experience-driven. Their marketing doesn't concern itself with experience. Their value chain is devoid of it.

What is the real challenge here, then? The fact that there are a lot of micro-entrepreneurs and startups resolved to make money out of making something better, easier and more fun for consumers, or the fact that our branding playbooks suck because they haven't been updated for the past 75 years, ever since the industrialisation happened?

The real innovation of the collaborative economy is not that people are - brace yourself - sharing, bartering, swapping, renting, lending and collaborating, because they have been doing that since the dawn of time. The real innovation is that the collaborative economy created a market for superior customer experience. Instead of competition based on price, production cost, distribution, and advertising communication, brands - oh the horror - need to compete based on the customer experience they provide. This is when innovation of the collaborative economy became truly disruptive.

It certainly helps that there is a lot of opportunity for disruption. There are 1 billion cars in the world. 740 million of them are occupied by just one person. The average car is used one hour per day. On average, our homes are filled with $3000 worth of unused items. Forty percent of human food goes to waste.

This waste is a direct result of the 75 years of branding being done in a certain way. This mode of branding persuaded, inspired and nudged us into acquiring more, more, and then some more. We became senseless hoarders without conscience. If that sounds harsh, look up the most recent data on global warming, energy sustainability and economic crisis.

The reality of this world, combined with our accumulated, idle assets and skills, and spurred by trust and connectivity coming from digital technology, created a context for economic exchange that's neither based on production nor on knowledge. Instead, it revolves around socio-economic exchange that happens directly between individuals, instead of exchange that takes place between businesses and consumers.

This is when the situation gets hairy for brands. Traditionally, they were mediators between producers and consumers, making producers more attractive to consumers and convincing consumers that they will be prettier, stronger, smarter because of products and services that producers create. Today, all we need to make a decision is a review, a photo and a community endorsement. So what happens to brands when the fastest growing form of economic exchange doesn't need mediation anymore? What is the role of brands in a collaborative economy (assuming there is one)?

This is a valid question. The current global economic landscape is interspersed with "traditional" companies, digital-first businesses, and collaborative economy start-ups. All of these diverse organisational forms revolve around different value chains. Industrial-era companies have value chains optimised for production and distribution. Digital companies have value chains optimised for service and information. Collaborative economy startups have value chains that optimise a marketplace. For example, in the retail market, there are traditional retailers like GAP or Target. They compete with digital-first retailers like Of A Kind, Zady or aggregators like Shopbop and Net-a-Porter. All of them now compete with retail marketplaces like Threadflip, Rent the Runaway or Walk In My Closet.

We, advertising professionals, do not need to answer the question of brand relevancy by predicting which economic model is going to win. The much more pressing question for us is how we can help prevent our clients from falling in the trap of the Innovator's Dilemma (when new technologies cause firms to fail), help them see that the collaborative economy is not just a "movement," and make them competitive in this complex landscape. For this, we need a new branding playbook.

The good news is that a roadmap to the new branding playbook is already laid our for us. There is no-one we can learn more from than those who disrupt our clients' businesses. The collaborative economy startups hand us the manual for success. This manual is a tool for brands to identify new branding practices and growth opportunities in collaborative marketplaces.

Grouped together, these new branding practices fall under one of four categories.

Add an existing marketplace

Brand's traditional, legacy business is going to be more valuable to consumers if we add an already existing marketplace to it. TaskRabbit is a marketplace for time, skills and knowledge, and, not accidentally, the most popular task there is assembling IKEA furniture. (I can personally attest to this). Loads of people do not want the fear and loathing of IKEA manuals. They would rather pay someone to go through the ordeal. Right therein lies an opportunity for IKEA. IKEA should own the "IKEA-assembling skills" marketplace on TaskRabbit. The option of having a TaskRabbit individual should be part of every online and in-store order, all bidding already done by IKEA. The retailer then delivers to your door both the furniture and the person who will assemble it.

Create a new marketplace

Brands are going to be more valuable to consumers if they create some sort of new value that did not exist before. New value usually comes out of connecting supply, provided by the brand, with customer demand in some new way. A few years ago, Peugeot unveiled "Mu," a rental service available in 70 European cities. Peugeot rents its customisable vehicles, along with scooters and bikes. This car manufacturer realised that its customers are engaging in car sharing behaviour, with the brand or without it. In a savvy move, it adjusted its supply to its customers' shifting demands.

In a slightly different vein, Patagonia partnered up with eBay to create a redistribution market for its pre-owned jackets, fleeces, gear, shoes, sweaters and other outdoors items. Patagonia customers can sell their ski pants, or buy a ski helmet on eBay, under Patagonia's brand. By expanding its product offerings into pre-owned goods, Patagonia effectively expanded its market, reached more consumers, and encouraged more economic transactions around its products. Since then, retail brands are starting to embrace the trend: H&M and British retailer ASOS crated their own online marketplaces.

Design for exchange

Brands are going to become *critically* valuable to consumers if consumers invest their own time and resources in them. In this scenario, consumers define their brand experience by adjusting brand product and services to their own needs and likes. Big, upscale US retailer Nordstorm partnered with TOMS shoes to inspire its customers to design new TOMS. Nordstorm attracts affluent customers who are looking for something more than just mass-produced clothes. They seek unique, elevated designs that are going to set them apart from their peers. Intimate knowledge of its customers allowed Nordstorm to come up with the initiative that responds to their needs in the best possible way. Nordstorm inspired its customers both to express their creativity through shoe design (and to own it), and to feel good about being part of a larger, meaningful humanitarian initiative.

Lincoln Motors tapped into customer insight in a similar way. Knowing that people who gravitate toward Lincoln cars like exclusive, highly personalised, unique experiences, it partnered with CustomeMade, a 3D hardware shop, to create matching jewellery for new owners of Lincoln vehicles. In this way, it rewarded its customers via the innovative, next-gen symbolic status recognition.

Disrupt business you are in

Brands create the most value when they reinvent their business by identifying and serving an unmet customer need. The fact that they modified their value chain so it diverges from their industry standard allows them to propel themselves ahead of their competition for the long-term. Walmart has now been suffering Amazon's online domination for years. The biggest US bricks-and-mortar retailer finally decided to do something about it. It transformed its value chain into a hybrid online/offline/collaborative economy model, where merchandise ordered on Walmart.com can be drop-shipped for same-day pickup at local stores. Additionally, Walmart incentivised customers shopping in its physical locations to serve as couriers, dropping off merchandise ordered online to those who live nearby. For their effort, they get a shopping discount.

Not to be outdone, Google quickly created Google Shopping Express that mobilises local merchants to deliver goods ordered online via Google Shopping. Rapid delivery has proven to be an unmet customer need that served to spur innovation and turn market competition into customer gain.

All these new branding directions are aimed at one, single-minded goal: amplifying customer experience. Make it better. Make it more complete, A-to-Z. Close the value loop. Provide consistent quality. Put customer convenience first. Be useful. Be interesting and stay clear of one-size-fits-all experiences. Allow people to share (people love sharing!). Add value in every customer interaction. Focus on unmet needs, and be one step ahead.

Brands who implement this kind of thinking have nothing to fear in the collaborative economy. They already behave according to its principles of generosity, transparency, sustainability and utility. Marketplace, design and disruption are the new branding playbook, and with it, collaborative economy can only make your brand grow.

Connected Devices, Disconnected Fans. Finding Emotional Resonance in Real-time Marketing

By Jon Burkhart

I've been helping brands be more culturally relevant for years and still I think they're shouting at people. The difference now is that they're choosing big echo chambers to shout in – like the Super Bowl and the Oscars - where at least a small percentage of people will notice. This is a flagrant foul in my opinion. The data is at our disposal for us to make real, emotional connections with fans through all manner of connected devices. What you're about to skim-read is an honest and purposefully disjointed look to a future where people connect with brands on an emotional level in real-time. Let's start with a quote from someone smarter than me:

"The winners will be those that respond in simple, creative, and more rewarding ways. Only the simplest, most human ideas travel well, and that's as true between platforms as it is between cultures. The increasingly rare companies and agencies that find those simple human truths and are able to bring them to life in astonishingly creative ways will thrive because creativity rewards the viewer and user - from utility to entertainment to EMOTIONAL CONNECTION."

John Patroulis, chief creative officer, BBH New York

Six Stage-Setting Facts On My Quest To Emotionally Connect With Fans In Real-time

1. Humans have always been real-time.
2. Marketing has always struggled to be real-time.
3. Humans have always craved transparency.
4. Marketing has always had a hidden agenda.
5. Humans are inherently emotional beings made to connect with one another
6. Marketing that makes a deep emotional connection is hard, but is the only way forward in a consumer-centric world.

Two Years Later, Real-Time Marketing Has Stopped Dunking But It's Still In The Dark

At SXSW this year, Content Strategy author Kristina Halvorson retold the story of the "Dunk In The Dark" Oreo Super Bowl tweet in a brilliant, never-told-before way. She ripped the piss out of it. She showed ridiculous headlines claiming that a simple press ad (albeit approved and released in 11 minutes after a Super Bowl blackout) revolutionised marketing. And this Cannes Lion winning tweet only took 13 people to create. She then revealed that only 0.008% of people on Twitter retweeted it.

While I wanted to yell "preach it Kristina" in my natural Memphis gospel preacher accent, I opted for a non-verbal double fist-pump. Please check out her talk "Go Home, Marketing, You're Drunk" on Slideshare (http://bit.ly/MktgDrunk).

Brands, Stop Trying To Own Every Moment You Think I Care About

Brands must stop hijacking humanity by butting-in on public conversations they don't have a right to be in. They must also stop filling their content calendars with "moments" they need to own. Cue Twitter's new #OwnTheMoment tool. This is a tool that provides agencies and brands with suggestions of dates that they should try to create tweets for. Confession: I developed prototypes of this tool in 2012 with two different agencies. My version used real-time data and beautiful visualisations, but fast-forward two years and it's too late for a tool like this. Too many brands are now out there making noise on the same days. Twitter's tool will help brands add to the cacophony around hundreds of more and less serious events - like National Wart Removal Day and International Hug Your Lizard Day. It's highly likely that these brands won't have a right to talk about warts and lizards. If you use the tool, use it to know what moments are already owned and avoid these altogether.

Brands will now have to make strides to be ready for something new and unpredictable. Thank you, Twitter for killing off "planned spontaneity." That other social network, Facebook, is so sick of brands creating buzz kills that they've decided to change the algorithm to make it bloody expensive for them to annoy people who are just trying to chat to their friends.

My Urgent And Sometimes Genius Past: From World's First Real-Time Creativity Blog To….

There has been a lot written about real-time marketing in the last few years – both good and horribly bad. I have been totally consumed by it since 2009. This obsession led Grant Hunter and I to write a book called Newsjacking, (Thames and Hudson, 2013).

Five years ago, my mission was first and foremost to help brands create content that was more tailored to fan's interests. These were the days when a brand could create a Facebook page and build an audience to hundreds of thousands. Of course, we were all struggling then with short attention spans, but we were used to brands shouting at us. We were starting to find clever ways to avoid their messages.

We covered hundreds of examples in our book from forward-thinking brands that have found clever ways to reach fans with disruptive real-time content. There were clever apps from Heineken that helped you enjoy live football matches by making real-time predictions. There were even real-time responses that tried to help people in need. One that springs to mind is Farmville's daikon radish crop that raised a ton of cash for the tsunami in Japan. This special radish only grows in Japan, and it was added to the social game within hours.

.... Real-time Uneasiness With Opportunistic Hijacking Of The News

All these real-time fun and games were great. Some of it was meaningful. However, as we neared our deadline, I felt uneasy about brands often latching on to current events without any strategic reason for doing so. Unless you count being seen as quick and clever. In 2014, we need more from brands. If brands land on our radar at all, it's because they've found a way to make our lives easier or better.

Fortunately, I was allowed to add a final conclusion where I got to predict what's next. I felt strongly that real-time connections would be more meaningful in a world where brands were doing remarkable things. I included one of the first branded examples of a connected device – BakerTweet. My friends at London agency Poke hooked up an oven to Twitter so it would tweet when the iced buns were ready. I'm a sucker for baked goods and this was also the first connected device I'd heard of – other than a Cambridge professor who hooked the plants in his back garden up to Twitter so they'd tweet when they needed to be watered. I thought this was all about brands adding value and, dare I say it, (some) meaning. I knew this was just the beginning of technology providing real-time connections with people, places and things (edible and otherwise.)

RTM Present and Future: Understand Context And Help Us Stay Better Connected

Why? Because our entire lives are connected now. Our clothes, our shoes, our wrists – we're walking data points transmitting information every second. We're revealing our location and frame of mind to companies in exchange for personalised services.

The new world isn't one where we're actively checking our phones 23 times an hour. We're entering a world of passive connections. Things are happening naturally as we become human data transmitters. We're being fed what we want, when we want it. We don't have time for anything that's not tailored to our needs.

Does Your Real-Time Effort Connect With Fans Emotionally?

The variables aren't related to where we are. They're all about how we feel. What we're in the mood for. Fortunately we're constantly pumping out information about our feelings on social networks. Our purchasing decisions reveal this as well. The real-time variable is all about how we FEEL. The future of real-time marketing is all about EMOTIONAL CONNECTION. It's about hitting us with content that connects with a sense of pleasure or purpose.

20 Questions To Ask Before You Attempt To Connect Emotionally With Fans

So let's say that you're a brand and you're planning to create content on a regular basis that creates an emotional connection with fans. Would you mind if I asked you a few questions?

1. What do you stand for?
2. Why do you exist?
3. Have you tested this? Have you interrogated it to within an inch of its life?
4. Would people miss you if you were gone? What would they miss the most?
5. Do you know your customers? How well?
6. Do you know what they want? Do you know how they feel?
7. Do you know where they hang out?
8. At what point during the day do they want to hear from you?
9. Have they allowed you access to their real-time emotional and physical state?
10. How are you rewarding them for this privilege?
11. Do you think about what they want 4 times more than you promote your own stuff?

12. Have you thought about how this might involve an object that's not a smartphone?
13. How many fans do you feel you're on a first name basis with due to time spent?
14. How many could you buy a gift for?
15. How have you re-worked your product or service based on what your fans want?
16. Do your fans know the people behind the brand?
17. Would they want to go for a beer with anyone who worked for your company?
18. Have you met your fans face-to-face?
19. Have you won them over with your real-life charm?
20. Do they feel like they're a part of your family?

Real-time Customer-Centric Content: Predictive and Personalised.

Is It Predictive?

What if brands could predict the future and were ready to prepare us for it? We're all so busy that we need brands to be a few steps ahead of us. As Michael Schrage says in *Who Do You Want Your Customers to Become?* - "Solutions that merely please, serve, meet the needs/specs or delight customers don't go far enough. They represent yesterday's marketing and design paradigms. They're too rooted in the now... They misunderstand innovation's real impact – transforming customers."

What I like most about companies like Amazon and Google is that they go beyond providing customers with what they want when they want it. They've changed their customers, revolutionising the way they think and behave. Thanks to Amazon, people no longer buy anything without comparing it online and then asking friends on Facebook. Thanks to Google, we're all instant problem solvers, with an answer to every query we could ever dream of in seconds.

Is It Personalised? If so, how Personal is the connection?

Problem: marketing can be personalised – "Jon, we haven't seen you in a while..." but is it personal? Does it make intelligent attempts to connect with who I am? I want brands to use technology to help me feel more alive. I want it to help me feel better about myself. I want the digital world to be so intertwined with the physical world that we're actually humanising technology.

I'm asking brands to listen more and shout less. When I allow them to - in order to provide me more time for real-life friendships - I would like them to recommend what food I should buy tonight based on the fact that my Evernote app analysed my receipt and reported to my fitness app the bad news of my cheeseburger, Oreo shake and onion rings for lunch. This will help me be less fat and may give me more energy when I'm in hour seven of a workshop and my attendees are flagging.

Top Three Ways To Create More Meaningful Content In Real-Time

REALLY know who you're talking to

The data's out there -- their likes, dislikes, hopes, fears and dreams. This is the age of sharing. The tricky bit is getting an analyst to make real-time insights that can help you alter your course at a moment's notice.

Take the big leap from knowing your audience to caring about them.

I love it when brands start proving that there are real humans in their company who enjoy looking after fans. Customer service is a great way to win big here. J Crew sent a guy a new pair of trousers when he had a bike wreck on the way to an important meeting. Zappos sent a pair of shoes to a church when forgetfulness meant a bride was going to go barefoot down the aisle. It's all about brands being human.

Pretend that you're giving fans a gift that they'll never forget.

Gift-giving is a real talent. You have to know and care deeply about someone to be an expert at it. It requires constant listening and an unselfish mindset. If you really care about someone you wouldn't give them a crap novelty tie every year for Christmas. Google "Westjet Airlines" and "Christmas" and you'll see what it's like. The airline gave personalised gifts to everyone at Christmas, requiring each passenger to sit on Santa's lap and tell them what they wanted.

Pleasure: Does it give you any?

While some were getting excited about an Oreo tweet, I'd moved on to the possibilities of connecting with fans in a deeper way, as Budweiser Canada debuted its Hockey Light during the Super Bowl. Budweiser offered to install a red goal light synced to the scores of your favourite team. If you're not into hockey, you may not know that the red light's iconic flashing and horn sound accompanies every goal and is as emotionally charged as football announcers yelling "goooooooaaaaaaal!"

Problem: Does it solve one?

Sticking with the beer theme, SteadyServ Technologies is a startup that hooks up kegs at pubs with sensors that monitor beer levels. It's always been a bit of a guessing game when trying to figure out how much beer is left in a keg, but now the kegs are connected to their bar's Twitter account sending out status updates about how many pints of certain beers are left so you ensure you don't miss out on drinking your favourite pint.

Purpose: Is it meaningful in any way?

When was the last time a bit of real-time creativity made you cry? I was speaking at a conference with Laura Jordan Bambach recently and she showed me something that made me tear up just a tiny bit. Yahoo Japan has made it possible for children who are blind to search the web. It's a machine called Hands On Search. It's a cross between a computer and a 3D printer. Walk up to it and say "dinosaur" and it will find a picture from Yahoo search and print out a 3-D image.

MY ACTION PLAN: What can we do right now to stay emotionally connected?

My new platform (a blog for now – perhaps a meet-up and conference eventually) asks the world we live in – "Will that connect?" By that I mean a few different things:

Will that device connect to the internet and provide something that connects with us emotionally? If it's real-time content, will it connect with consumers in a meaningful, human way? I will rate each example 1-10 for Pleasure, Problem and Purpose.

Let's take today's blog post. Australian rules football channel FoxTel has created an Alert Shirt that uses wearable technology to help fans feel what's happening in the game in real-time. If a player is nervous before the game, they feel that. If someone suffers a bone-crushing tackle, they feel that in the shirt as well.

I rank this highly for Pleasure, as it creates a real-time experience of what it feels like to be on the pitch. It scores well for the other criteria as declining attendance rates for professional sports (Problem) means that you need to try harder to provide fans with a unique experience (Purpose) like this.

If you'd like to join me on my quest to make brands more focused on their customers by connecting with them emotionally, connect with me at jon@ realtimecontentlabs.com. Let's stop the madness one brand at a time.

FUTURE

Make Things People Want > Make People Want Things

By John V Willshire

Foreword, twice

It is two years, four months, twenty-one days, four hours and forty-seven minutes since I carefully marked out *Make Things People Want > Make People Want Things* in the visitors' book at *Clinic* in London.

I signed it *@willsh*. The @ symbol was first used to measure quantity, but is now helps measure quality (or indeed lack of). It tells you who made something, and invites you to connect with them instantly. It is a maker's mark with a living stream of consciousness.

The tools we use today to create, capture or communicate mean that the things we make are invariably linked to us, their creators, and also to the fixed moment in time when they were brought into being.

When we record the minutes and seconds so accurately, it is perhaps hard to think of anything as 'timeless' from now on. The ripples always start somewhere.

In this case, I shared a photo of it on Instagram; the image, date, time and place marked for as long as anyone can find that image file. Then I shared it on twitter, then the blog, then...

Wait, let's start earlier.

————————

It is two years, ten months, twenty days, one hour and thirty-two minutes since I resigned as Chief Innovation Officer at PHD in London, a position I'd held for some five years.

Do I recall this with such certainty because I posted a picture of my boss's reaction to the news on Instagram? No, of course not, what do you take me for? It's because I decided to resign on May 4th 2011. Star Wars Day. Shortly before lunch.

Reading that back, I'm torn between which of the two is worse.

Why resign? It was a great job, at a great agency. In truth, something bothered me about the world I worked in. I couldn't quite put my finger on it at the time, so instead I left to find out…

Four words, twice

It is two years, four months, and about twenty days since I sat down with some blank playing cards, a black fine point 1.0mm Sharpie, and stumbled upon a phrase that's changed my life:

Make Things People Want > Make People Want Things.

I can't even remember why I'd written *make, people, want,* and *things* on the cards in the first place. It doesn't really matter now. Perhaps that's one of the beguiling things about a good creative process; you discover things you weren't looking for.

Once discovered, once lodged in the conscious, it appears *Make Things People Want > Make People Want Things* is hard to shake off.

Perhaps, if *"the limits of our language are the limits of our world"*, then by this lingual slight of hand we can find ourselves transported to another world entirely.

This new world is a place where we can explore making things fit for purpose *right now*, rather than daubing fresh hieroglyphs on the tombs of brand gods people no longer worship. A place where we can discover new abilities and reclaim old responsibilities.

MTPW > MPWT is a bridge between realms, spanning a chasm against the background of the times we live in. For too long, most companies have been content to simply exploit existing demand, and now find themselves unable to change.

MTPW > MPWT serves as the working ethos for Smithery, helping those companies explore alternative ways to create new demand, being small and nimble enough to dodge between the silos, and shaping experiences and prototypes with clients as we go.

From my experience across the last eight hundred and seventy one days, I'd like to offer some ideas about these four simple words.

Four words, once.

i) Make
It is two years and a handful of weeks since I was sitting in a cottage in the Lake District, reading *The Craftsman* by Richard Sennett, the premise of which is the assertion that *"making is thinking"*. Why should such a simple idea be such a big deal?

Well, there was a distinction drawn between thinking and making in wider society during the last century. Perhaps most acutely, in the shift to become a knowledge economy we have held the act of thinking in ever-higher regard, separating the cerebral activities from manual endeavours, in order to justify the increasingly high value we now *must* place on knowledge.

In truth though, it is much harder to separate the two; as Joseph Brodsky put it, *"no honest craftsman or maker knows in the process of working whether he is making or creating"*. In all we do, we are likely to be simultaneously creating and perceiving.

Yet in marketing, the agency game is rigged, committed to creating divides and tension. Thinking is a nebulous commodity to be traded up-front; the dance of a thousand meetings where people in white-walled meeting rooms out-reckon each other into submission.

The relationship between client and agency is centred around when making might *start*, not when it can *stop*. Even when early prototypes are made, they're only shown in a glass walled room where respondents gorge on potato skins slightly less loaded than the questions.

Yet instead, we can create massive ongoing feedback loops that guide all of a company's work, much in the same way as a blacksmith might use the sounds, shapes and resistance of metal-on-metal when shaping his work.

Making in today's world is a much more useful form of *thinking*. When you keep doing things you've never done before, you become better at doing *anything* for the first time. By learning from failure, and honing our intuition, we can begin to thrive on uncertainty.

Make first, make quickly, make often, make where the world can see it, and you're more likely to make things well.

ii) Things
It is more than three years since I was at a conference in London where Matt Jones, then of the newly monikered BERG, talked about an idea he'd been exploring…

"I'm proposing that the technologies of rapid fabrication and pervasive networks are allowing the tangible and intangible to switch places and mingle"

A future where products become services, then products again, looping in and out of previously well-defined domains. The same network that makes the @ symbol into our maker's mark also starts to underpin that which we make, own, rent, or sell. A hoopy frood used to know where his towel was. Soon the towel will know where it's at all by itself.

So when I say '*Things*', it is a purposefully fuzzy description of potential outputs in this strange future. Not products, not services, not brands, not adverts. *Things* are something that all different arts of an organisation come together to realise. *Things* are remarkable, in the sense that people bother to pass a remark about them. *Things* could mean, well, just about *anything...*

Which is very useful. Because in disruptive times, established companies are often too caught up in the specifics of what they currently do to grasp and utilise the generalities of what they could do. Squint at a product, look obliquely at a service. What is it *really* doing? What else could do that? How would you build a subscription model, a freemium version, a paper prototype, a hand-cranked experience?

Working in this oblique way allows us to experiment in ways that are both relevant to a company's purpose, yet sufficiently removed enough from 'business as usual' to be of great value. It is an exploratory, creative form of innovation, and it unites different silos of a business together in new ways.

What's more, it helps generate authentic stories for a business; advertising isn't the thing you do, it's the story of the *things* you've done. And the more interesting the *things* are, the more you've pushed at these fuzzy boundaries, the more interested people will be.

iii) People
It must be a little over fifty-seven years since John McKitterick, a senior marketing manager at General Electric, wrote a piece for a marketing textbook. *"The principal task of the marketing function"*, he stated, *"is not so much to be skilful in making the customer do what suits the interests of the business as to be skilled in conceiving and then making the business do what suits the interests of the customer"*.

Being 'user-centric' has always been the marketer's job. Unfortunately, the tools used by marketers and their agencies have been largely made redundant by a fragmenting media landscape.

The consumer was considered as homogenous as the products a factory produced. The occupation of the industry was to design brands and advertising for average people, because the research we had told us that everyone *was* average. Yet the demographic profiles previously relied upon look like the thinnest of ciphers now.

There is no average anymore. Everyone, without exception, goes to an extreme here or there. Some people learn inordinate amounts about the craft beers they drink, or the artisan coffees they buy. Some people spend hours on forums working out the best couponing strategies. Some people make a living from shooting videos of toy unboxings.

People is a collective word describing an otherwise dissimilar group. Because people are weird. Brilliantly, loveably, diversely weird in a way that you'll never see if you think of them as mere 'consumers'.

Stop focusing too much on how to influence the individual (and by inference, everyone else just like them), and instead make the most of how we're a social species, much more likely to just copy each other, as Mark Earls explains so beautifully elsewhere in this book. It is the things *between* people that they use to make connections with each other that matter most.

To understand what these are, you have to build up a picture of diversity by talking to as many people as you can. This seems obvious, but it's remarkable how far away from actual people marketers and their agencies tend to be. And rather than boil research down into 'one key insight', find the things that make people different, highlight them and celebrate them.

Then, look for the connections between people, the strands that draw them together, their conversations, their shared activities. Look between people, not at them in isolation. That way, you'll stand a much better chance of making what they want.

iv) Want
It is nearly three quarters of a century since Maslow first published his *"Hierarchy of Needs"*. When people tend to talk about "consumer needs", I have a simple principle; it's not a need unless Maslow says it is. Everything else is just a *want*. As suits my belief, I've morphed Peter Doyle's *needs* framework into *three types of wants*.

Firstly, there are *Existing Wants*, where the market already exists (butter, current accounts). Secondly, there are *Latent Wants*, things that don't exist just yet, but they are pretty easy to spot by anyone (Dell IdeaStorm, My Starbucks Idea*)*. Thirdly, there are *Incipient Wants*, the things that nobody really saw coming, but 'couldn't live without' now they're here (Walkman, iPhone*)*.

Existing companies tend to spend a disproportionate amount of time working on something that serves as an *Existing Wants*, and fixating on the six other things exactly like it. There's a reason for this. Theodore Levitt (1960) highlighted the story of the US railroads, who had assumed themselves to be in the railroad business, not the transportation business. They let in a new generation of companies, the airlines, who have come to dominate the nation's transport infrastructure.

Failings of this type, pointed Levitt, always lie with the incumbent businesses; *"To survive, they themselves will have to plot the obsolescence of what now produces their livelihood"*. They're often too busy looking locally at the competition, rather than at the wider landscape. You must look for the businesses that will make you obsolete.

Because right now, the start-up capitals of the world are filled with the brightest talent looking for a way to create new forms of business, as Ana Andjelic rightly highlights in her contribution to this book. If there's any established business in the world that doesn't believe they're being targeted in this way, they're not looking hard enough.

It is a highly useful discipline to identify whether you're working on an *Existing, Latent or Incipient Want* by drawing out a physical map. You can start to fill in the spaces where other people are doing things. Are there any start-ups who've spotted this easy, latent idea, and are trying to realise it in a new way? Any groups of potential customers making their own version? Or if it's truly an incipient want, what's stopped people getting to it before? What makes this special? Who's tried and failed?

Maps like these can be your best guide to discovering what people want, not just what you and your closest rivals want to sell to them.

Four words, two worlds
This phrase has given me a useful degree of clarity in the work that I do now, just by following four simple principles:

    i)   use *making* as thinking
    ii) be purposefully fuzzy with *things*
    iii) remember that there are no average *people*
    iv) make a map to discover an incipient *want*

And whilst it is only fifteen minutes since you began reading this exploration of *Make Things People Want > Make People Want Things*, I hope these principles prove to be just as useful for you. The ripples always start somewhere.

This used to be the Future

By Flo Heiss

Monday
here we go, c'mon
I press the button on the coffee machine. Two pods.

The business editor on the BBC Breakfast News is now standing. She used to sit on a barstool. They introduced full bleed pictures as backdrops with a little bit of blurring bottom right. It might be quite nice to blur the whole picture? Or would that look weird? They blurred out Watson's and Holmes's face in turn in a drunken scene last night on Sherlock. So maybe not a good look for the BBC News.

Someone is pulling a bin up the lane. Monday is bin day. A car drives past. It's still dark. Big shadows of the bin and puller are projected onto the wall of the thatched house. Massive shadows. All moving and overlapping. A bit like that famous shadow scene in Murnau's Nosferatu. Only with. Erm. Bins.

The woman with the wet hair on the bus is putting her seatbelt on. She has that blue Cath Kidston bag with white dots. Same one. Every day.

Train. Interesting how everyone reads the same stuff. Free newspapers they've been given. Well actually not all people. But quite a few. We seem to be happy to let ourselves be dictated by someone else's choice. I quite like to put the TV on sometimes and just watch whatever is on. All this interactiveness and digital choice is exhausting. It's nice to let yourself be sucked into dross sometimes. Sometimes.

Why is everything a hack now? Isn't hacking just making things, being inventive? Why is this a thing? Do we need a label for making things? Maybe we do so we feel we have permission to do something that otherwise won't immediately be recognisable as real work.

Tuesday

do it
do it
do it

First we had microsites, then Facebook pages and now it's suggestive hashtags in ads. In a way I preferred the microsites (yes, I said microsites) - at least there was some time and love spent on them. Crafting. Filming. Animating. Now a hashtag is just a link to words. It's more real and immediate, but maybe also less interesting?

This train is now ready to depart. Please stand clear of the doors.

I see a pretty, meandering country lane. The scene is spoilt by a white van parked under a tree. Or is it spoilt? Maybe the van is what makes the picture interesting? Just like I always find myself drawn to the washed up rubbish on a beach, it's always more interesting, I think, in any type of work, be it a painting, a photo or a design to corrupt the beauty a little with something that sticks out. Something that tweaks normality a little. Could that be the key to creating fresh work? A tweaking of the everyday? New work. We are all after it all the time. And truly new work can be made.

If it's made now, even if it's based on an old idea, whatever you are making will be new because it is something made now and it will be different because YOU are making it. Everything you do is new. It's not true that everything has been done before. NOTHING has been done before the way you are doing it.

There's a danger that nothing actually gets made anymore because it's not new enough. Make it anyway. It will be good. It will be different. It will be new.

It happens so often that fresh, sad, silly, surprising, different, crazy, risky, stupid, ideas get killed by a technicality or a clever fact before they even are allowed to live and develop and exist. Facts kill ideas.

Things only exist if they exist.

There is a peculiar light this morning. It's been raining really hard and the clouds are still there but moving really fast. Trying to clear themselves away. From somewhere the sunlight is hitting the lawns and this combination of Turner sky and Gursky land looks really beautiful.

I have to concentrate hard to see all the black barnacle like satellite dishes sucked to the walls on the rows and rows of houses. Once you've seen them you can't un-see them. Odd growth on brick. Everywhere. Bringing distraction and desire.

Wednesday

pump up the volume

Isn't it strange that we put the crackling of a vinyl record onto a streaming sound file? That we use 70s filters to make our photos less perfect? We seem to have a craving for imperfection in our auto-tuned lives. Perfection is boring.

A big murder of crows is swarming around leafless trees to make their nests. What's that Tom Waits track with the crows barking in the background. I think it's on The Black Rider album (Flash Pan Hunter/Intro – looked it up). I wonder if anyone will ever persuade him to use his music in advertising. I hope not. Bob Greenberg told me a story (he tells very many brilliant stories) about people having their voice trademarked (this story might not be true, who knows, does it matter?). He is somehow involved in that. Tom Waits is one of the people who has had their voice copyrighted. In a way his voice is his biggest asset. Very clever. Also a little creepy. Especially if you think that a person's voice is protected after their death. But it makes total sense. Actors can be recreated visually to star in films. So I'm sure there will be / is technology to create an artificial voice that sounds exactly like someone. Combine that with the advance of robot technology and we are one step closer to eternal life (death).

Thursday

pump up the volume

Yo hobo humpin slobo babe...
Placebo Innovation. What a great summation of making us feel better by tinkering around and actually not doing anything (from Benjamin Bratton's brilliant anti TED - TED talk).

A sea of people waiting at Kings Cross looking up at the departure board. I'm in it. We are all dressed in black. Everyone has chosen to do so. Why is that? Is it the easier choice? I silently applaud the few red coats, the occasional flash of purple or yellow. Hat. Scarf. This is the second decade of the 21st century. Isn't this supposed to be the future? With silver and gold metallic clothing? No one is hovering. No one is teleporting. Shame really.

What has happened to the great promise of clever, behaviourally driven online advertising? Amazon reminds me that I have just put a camera on my wish list in every single banner on every single web page I go to. Yes, I know. Thank you Amazon. I'm not a goldfish.

Friday

dance dance

I'm reading Max Ernst whilst listening to Metallica. Make of that what you will.
A text conversation with Graham Wood

GW: Natively online digital innovations
FH: 360 Integrations
GW: 720 destruction
FH: Level 42
GW: Shalamar

Remember 360° advertising? Or integrated advertising I think it was called then. It used to be the future. What happened? I would love to see design and advertising come together again as friends. Possibly even coming from the same place. Would that be too difficult? It's not that long ago that designers made advertising and advertising creatives designed. It's curious that in a time of supposed convergence, disciplines drift further apart. A sea of specialists and no generalist in sight. Could we describe someone as a generalist and not mean it as an insult?

There is a wonderful short essay in Brian Eno's book "A Year With Swollen Appendices" about pretension and how children learn through pretending to be something/someone they are not. For kids it's normal to pretend. Why is it that pretention is such a dismissive word? Pretenders are those who at least have a go at something. Try something out and learn, you pretentious generalist!

I was recently at a talk by Danny Boyle (about his film Trance) where he passionately spoke about the time when he made Shallow Grave and how his innocence, and the fact that he was pretending to be a director, made it so much better a film (and how he misses that ignorance now). The beauty of ignorance.

Technology presents endless options. Make decisions and keep it simple. Try this for a change: Make something, anything, and see if it leads to an idea. It's the opposite process to having an idea first and then spending ages trying to make it. Be receptive, trusting, and allow yourself to be vulnerable to your own ideas.

Are we all feasting on the same all-you-can-eat creative buffet? What happens if no one actually creates anything anymore? What if we have hashtagged the fuck out of every last single ounce of existing creative work?

Mephistoles said:
Ich sag es dir: ein Kerl, der spekuliert,
Ist wie ein Tier, auf dürrer Heide
Von einem bösen Geist im Kreis herumgeführt,
Und ringsumher liegt schöne grüne Weide.

A chap who speculates - let this be said -
Is very like a beast on moorland dry,
That by some evil spirit round and round is led,
While fair, green pastures round about him lie.

Or in Elvis' words: A little less conversation, a little more action please!

But, you know, what the fuck do I know.

Proving MC Hammer Wrong

By Tim Buesing

Almost 23 years ago, a wise man named Stanley Kirk Burrell penned the following words:
So wave your hands in the air
Bust a few moves
Run your fingers through your hair
Look, man - You either work hard or you might as well quit.
You can't touch this!

THE GOLDEN WEB

At the time of his biggest hit 'U Can't Touch This' Stan, better known as MC Hammer, was right on the money. We couldn't touch him, his dazzling leg-wear, or his dancing skills. The same was true for the web, invented only a year earlier. Back in 'Hammertime' you accessed digital web pages from a distance, via a proxy. We employed a boxy mouse that had been invented in 1963, a keyboard, or alternatively a stylus plus a graphic tablet. And touching a screen during a creative review only led to annoyed glances from the art directors. After all, who wanted to have their display full of smudges and fingerprints?

THE NEW WEB

Fast forward to today and we are able touch, blink, talk, walk and bump our way through the same web. In some instances it suffices to merely hover over a screen, using so called 'air gestures'. And some of us are already experimenting with using brainwaves to navigate.

Initially we had imagined the web to be a 'better TV'. But instead it just continued to become a much better web. It became ubiquitous and something we now take for granted and consider a human right to access. We do access it whenever, wherever and for as long as we can. And a lot of our interactions now happen through touch.

AT THE TOUCH OF A FINGER

Our world has embraced smart phones and tablets with unprecedented speed. By the end of 2014 we will have more mobile phones on this planet than humans. And through these devices we have learnt and integrated touch gestures into our lives.

We like to tap our mobile phone and tablet apps. And we prefer them over desktop computers and keyboards. Microsoft Surfaces are hybrid computers that offer both keyboard and touch screen. But their users instinctively prefer to touch the display. They bypass the keyboard and grasp the screen like a tablet. This behaviour happens even when they have to perform more complicated tasks like filling out forms.

So evidently there's a strong appeal to 'just grab and touch'. Touch delivers a more gratifying experience of what's in front of us. Technology and the interface fade into the background. We can focus on the emotional quality of our activity. We emphatically flick, tap, swipe, pinch, nudge, punch and press. This is especially true for social media apps. Our thumbs flick through Twitter and Pinterest streams. And this casual gesture underscores our emotional state. We scan the abundance of content, let it float by, sometimes stop and double tap to open or 'Like' an item. And thus we feel more connected, more in touch with news from our friends and family. It's no wonder we feel closer to their content. Touch is a more intimate and direct gesture than clicking and dragging with a mouse.

Have you seen the video of a baby girl getting frustrated by a paper magazine? The one-year old is confused because she can't tap and swipe the pages like she would on a tablet. In a similar fashion, we adults get annoyed when a brand hasn't yet adapted their website to mobile. Its desktop sized site, images and copy shrinks to tiny proportions. It forces us to scroll, pinch and zoom. Honestly, who do these shmucks think they are? As Sir Ken Robinson observed, we are not a very patient species: *"Come on, I don't have all minute!"*.

POINTING BACK TO US

So what consequences does this have for our profession and industry?

First, we have to learn a lot of new tricks. There is no way back. People won't return to liking a mouse or keyboard more. When given a choice people will prefer touching. That's why mobile expert Josh Clark states that 'every desktop UI should be designed for touch now'.

That means we definitely have to grow our skill-sets to keep building great digital experiences. User Interface (UI), Interaction and User Experience (UX) design now require a prominent place in our teams. Because these skills address how customers solve problems, entertain themselves, shop and communicate with others. And so the rise of touch, and to a lesser extent voice and gesture, changes what defines a good user and customer experience.

Do you know the average finger tip size in square pixels? Just look at it. Not sure? Even mobile touch screen manufacturers can't quite agree on how much space our fingers need to get working. Their interface recommendations range from 28 (Nokia) to 44 square pixels (Apple).

Or how about navigation items: would you place them at the top or at the bottom? Convention says you place them at the top, from left to right, in easy reach of a mouse. But tablet and phone users would prefer to see them at the bottom, where their hands come to rest.

Mouse users also don't tire as much when buttons are spread out across the screen. But touch screen users feel the pain - they like to tap within comfort zones. So remember that your branded app will only become a favourite if it doesn't force fingers into all kind of hooks and pretzels.

Second, we need to come up with ideas that work with this preference for touch. We know how to present a crisp image and a concise headline together. We know how to write a story that is bold and engaging. Those formats are key to expressing creative ideas. But now the audience wants to touch the content. And they want to do it on a wide range of gadgets and devices. Maybe you thought the new practice of responsive web design was going to take care of that? What you might have forgotten is that it moves the content around, rearranges, stacks and even crops images. If you aren't careful this might actually change the focus of our ideas. Not all creatives are aware of this. And so they might concentrate on a linear execution, checking it only on that perfect TV screen or wide-screen computer display. Yet their creative work will get displayed in a myriad of different layouts. And for all those it absolutely has to be 'built for touch'.

Third, we will only be successful working hand-in-hand with our clients. We agencies are able to react to this change in media use. But only when our clients understand the value and extra effort required. So the smarter agencies team up with clients, sketching and working on ideas together, owning the problem as much as its solution. Delivering a design on a client's personal phone or tablet can work miracles, creating a deeper bond with the work. And for us agencies it can be gratifying to see clients interact one-on-one with our ideas.

THROW UP YOUR HANDS?

Despite all this new complexity, this is no time for hand-wringing. We just have to grasp how to both come up with, as well as present, a great idea for touch. Give it a shape that the audience can tap, touch, nudge and manipulate. Or speak to. Or gesture at. And sometimes it will be a combination of all these inputs, used in one consecutive session. After all, the same customer can interact with the same brand in various ways. This can depend on context, mood, time of day, whether alone or in company and where the customer is.

William Gibson once quipped: "The future is already here, it is just not very evenly distributed." So let's look at recent creative work that points in the right direction:

In my own practice I have used touch not only as an input method but also as a metaphor: WWF wanted to lobby attendees of the Copenhagen Climate Summit. We chose a mobile voting app in which WWF supporters could spin a virtual dynamo on their phone screens. With their fingers the users created enough energy to send their vote for action to Denmark, directly from their individual location.

Another fellow Creative Social agency B-reel and mobile phone company 3 produced web video conferences that used 'see-through' touch screens. The sales agents touched a screen in front of them, moving phones and features around. At the same time they would talk and interact live with the customers, responding to their requests. The instant and simultaneous character led to a shared touch screen experience.

Audi has already transformed several showrooms in London, Berlin and Beijing into spaces where visitors' touch, movements and gestures define their experience. The 'built for touch' idea permeates these 'Audi Cities', right up to the final sales moment.

OUR FINGERS IN EVERY PIE

Looking ahead, 'touch' will become the preferred interface for almost any real life situation involving computers and screens. So how can we create more brand videos that customers want to literally get their hands on? Or projections, apps and kiosk screens that entice punters to tap, touch and caress them?

MC Hammer again gives us a clue by rapping "either work hard or you might as well quit." Our CS friends from rehabstudio did just that and produced a concept for personalised window shopping. In their future vision punters will be able to casually flick through and try different looks right on the shop windows. Selecting and purchasing will go hand in hand with the always-on mobile phone.

So keep on working hard and 'think touch first': picture the user with a tablet or phone, out and about or on the couch, swiping and tapping. Ask yourself whether your work would survive in this situation. Watch real people use a prototype of your idea. Keep on testing and interrogating, then improve and redeploy. If you work for a tech brand, try to get access to its engineering squad and prototypes. Tinker with the latest screens and input devices. And if you can afford the time, work with universities, start-ups and publishers to gain a broader understanding of this new interface world. In the end we all want to prove Hammer wrong, standing tall with our phones and tablets in hand, and say that we can and will be able to touch this!

Money Can't Buy Me Love?

By Alex Lavery

Introduction

Music connects at the deepest emotional level, evoking feelings and driving behaviours that are impossible to deny.

For brands that seek to build positive associations with an audience or even better, influence people's behaviour, this is marketing gold dust.

And yet, despite the millions (billions?) of pounds spent on music activity, there have been many instances of one-hit music marketing wonders but very few examples of ongoing, successful tie-ups. It seems that Lennon and McCartney had a point with 'Money Can't Buy Me Love'.

Why is that?

Music is often applied at a very generic and superficial level, young people like it, it's contemporary, it's cool, it's mass. So just add my brand logo onto the music act, property or platform and hey presto, I'm cool.

It's complex (the music eco-system and the management and rights structure) with dozens of stakeholders between a brand execution using music and an artist granting approval.

It's also just one part of the overall brand marketing mix and needs to work efficiently with the other channels and activities of a campaign.

There are a lot of brands doing things in the music space and so, unless you are doing something very unique and distinctive, it takes time to own your idea or territory in music. Time which most brand managers cannot afford to wait for to yield results.

But get it right and the rewards will be big. How many of your marketing activities have the ability to make people smile, sigh, cry, feel good or nostalgic, jump up and down or shout Knees Up Mother Brown?

And how much of your brand equity can be instantly associated with your brand and conjure a rich mental picture of its creative world with just a couple of seconds of a few notes, even whilst your target might be bombarded by a myriad of other tasks and distractions (as is usually the norm in our modern world).

Getting It Right

To get it right, you need to apply a more structured, strategic approach, with a long-term commitment to music, carefully integrated across the full marketing programme.

And that starts with a clear marketing objective for the music activity to address. As has already been stated, far too often music activity happens simply because it appeals to a younger demographic and is seen as a source of cool for the brand. That is simply way too vague and general a reason for marketing activity in this day and age. People are looking for so much more from their brands, a depth of meaning and identity, distinctive values and a clear point of view. Sticking your logo on the latest mega-star's tour is probably worse than doing nothing. It stinks of soul-less, mindless, idea-less marketing (lots of money but no credibility).

With a clear understanding of what you want your brand to stand for and clarity on the marketing objective (including target audience) that the activity is designed to address, it is possible to build music solutions that are both distinctive and effective.

The Right Type Of Music

So, what help is there for brands that want to make the right choices in music?

One route is the use of data derived from consumer music consumption and behaviour, offering detailed insight into what music and which artists have the most reverence for a target demographic. Sources such as Music Metric or Echo Nest provide real time access to music artists' social activity (fans, likes, dislikes), sales, radio plays, illegal downloads and streamed plays. This detail can provide demographic specifics including location, age and gender. For example, it is possible to search for artists most popular with girls aged between seventeen and nineteen; which cities have the most fans in that age group; and which social or music platforms have the most fan activity.

But data tends to drive to broad demographic choices and often popular, mainstream music acts.

However, there is the opportunity to be more targeted in your choice of music. To take a psychographic (rather than demographic) approach. To look at the 'why' rather than just 'who'.

The benefit of this approach is that you connect with the real, underlying drivers of a person's music choice, the psychological drivers and motivators, linked to our deepest values and desires as human beings.

For brands, this is increasingly important because the proliferation of choice means that basic functional and economic benefits are covered (many times over) and therefore in saturated categories, to differentiate, brands need to offer something else; distinctive values and beliefs that talk to the deeper motivations and identity desires of people.

By being clear what a brand stands for and by implication the type of person that this would appeal to, they can connect at a much more meaningful level, becoming a strong ally to people and their deepest aims and goals in life, not just a product or brand that gets bought because they like it, or it meets a basic functional need. So for example, Apple does not simply help people to write a report or listen to music, it meets a fundamental need to express an individual's creative nature. Harley Davidson doesn't just help someone get from A to B, it meets (mostly) men's (especially the middle aged variety) need to experience and to express their freedom.

And this is where music can play a crucial role.

There are areas of study in the field of music psychology dedicated to the categorisation of personality types by genres of music. This burgeoning field of study has developed by examining the preferences of thousands of music listeners and evaluating their self-reported affinity to selections of music. The results of these studies have allowed psychologists to select fourteen music genres to encompass all known types and styles of music for scientific purposes.

These are:

1. Blues
2. Jazz
3. Classical
4. Folk
5. Rock
6. Alternative
7. Heavy Metal
8. Country
9. Soundtracks
10. Religious
11. Pop
12. Rap / Hip-Hop
13. Soul / Funk
14. Electronica / Dance

These genres have been sorted into four distinct categories based upon their common musical attributes:

1. Energetic & Rhythmic;
2. Upbeat & Conventional;
3. Reflective & Complex; and
4. Intense & Rebellious.

This categorisation of music genres has been linked back to the wider study of personality types, and finds that the genre-based music preferences of test subjects speak volumes about dominant aspects of their personalities. This means that music selections for marketing purposes can target specific personality traits and tap directly into a listener's deepest psychological drivers and desires through a carefully conceived and curated choice of music. This means connecting with your target demographic at a subconscious and much more fundamental and meaningful level.

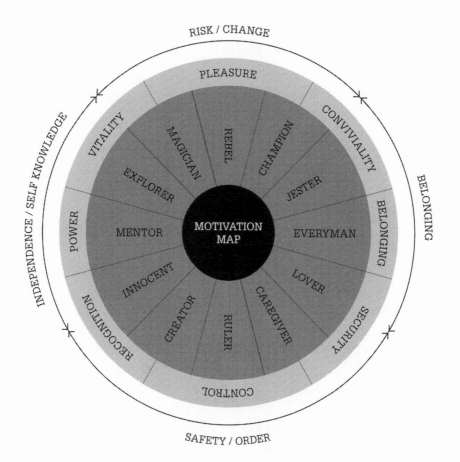

It is not as simplistic as just picking a genre and then being consistent in your application and use of this genre across your marketing activity. Though, that would be a good start. You also need to understand the layers of human meaning that lie beneath the genre, which is acting as a useful, simple headline summary of the multiple aspects that make up the personality contained within it, which is essentially a musical archetype. This area of psychological study is too vast to debate fully here but this kind of approach, looking at the 'why' rather than just 'who' is unquestionably of huge value in building sharp and distinctive brand personas and connecting more deeply with consumers.

This approach also has the benefit of moving away from the current, rather predictable, approach of jumping on the latest 'popular' act or song. By understanding the core elements that make up a piece of music, or the music behind particular cultural 'scenes' to appeal to a specific type of person, a brand is suddenly free to make much more interesting choices.

To illustrate the thinking, here are a couple of examples of brands that have carefully used their choice of music to reinforce specific desired values.

British Airways' association with an adaptation of the Flower Duet from Léo Delibes' opera *Lakmé*, appeals to a listener's sense of Security and Control, both important qualities for an airline (especially one as large and traditional as BA) to own in their passengers' minds and fulfil the desire of Safety and Order, as well as delivering a touch of Superiority. Established through big budget TV advertising it has since been used consistently over a very long period, across multiple touch points, not least in the BA cabins during key moments where passengers look for reassurance: the take-off and landing.

Another good example of a brand that has used music in their advertising to underpin the essential emotional values at the heart of its identity is the British high street retailer, John Lewis. Their careful commissioning of updated versions of well known, nostalgic songs featuring contemporary and usually popular vocalists has built a strong and distinctive identity appealing to a listeners sense of belonging (within the context of the relationships associated with couples and families) through a message that oozes reliability, warmth and caring. At the same time, these songs have generated added buzz around the advertising event, creating anticipation for what will be next. The songs themselves have sometimes performed well in the UK music charts, scoring number one chart positions on a couple of occasions. The music has become an integral part of the overall creative idea. While spend on music for each of these campaigns is significant, in the hundreds of thousands, the ROI is significant because they have taken care to build strong and own-able music equity and planned meticulously to make sure that they build the buzz and then work the subsequent opportunities hard across multiple channels. The music element of their Christmas campaign is only one part of the marketing mix but it's undoubtedly been a key part of their success as John Lewis, unlike many high street retailers, have enjoyed positive growth over a number of trading periods.

Real Vision and Commitment For The Long Term

Red Bull have a very strong reputation within music in the form of the Red Bull Music Academy (RBMA). That comes from their very clear vision and strategy, followed relentlessly over many years.

At the heart of their activity is a strategy based on building and continuously updating the latest generation of highly credible brand ambassadors. A key source of brand advocates, cultural experts and a source of highly relevant content.

In its own words, "The result is an exchange of inspiration that is as unpredictable as it is hard to define. Ideas are bounced around 24/7, refreshing new sounds emerge and true bonds are forged beyond music."

I was lucky enough to experience the RBMA first hand as a participant in Dublin in 2000. This was my first adult experience of a brand giving me something that I truly cared about. I was introduced to likeminded music peers from around the world, which subsequently became a network, opening up the opportunity to travel and to DJ. A raft of icons from the world of music also informally shared their life experiences with us, many of which were awe-inspiring, from the likes of Roger Linn and Dave Smith, pioneers of synthesis and other music technologies, and David Rodigan, a DJ like no other. Many of these icons offered support and contacts to participants, a potential leg up in the music business. The RBMA network has since blossomed into the most credible global property associated with underground music. Guest speakers now include the who's who in music from James Murphy to Bootsy Collins, Giorgio Moroder to Philip Glass to Rza. Aside from annual academies around the world, RBMA lend their brand to regular club and live music events. Content from academies and music events all tie back to a digital platform including RBMA radio and guest speaker interview footage from all academy events.

In terms of investment, the early academies received up to €150,000, which increased incrementally over years to millions. The academy now has a multi million budget. Interestingly, RBMA generates revenue from other brands wanting a piece of the action. Content generated is also monetised through Red Bull Media syndicating the content globally across various channels, including TV and Radio shows. This content is also available for all Red Bull markets to leverage locally through their own comms, making RBMA a content hopper.

Obviously the Red Bull brand has grown extensively over the past sixteen years, which is also a factor to consider for affordability.

ROI was difficult to measure as the primary objective of building real life connections is hard to quantify. Nor was any official process in place to attempt such measurement. Over time, the RBMA network has grown and alumni include music success stories ranging from recording artists, producers (Aloe Blacc, Katy B, Mr Hudson, Pilooski) a raft of radio presenters and of course, hundreds of DJs, dozens of which are headliners or residents at international or local music events.

More recently, the RBMA digital platform has started providing data to inform ROI around its digital content. Media deals for syndication of RBMA content will continue to be another indicator for Red Bull Media.

If footfall was measured, numbers would be huge related to attendance of RBMA related events globally, but again, this isn't being measured as it's not the point.

A final insight is the love given back to RBMA for its support to music. Speakers come back year after year as they are inspired by the event, the people it draws and the community it builds. The same speakers who perform as DJ's or artists waiver performance fees during the academy to perform alongside the participants for the love of music. This point shows that the intention of making connections comes full circle from participants to speakers, forming a supportive and authentic network.

While I may not be particularly fond of the Red Bull product, I'll be a hard core brand ambassador forever in appreciation of the inspiration and help on my way in the music business which RBMA gave me.

Conclusion

So in conclusion, the huge opportunities to use the deep emotional connections offered by music are sitting right in front of us. And with a more considered and strategic approach, the real potential from music marketing can be achieved by brands. I believe that you need to build your approach around 3 core elements to make sure that this happens – a deep and clear brief, a psychological model to build the right music choices for each particular brand and target, and an integrated planning approach that builds a cohesive multi-channel music plan that connects with the audience's life at optimal moments and is tied into the overall brand marketing activity to optimise opportunities for synergies and amplification.

And I think that's a much smarter way to build effective and inspiring music solutions because otherwise you might just find that, despite your target audience's deep passion for music, 'Money (Alone) Can't Buy Me Love'.

Replicators, Fearlessness and You

By James Stewart

We were promised jetpacks.

They're just about here, in a manner of speaking. And while *owning* one should be extraordinary, I want to talk about the way in which the veritable jetpack is going to affect your creative life.

Sure, *actual* jetpacks aren't coming (sorry to get your hopes up) but the type of future we once imagined coming alongside jetpacks and flying cars *is* on the way. It's a future that's defined by an ecosystem of things that seamlessly work together and make life a whole lot better. That ecosystem, that future? That future *is* within grasp.

Scroll through the pages of Gizmodo or the offerings over on Kickstarter and you'll find a glut of intriguing technologies, from 4K 3D TVs to gesture based wearables. There's rarely a day that goes by that doesn't include me staring slack jawed and wide eyed at some new awesome thing. (On that note, I got a chance to "drive" the self-driving Google car (very fast) at TED which was quite amazing. It was also easy to see how this would be good for advertising – watch TV while someone else drives.)

For the most part, the development of this new tech has been in silos. One car company comes up with a proprietary navigation system. Microsoft develops Kinect. Makerbot introduces affordable 3D printing.

What's about to change – in fact, what *is* already happening, is that these disparate technologies are becoming a whole lot less disparate. They're starting to connect with each other and pretty soon, you'll be thinking more about what you want to do than who has the technology to make that happen. Think about this…

- Today we've got Bluetooth speakers, wireless headphones and connected watches. Within a decade, we won't have individual pieces. Instead, we'll be surrounded by an entire Bluetooth zone. Want to watch a movie? You won't pick up a phone, you'll tap into your zone and project the image right in front of you.
- Today we've got texting, video chat and voice data. Soon, we won't think about the platform we're using, we'll just communicate. We'll say what we want to communicate and to whom – that person will then choose *how* they'll receive that information. It could be a phone conversation. It could be a text message. It could be something we haven't thought of yet (Side note: In a way, we're already preparing kids for this in schools. The shift is on to move from the physical process of writing/spelling to the context-based process of communicating an idea).
- Consider those 3D printers. Today, they're just out of reach for the mass market. Tomorrow, they'll be the basis for everything, whether it's a replacement part or a replacement heart. The existence of the interconnected internet and cheaper hardware means we'll be able to make anything for anything. Think forward far enough and you can see the possibility that 3D printers could easily become the Star Trek replicator...or even transporter.

The most fascinating part of our future isn't that it's lined by unheard of technology, it's that the foundation for this convergence of things into a seamless ecosystem already exists. We see this pattern again and again in current technology and you need to be fearless of this future. Photography led to film, then digital. Horse and buggies were superseded by a buggie with an engine. Screens became touch-screens, which became environments controlled by hand movements and voice commands. Our

360° future has many of the pieces in place that will form the foundation of our future. Those pieces are just in the nascent forms.

So. What? What does this educated guess at our future mean to you?

If we're about to cross that line from proprietary technology silos to an interconnected series of ecosystems, you need to start thinking about how you can create for, mine and fund those ecosystems. For example, instead of simply creating a smartphone app, you want to think about a smartphone app that connects to a wearable that talks to an iBeacon that relates to a physical installation.

"Creating" for the future is going to be a lot of fun, and in a way, it's already begun. The shift from "brands" to "brand experiences" is going to be accelerated (and hopefully, improved) by this integration. It won't be a "social media" campaign or an "above the line" campaign. It'll be the answer to the question – *how does the promise of the brand stay with you wherever you go?* My film company pitched a client on the idea of replacing the seats of a movie theatre with the seats of its luxury car brand. We proposed creating a short film that played with the trailers, a film in which the audience could use their own smartphones to affect the outcome. It's early days, but this sort of integrating into people's lives and what they do is going to happen more and more. That can be a promotional experience like the film we proposed, holographic way-finding systems that send data to a phone, or simply the ability to say "Hey Siri, find me a restaurant," then looking up from the phone to see digital signage flashing at locations with sight.

We're going to need to get paid for the work we do and that payment won't come in the traditional ways. Today, we bill for our work, but as we continue to monetise data, the model will shift from paying for work to paying for action. 15 years ago, the dotcom crash happened because we tried to apply old financial models to the technology frontier. Then Google came along and demonstrated how data could make money. Amazon started generating revenue by becoming the backend to the Internet. As we move forward, even these relatively new models are shifting. Google is taking data to the personal level. The purchase of Nest shows that they're thinking about this integrated ecosystem and how to make money from it. Expect more and more of these types of acquisition as we all explore how to make sense of the future.

Technology can still be expensive, which is why advertising should continue to do what is has historically done very well – fund the future. Advertising built the infrastructure for TV, keeping costs reasonable and getting sets into homes. Advertising expanded the smartphone and tablet markets, using data mining as a way to create revenue and subsidise the cost of the amazing little computers in our pockets. We'll be counted on going forward, financing the base technology for things like those Bluetooth zones. In a sense, we'll be responsible for setting up the ecosystems in exchange for data that we can use to tell and sell our stories.

The future isn't about reddit or Facebook. It's not about iPads and Oculus Rifts. The hardware and software will be there, but it'll be integrated into customised experiences. At retail, that'll mean that the next generation of iBeacon will generate a personalised shopping experience. At home, that will mean more efficient everything, whether that's air conditioning profiles or lighting connected to the RFID in your phone. The promise is that it will all work together, and it's up to us to fearlessly find new and compelling ways to turn those ecosystems into great storytelling.

And jetpacks. Hopefully, there will finally be jetpacks.

Room 101

Alex Lavery

I would consign the last minute consideration for music used in advertising. When considered during the planning process, music can deliver so much more, including value for money. When left to the last minute, too often subjective panic decisions are made at a cost to the effectiveness music can accomplish.

Ana Andjelic

The label "provocateur" belongs perfectly to Room 101. In advertising, too often we come across professionals who claim to be provocateurs. Here, we yet again encounter the problem of *saying* vs. *doing*. The biggest provocateurs in the industry don't feel the need to personally brand themselves as such. They allow their thinking, writing and their work to speak for them, and through it, they provoke others - in a humble, hard-working way - to think, write and do more creative, interesting and smarter things. But if someone calls herself or himself a provocateur, they most certainly are not. They just want attention. Room 101 is for them.

Anders Gustafsson

Let's schedule 90% of our regroups in there.

Anders Sjostedt

I'd probably consign advertising to room 101. That a big chunk of the world's most brilliant minds spend most of their time crafting messages to convince the rest of the world that one physically (or globally) damaging product is better than another (similarly damaging one) is, and should be, quite unsettling.

Ben Cooper

It would have to be acronym 'ATL', and 'BTL'. For those fortunate enough not to know them, it's 'above the line' and 'below the line', and for some reason 'ATL' is supposedly more important; this includes TV, radio and billboards. No human on planet earth is delineating their media consumption in that way, and never has. Die ATL and BTL... you're not welcome in anyone's world.

Bridget Jung

I'd put 'banner ads' into Room 101 without hesitation. *«It's more likely you will survive a plane crash or win the lottery than click a banner ad»**. In addition to simply being inefficient, generally speaking they're pretty damn ugly and serve as a reminder of the dark ages of digital advertising. *http://read.bi/LyIz6e

Carl W. Jones

I would consign the word 'ego' into room 101. For me it has no place in advertising as it clouds and interrupts the creative process. I believe superior artistry would arise if the same energy put into the 'ego' was directed into ideation and craft.

Daniele Fiandaca

I would consign the word 'consumer' into room 101. For me it has no place in briefs - not only does it dehumanise our audience, it also does not describe what the audience are doing when we are communicating with them. I believe that if every agency banned the world consumer from their communications briefs, we would get far more effective and far more human communications strategies.

Dave Bedwood

I would consign the word 'storytelling' to room 101. It's used by a load of numpties in digital who think they've discovered the secret of great work, and are kindly sharing their sharp insight with us all. All the while the rest of the world has been doing it for 3,000 years. Pathetic. What makes it even worse is that there's a clip on youtube of me doing this very thing. I want to kill myself. The End.

Dave Birss
I detest the term 'ideation'. I'm hearing it more and more these days and it makes me sick-up a little in my mouth every time. (I hate it almost as much as I hate the term 'brainstorm'. Which I hate just a little bit less than actually being forced to endure a brainstorm). 'Ideation' is such a piece of American corporate ballyhoo that I can't associate it with truly liberated creative thinking. The word feels safe and sanitised, much like the ideas that it leads to.

Erkki Izarra
I would consign bad breath into room 101. Next time you go over someone's shoulder to look at whatever is on the screen, take a mint or keep a distance. Being French is not an excuse.

Flo Heiss
My biggest hate in advertising and life in general is putting a king size cover on a king size duvet, that's what I'd like to put into room 101. I demand an innovation hack!

Gareth Kay
I'd consign the word brand. It's the most misused word in business. It's not something we create, do or own. And nor is there such a thing as the 'brand' campaign.

Jake Attree
How slow advertising can be deserves to be in room 101. Too many processes and people kill momentum. We should start questioning why stuff takes as long as it does and work out how to change that.

James Cooper
If you had asked me five or six years ago my 101 would have been 'viral'. Now it's another word that has become equally nauseous for me;

'innovation'. The 'I' word, I can barely bring myself to say it any more, has become a term bandied about by agencies (and everyone else) as a remedy for all ills. People say they want to be innovative or do innovative things without having a notion of what that actually means. What it really means is doing something that has not been done before. Really sitting down and thinking about something and getting scared.

James Stewart

I would like to ban the word CONTENT. What we do is storytelling, often emotional, sometimes funny, but ALWAYS well crafted communication. To call it "content" is to make it generic, marginalise it and commoditise it. Our work doesn't "cover the black", it takes our audience on a journey that enriches their life through a product, lifestyle and aspiration. Or, dare I say…Dream. Please send "content" away to the place in creative hell where we sent "paradigm" and "zeitgeist".

James Kirk

I would banish bad internships to Room 101. Having experienced the damage they can do to a young creative, I would make sure that every internship is paid reasonably and allows the individual an opportunity to grow and take something positive away from it. It's true that every intern is responsible for how much they get out of the experience, but they must be given a fair chance. If a company can't provide that then they shouldn't run an internship programme.

James Wallman

I hate the way advertising people say "consumer" instead of saying person. I think that's the same as saying "pizza" while meaning Italian food. Sure, people consume. And sure, pizza is an important part of Italy's food culture. But if you thought pizza was all you need to know about Italian food, you'd miss out on cappuccino, gelato, gianduja. It's the same when you say "consumer". Do that and you might miss out on the frothy, the frozen, and maybe even the gooey bits that make up real people.

Jana Savic Rastovac

I would consign the word 'testing' into room 101. Testing of creative work feels like measuring poetry (remember Dead Poets Society?) - wrong. Testing should stay at the beginning of a creative process, as a valuable tool for setting the right paths in thinking about our brands, but never ever in the last phases of creative processes, as it is responsible for the big graveyard of ideas.

John V Willshire

To be honest, I'm reluctant to put anything into room 101. It is symptomatic of this industry, and perhaps society more generally, that we must operate at extremes, and stick steadfastly to these views despite all evidence or changing circumstances. I don't believe it is a question of what is right or wrong, it is simply a question of what is most appropriate for the circumstances. For this reason then, if I'm am forced to consign anything to Room 101, then it is any dogma which the industry too readily adopts.

Jon Barnes

I would put businesses which don't put a genuine focus on developing their organisation's culture into room 101. Businesses are built by people and can therefore only be successful if they put the same commitment and effort into fostering environments that focus on personal growth, as they do into strategies and Keynote presentations. *'Culture eats strategy for breakfast'* - Peter Drucker.

Jon Burkhart

That's easy. I would banish the phrase "real-time marketing" to Room 101. No-one needs the pressure to be doing stuff in real-time because this makes brands hyperactive and desperate. It makes them forget about thinking strategically. It makes them impulsive. Many people have suggested words like "right-time" and "relevance." They've changed "always on" to "always ready." I agree with all of this. I just think the answers lie in a double embrace of customer data and innovation around connected devices. Real-time marketing is tough, as it requires organisational change that very few brands are ready to adopt. Sure, news media outlets think this way but getting a brand to do this even in a token-way is extremely tough. I am thrilled by this challenge. Watch this space.

Julian Cole

Nike+, I think the example of an agency coming up with a product was the anomaly. After Nike + all these agencies thought that they needed to start creating labs and innovation units to make products. This was all a distraction to the job that was at hand which is helping communicate a brand's message on <u>scale</u>. Unless it is creating a product for a PR story there is really no reason that communications agencies need to be getting into the product design world

Laura Jordan Bambach

I would throw with joy the pollution that passes for a lot of digital advertising these days into Room 101. It's become a volume game where creativity has been replaced by targeting, and that delivers diminishing returns. No more making shit to add to the world of shit - there's too much information out there already and I for one am drowning.

Mark Earls

The thing I'd consign to room 101 is "brand": it's a flabby word that we all tend to use to avoid being clear what we're on about – or as an inducement to get someone else to do what we want them to (which is normally not that interesting) or stop them doing something we don't agree with. It also tends to involve a bit of a power trip – we are powerful, the punters are weak and stupid. Seems we imagine that what matters is the consumer's view (worship) of the brand when in truth most lives are concerned with other people, not brands or things. "Brand" is lazy and silly and distracts our attention from doing what really matters – good stuff that touches people and helps them interact better with each other.

Marc Lewis

I would consign advertising into room 101. I know that I'm supposed to pick something from advertising, but the word itself has seriously negative vibes because it tends to hypnotise creative people into thinking about the act of communicating before the act of problem solving. Our jobs should not be to produce stuff just to fill up space on TV, radio, print, outdoor or digital. Our jobs should be to create value between communities and then to communicate our ideas in the most interesting ways possible.

Mark Anderson

What would I like to put into Room 101? Lazy Thinking and a "that'll do" approach. Our job is to continually push until we get the idea we truly believe in. It helps when we have clients who understand this, where the relationship is developed enough for an agency to put in the call and say, "Hey, we need another 24 hours". But sometimes there isn't another 24 hours… so *we* need to put in a little extra – burn the midnight oil. Don't let lack of effort define the end result. So, next time the pain comes, don't stop. Flip your idea upside down, sideways, back to front. Throw it against a wall. Don't be afraid to start all over again. And never say, "That'll do".

Patrick Collister

The word 'storytelling' should be banned. If you manage a famous FMCG brand, then maybe you do have stories to tell. If you are looking after an unglamorous product, you don't. I wish marketers and media agencies would wise up as to what a brand is and isn't. C'mon, how many stories about haemorrhoids do you really want to be told? Preparation H think the answer is probably none. And they're right. That doesn't mean they don't have a damn good business. They do.

Pierre Odendaal

I would consign 'focus groups' to room 101. For me they have no place in Advertising, and Communications for that matter. Seems since this got incorporated into the creative mix, creativity has been dumbed down to stats and numbers and the true, real essence of creativity has been diluted or even lost. If we were to lose this aspect in the creative mix I am convinced there would be much better storytelling taking place.

Sam Ball

There is no point hating anything in advertising, its not that important. Saying that, I would stick anything that gets in the way of having fun into room 101. Specifically client and agency people who have the ability to suck the energy out of the room. You know the type: the dower faced, cowardly ones who shoot the great ideas down, fuck every last one of them.

Seb Royce

I hate 'chemistry meetings' or at least what they have become. The idea of getting to know the people you might work with is a great one but now they have become a 'pitch before the pitch', which is ridiculous. Chemistry meetings should be about chatting over a meal or a drink, or both – seeing if you get on. And never involve any kind of presentation whatsoever.

Scott Morrison

I would consign the words 'space' and 'piece' into room 101 unless they form part of a brief from NASA. Jargonistas talk about operating in the 'X space' or 'there's the whole Y piece around this' or even 'there's a whole C piece around this A space'. No there's not. Please don't use either of those words in my...erm...vicinity. Thank you.

Steve Clayton

I believe we could all do without discounted media bundles. Campaigns are designed to live, communicate and perform in certain spaces. The target audience is considered from the moment we sharpen our pencils and then the client drops some obscure media bomb on you just because they feel that they're getting it cheap - I could tear my hair out

Tim Buesing

My *Room 101* would be filled with adland's egos and 'big swinging dicks'. They often get in the way of great work and (not surprisingly) turn talented female creatives off the industry.

Vladimir Ćosić

I would consign the phrase 'focus group testing' into room 101. The only way to 'test' the idea is to bring it to life and make it happen. In ten years of working in advertising, I have never experienced true benefits of these kind of tests - but have seen so many ideas crippled or killed; and, is there a more sad thing than the idea buried before it really came to life? Just try to imagine Robert Crumb comic books, Sopranos, Rage Against The Machine songs, Shakespeare's Hamlet or Hitchcock's Psycho being tested on focus groups before seeing the daylight? What a short and sad 'History of Art' that would be.

Appendix: Author Biogs

Alex Lavery, Partner & Creative Director, P&S
Alex (@pitchandsync) has a passion for music in all shapes and forms, which led to founding P&S where he is now partner and creative director. The best piece of advice he has ever been given was by Joyce Ryland, his grandmother "Be true to yourself and go after what you believe in."

Ana Andjelic, Group Strategy Director, Spring Studios
Ana (@andjelicaaa) currently works as the Group Strategy Director at Spring Studios, a next-gen agency specializing in design-focused brands. The best piece of advice Ana has ever been given is to count to 20 before reacting, by her beloved former manager, Nicole Victor. She follows it sporadically.

Anders Gustafsson, Creative Director, TBWA \ Media Arts Lab
Anders (@agcdmal) lives in Los Angeles and works with Apple. The best piece of advice came from his grandma who told him "Remember that you do what you want to do".

Anders Sjostedt, Partnership Director, Hyper Island
Anders (@anderssjostedt) is currently Partnership Director at the digital media school Hyper Island, working with brands such as IKEA and with agencies in Europe and the US. The best piece of advice he was ever given was from a teacher at his management school who told him: "Always treat everyone better than they deserve."

Ben Cooper, Group Innovation Director, M&C Saatchi Sydney
Ben (@benhamin) is currently Group Innovation Director at M&C Saatchi Sydney. The best piece of advice he's received is from Tom Uglow who said "Recruit people who are curious and passionate first (skill set 2nd)' and it works every time".

Bridget Jung, Chief Creative Officer, DigitasLBi Paris
Bridget (@bridoo) is currently Chief Creative Officer at DigitasLBi Paris. The best piece of advice she ever received was from her old boss and friend Mark Beeching, who encouraged her to always 'risk being wrong'.

Carl W. Jones. Assistant Professor, Faculty of Design at OCAD University, Toronto. Pop Culture Engineer in Miami Ad School, Mexico City.
Carl (@carlwjones) present goal is to advance advertising creation through the application of advertising theory and marketing semiotics. The best advice he ever read was from Leo Burnett "When you reach for the stars you may not quite get there, but you won't come up with a handful of mud either".

Daniele Fiandaca, Co-founder, Creative Social
Daniele (@yellif) is one of the co-founders of Creative Social, which he has been building with Mark Chalmers for over a decade. He also runs his own consultancy as well as working with Hyper Island as an ongoing Masterclass speaker and Course Leader. The best advice he was ever given was from a blogpost by Dave Trott, when he wrote 'Better to be wrong and interesting than right and boring'.

Dave Bedwood, Creative Director, M&C Saatchi
Dave (@dbedwood) is currently Creative Director at M&C Saatchi. The best advice he was ever given was by the Dalai Lama "If one isn't that interesting, then one should lie".

Dave Birss, Founder of Additive and OneDayCodeSchool.com, Editor at Large, The Drum
Dave (@davebirss) has what's known as a 'portfolio career'. The best piece of advice he ever received was 'If you don't enjoy creating it, nobody will enjoy what you've created'. He was miserable when he wrote this paragraph.

Erkki Izarra, Director, Portfolio Marketability & Propositions, Microsoft
Erkki (@erkkiizarra) is currently Director of Portfolio Marketability at Microsoft. The best encouragement he was ever given was by his former boss Ami Hasan who said "It's often easier to ask for forgiveness, than to ask for a permission".

Flo Heiss, Studio Heiss
Bavarian born Flo (@floheiss) is founder of his own Creative Design studio called Studio Heiss. The best piece of advice he was ever given was from his dad who told him "I don't think you are good enough to work for the German Railway".

Gareth Kay, founding partner, Zeus Jones San Francisco
Gareth (@garethk) is a strategist by trade. Zeus Jones San Francisco opened its doors on March 1, 2014 with the ambition to help businesses and brands rediscover their imagination. The best advice he was given came from the BBC TV show Why Don't You, which was on every morning in Gareth's school holidays. Its advice was a challenge: "Why Don't You Just Switch Off Your Television Set And Go Out And Do Something Less Boring Instead?"

Jake Attree, Creative, Dare
Jake (@JakeAttree) is currently a Creative at Dare, Campaign's digital agency of the decade, where he started on the Dare School grad program after doing a Masters at

Hyper Island, Manchester. The best piece of advice he has ever given was from his Dad: "Don't stay in a comfort zone."

James Cooper, Head of Creative, Betaworks
James (@koopstakov) helps betaworks products partner up with brands and agencies to make cool stuff. The best piece of advice which he read somehwere was "If it was easy it would be easy".

James Kirk, Creative Director, Breed & Craft
James (@otherJamesKirk) is currently Creative Director at Breed & Craft, a new type of creative agency. The best advice he's been given is 'If you can't do great things, do small things in a great way'.

James Stewart, Chief Content Creator, Geneva Film Co.
James (@jamesstewart3D) is an award-winning director, storyteller, artist, digital innovator and multi-platform visual designer whose work ranges from mobile to giant screen, and from commercials to stereoscopic 3D museum installations.

James Wallman, trend forecaster, journalist, presenter, author
James (@JamesWallman) has a rare ability to read, reflect, and define the Zeitgeist - as seen in his new book, *Stuffocation*. The best piece of advice he has ever been given? His old school motto: *omnia vinces perseverando* – you will conquer all things through perseverance.

Jana Savic Rastovac, Creative Director, McCann Belgrade
Jana (@janasavic) is Creative Director at McCann Belgrade, leading a team of wonderful people responsible for handling the biggest international and domestic brands in the market and winning the first ever Cannes Lion for their home country, Serbia, in 2011. Best piece of advice ever was given to her by her first mentor: "Never be late".

John V Willshire, Founder, Smithery
John (@willsh) is founder of Smithery, a Product and Marketing Innovation studio. The best advice he ever was given was that to get on in business, he'd have to specialise in something. He has yet to follow this advice.

Jon Barnes, Relationship Manager, Hyper Island.
Jon (@jonathanlbarnes) is currently Relationship Manager at Hyper Island, an organisation which helps businesses and people learn how to embrace change. The best advice he was ever given was on a Humans Of New York post which said *'Keep travelling, even if you need a loan'*.

Jon Burkhart, Content Strategist, Copywriter, Author
Jon (@jonburkhart) is a content strategist and copywriter who helps brands and agencies kick-start their real-time content creation efforts by building 'brand newsrooms' for them.

Julian Cole, Head of Comms Planning, BBH NY

Julian (@juliancole) is the Head of Communications Planning at BBH where he leads Communication Planning across PlayStation, Axe, Johnnie Walker, Baileys, Sharpie and Vaseline.

Laura Jordan Bambach, Creative Partner, Mr President / President D&AD

Laura (@laurajaybee) is currently Creative Partner at nimble creative agency Mr President; and President of D&AD. The best piece of advice she was ever given was from her English master, who said "Only boring people get bored".

Marc Lewis, Dean, School of Communication Arts

Marc (@SCA2Dean) is currently the Dean at School of Communication Arts, the leading school for aspiring creative talent. The best advice he was ever given was from the title of an early 1980s children's television programme called, *"Why Don't You Just Switch Off Your Television Set and Go Out and Do Something Less Boring Instead?"* Great advice!

Mark Anderson, Co-founder and Managing Director at We Love Digital

Mark Anderson is Co-founder and Managing Director at We Love Digital – an agency that has grown exponentially in the last 6 years, with offices in both the UK and Denmark. The best advice he has ever been given was from an old colleague who said "Work hard and fast, be brilliant or get the fuck out!"

Mark Earls, Founder, Herd Consulting

Mark (@herdmeister) writes books, gives talks and runs HERD Consulting independently out of London. The best professional advice he ever heard was from an interview with novelist Kurt Vonnegut, just before he died. "Join a gang – any gang". Which is why he still fronts a ska-band when he can. If not, he'd rather be fishing or watching cricket somewhere hot and sunny.

Patrick Collister, Head of Design, Google Zoo NACE

Patrick (@directnewideas) is currently Head of Design, Google Zoo NACE. Best piece of advice: "Don't take yourself seriously. No-one else will if you do".

Pierre Odendaal, Chief Creative Officer, McCann Johannesburg and McCann Worldgroup Africa.

Pierre (@pierre_o) is currently Chief Creative Officer at McCann, the world's largest Advertising network.

Sam Ball, Creative Partner, Lean Mean Fighting Machine.

Sam (@samuelball) is Creative Director at M&C Saatchi, London. It sounds bad but he can't remember a single specific piece of enlightening advice anyone has given him about advertising. If he has to sum up the lessons he has learnt it would be "If you not having fun you're not doing it right".

Scott Morrison, Founder, The Business Accelerator

Scott (@IAccelerateU) is the Founder of 'The Business Accelerator' and helps businesses to adapt and respond to the massive opportunities that the post-recession market place presents by leveraging innovation and acceleration partnerships. His best advice was from a friend who'd spent a lot of time with Marvin Gaye in his final years. Marvin used to say "Give everyone 5 minutes".

Seb Royce, Chief Creative Officer, Rockabox

Seb (@sebroyce) is currently Chief Creative Officer at Rockabox, a new breed of company pioneering video content production, tech and distribution. The best advice he was ever given in advertising was by his Group Head at Ogilvy (his first job) who said 'Never take yourself too seriously....'.

Steve Clayton, Associate Creative Director, McCann

Steve has been at McCann Johannesburg since the beginning of 2012 as the Associate Creative Director.

Tim Buesing, Creative Director, Reactive

Tim (@tbuesing) is currently Creative Director of Reactive, an independent digital agency network with offices in 4 countries. The best advice he ever received was from Olaf Czeschner during his time at Razorfish: "Never stop doing what you love."

Vladimir Ćosić, Creative Director, McCann Belgrade

Vladimir (@gruntoslomni) is currently Creative Director at McCann Belgrade, the first and so far the only serbian agency to win the Cannes Lion. The best advice he was ever given was from his university professor Nebojša Pajkić, who said "In order to call himself a screenwriter, one must write at least 10 pages of scenario each day, till the end of his life".

The Creative Social
Roll of Honour

You become an Official Social by attending one of our global events. In honour of a decade of Creative Social, here is a list of all our Socials (and the events they have attended):

Where:

AM = Amsterdam	*HE = Helsinki*	*SE = Seattle*
AN = Antwerp	*LV = Las Vegas*	*SF = San Francisco*
BA= Barcelona	*LO = London*	*SH = Shanghai*
BE = Beirut	*MO = Montreal*	*SP = Sao Paolo*
BN = Berlin	*NY = New York*	*ST = Stockholm*
FL = Florence	*PA = Paris*	*TO = Tokyo*

Aaron Griffiths	NY
Adam Kerj	LV
Akihito Abe	TO
Alessandra Lariu	BA / ST / NY / BE / LO / SH / SF / PA / BN
Alex Lavery	HE
Alistair Campbell	HA / BE
Anders Gustafsson	FL / AN / PA / LV / TO / SE
Anders Wahlquist	FL / AN / SF / AM / BE
Andre Matterazzo	AN
Antero Jokinen	HE
Andy Sandoz	AM / LO / NY
Angel Herraiz	BA / NY / LO

Barry Brand	BE / HA / TO / SE / MO
Becky Power	HE / LO / HA / BE / PA / AN / AM
Ben Clapp	LO
Benjamin Palmer	BE / AM / PA / LO / NY
Beth Ryan	NY
Björn Kummeneje	HE / MO
Björn Höglund	AN / SP / LO / ST
Bo Hellberg	BE / PA / AM / LO / TO / HE
Bob Mackintosh	SH
Bram Oorthuizen	BE / FL
Brandon Waterman	SE
Bridget Jung	TO / HA / AM
Carl Jones	MO / LV
Chris Barrett	AM
Chris Baylis	AM / BA / FL / SH / AN / LO
Chris Clarke	LO / HA / BE / FL / SP / BE / NY / BA / ST
Christine Turner	PA
Corinna Falusi	PA / BA
Cyrus Vantoch-Wood	ST / BA / NY / LO / SP
Daljit Singh	LO
Daniela Michelon	LO / HA / BE
Daniel Jordan Bambach	NY / HE / BA
Daniel Kormann	AM
Daniele Fiandaca	AM / ST / BA / NY / BE / LO / SP / FL / SH / AN / SF / PA / LV / BE / HA / TO / HE
Daniel Richau	LO
Danusch Mahmoudi	TO / LO / HA / LV / AN / FL / SP / BE / NY
Darrell Wilkins	LV / BE / HA / LO
Daryl Arnold	SH
Dave Bedwood	BE / BN / LO / PA / SF / SP / TO
David Godycki	HA
David Morgan	TO
Dick Buschman	AM / BE / HA

Dirk Eschenbacher	SH / TO
Domenico Massareto	SP
Doug Schiff	TO
Ed Robinson	HE / SH / FL
Edou Pou	BA
Edward Bishop	BN
Eduardo de Felipe	LO / BE
Eduardo Marques	SE
Elizabeth Valleau	PA / BE
Eka Ruola	HE
Emil Lanne	NY
Emmanuel Saccoccini	SE / AM / LV
Enric Nel-lo	BA
Erkki Izzara	SE / HE / TO
Erik Holmdahl	PA / SP / NY / BA / ST / AM
Erwin Jansen	ST / BA / NY / AN / SF / BE /
Fabio Costa	PA
Fabio Simoes	PA / SF / SP / BE / NY
Fanny Krivoy	LO
Fernanda Romano	BE / LV / LO / SF / AN / SP / BE
Flo Heiss	AM / BA / NY / BE / LO / AN / SF / HA / BE
Florian Schmitt	LO
Fredrik Carlstrom	PA
Fredrick Aven	BE / SF / FL
Fredrick Bonn	HE
Fredrik Heghammar	SF
Fredrik Thorsen	SE
Friedrich Von Zitzewitz	SF
Gavin Gordon Rodgers	SH / AN / PA / LO / MO
Gemma Butler	LO / PA / AN / SH
Geoff Tehan	HA / MO
George Prest	HA
Graham Fink	FL / SH / AN / SF / PA / LO / BE / TO

Graham MacInnes	SE
Guillermo Vega	SP / AN / AM / HA
Gustav Martner	BE / NY / BA / ST / AM
Ian Kerrigan	HE
Ignacio Oreamuno	AM
Jackson Murphy	SE
James Cooper	AM / ST / BA / NY / BE / LO / SH / SF / PA / LV / BE
James Goode	SE / TO / LO / AM
James Stewart	LV / HA / TO / MO
Janet Kestin	AN
Jim Haven	SE / AN / SH / FL
Joakim Borgström	AM / ST / BA / SP / SF
Johnny Vulkan	BE / NY
Jon Sharpe	FL / AN / SF
Jonas Hedeback	FL / SP / LO / BE / NY /
Jose Carlos Mariategui	LO
Jurgen Prause	LV
Kenneth Pederson	ST
Kosuke Hashijima	TO
Lars Bastholm	NY / SF / LV / SE / SH
Laura Jordan Bambach	HE / LO / HA / LV / PA / AN / BN / NY / BA
Liz Sivell	SP / SH / LO / LV / BE / HA / TO / HE
Louisa St. Pierre	SE / NY
Lyndon Hale	BA / NY
Mariota Essery	LV / PA
Mark Anderson	AM /
Mark Chalmers	AM / ST / BA / NY / BE / LO / SP / FL / SH / AN / SF / PA / LV / BE / HA / TO / HE / SE
Mark Cridge	BA / ST / AM
Mark Earls	PA / LO
Markus Maczey	HE / TO / AM / SF / AN / SH / MO
Martin Baillie	AM
Martin Cedergren	LO / ST

Mary Lee Copeland	SF
Mateus Braga	SP
Mathew O'Rourke	SF
Matias Palm Jensen	PA / SF / LO / BA / ST / AM
Matt Powell	AM / AN / LO / BE / NY / BA
Matthias Schmidt	SH
Mauricio Mazzariol	SP
Mauro Cavalletti	SF / PA / AM / BE
Max Jones	BA / ST / AM
Mervyn Den Tam	BE / HA / TO / AM / LV
Michael Frank	SP
Michel Lent Schwartzman	SP
Mike Williams	HE / AN / BN / AM / LO
Nathan Cooper	SF / TO
Natalie Lam	TO / HA / BE
Nick Hamilton	PA / SF / AN / FL
Nicke Bergström	AM / ST / BA / NY / BE / LO / AN / SF
Nitin Mistry	ST
Olli Siren	HE
Olly Robinson	BE / NY
Pablo Marques	FL / AN / PA / BE / LO
Paulo Bernini	TO
Patrick Gardner	BN / SP / FL / AN / PA / SE
Paul Banham	LO / BE / BA
Pedro Gravena	SP
Pelle Nilsson	SE
Peter Martin	SE
Pete Petrella	HE / LO / HA / PA
Petter Westlund	LO
Phil Wilce	SE
Piero Frescobaldi	BE / FL / HE / LO / SE / SF / SP
Pierre Odendaal	AM / LO
PJ Pereira	TO / LV / SF

Rafa Soto	BA / BE / SP / SH / AN / SF / PA / BE
Raphael Vasconcellos	SP
Rei Inamoto	SH / SF
Ricardo Figueira	TO / LO
Ricardo Frescobaldi	BE
Rick Webb	NY
Rik Van der Eng	BE / LO / FL
Rodrigo Teco	SP
Rogier Vijverberg	HE / HA / AM
Russ Tucker	BA
Sam Ball	TO / LO / AM / PA / SP / BE / NY / BA / SH / BN
Sam De Volder	BA / NY / BE / LO / FL / AN / SF / PA / AM / HA
Sascha Portisch	AM
Scott Clarke	FL
Scott Rodgers	SE / TO / BE / AM / SF / SH / LO / NY / BA / ST / AM
Senta Slingerland	HE
Seb Royce	AM/ BE
Simon Sankarayya	HA / LV
Simon Waterfall	LO
Sonja Loth	AM
Steve Lawler	TO
Stuart Peddie	LO / BE
Ted Persson	SP / SH / AN / SF / AM / BE / HA / SE
Tim Fouhy	LV
Tim O'Neill	LV
Tim Rodgers	LV / LO
Tobias Gaertner	AM / BA / BE / BE / FL / HA / LO / SF / SH / ST
Todd Krugman	TO
Tom Bazeley	LO / AM
Tom Evans	TO / LO / HA / BE / AN / SH / SP / BE
Tom Sacchi	AN / LO / LV / BE
Tony Hogqvist	BN / SP / FL / SH / BE / SE
Tony Sajdak	HE / SF / FL

Vincent Jansen	FL / AN / PA / AM
Vivian Rosenthal	PA
Wayne Arnold	AM / ST
Wain Choi	TO
Wesley Ter Haar	SE
Will Hyde	SE
Will McGinness	SF / NY / BA / ST
Yann Kretz	LO / PA
Yannis Marcou	AM

We salute you ;)

Made in the USA
Middletown, DE
10 January 2015